Learning Apache Spark 2

Process big data with the speed of light!

Muhammad Asif Abbasi

BIRMINGHAM - MUMBAI

Learning Apache Spark 2

First published: March 2017

Production reference: 1240317

Published by Packt Publishing Ltd.
Livery Place
35 Livery Street
Birmingham
B3 2PB, UK.

ISBN 978-1-78588-513-6
www.packtpub.com

Credits

Authors

Muhammad Asif Abbasi

Reviewers

Prashant Verma

Commissioning Editor

Veena Pagare

Acquisition Editor

Tushar Gupta

Content Development Editor

Mayur Pawanikar

Technical Editor

Karan Thakkar

Copy Editor

Safis Editing

Project Coordinator

Nidhi Joshi

Proofreader

Safis Editing

Indexer

Tejal Daruwale Soni

Graphics

Tania Dutta

Production Coordinator

Nilesh Mohite

About the Author

Muhammad Asif Abbasi has worked in the industry for over 15 years in a variety of roles from engineering solutions to selling solutions and everything in between. Asif is currently working with SAS a market leader in Analytic Solutions as a Principal Business Solutions Manager for the Global Technologies Practice. Based in London, Asif has vast experience in consulting for major organizations and industries across the globe, and running proof-of-concepts across various industries including but not limited to telecommunications, manufacturing, retail, finance, services, utilities and government. Asif is an Oracle Certified Java EE 5 Enterprise architect, Teradata Certified Master, PMP, Hortonworks Hadoop Certified developer, and administrator. Asif also holds a Master's degree in Computer Science and Business Administration.

About the Reviewers

Prashant Verma started his IT carrier in 2011 as a Java developer in Ericsson working in telecom domain. After couple of years of JAVA EE experience, he moved into Big Data domain, and has worked on almost all the popular big data technologies, such as Hadoop, Spark, Flume, Mongo, Cassandra,etc. He has also played with Scala. Currently, He works with QA Infotech as Lead Data Enginner, working on solving e-Learning problems using analytics and machine learning.

Prashant has also worked on *Apache Spark for Java Developers, Packt* as a Technical Reviewer.

I want to thank Packt Publishing for giving me the chance to review the book as well as my employer and my family for their patience while I was busy working on this book.

www.packtpub.com

For support files and downloads related to your book, please visit www.PacktPub.com.

Did you know that Packt offers eBook versions of every book published, with PDF and ePub files available? You can upgrade to the eBook version at www.PacktPub.com and as a print book customer, you are entitled to a discount on the eBook copy. Get in touch with us at service@packtpub.com for more details.

At www.PacktPub.com, you can also read a collection of free technical articles, sign up for a range of free newsletters and receive exclusive discounts and offers on Packt books and eBooks.

https://www.packtpub.com/mapt

Get the most in-demand software skills with Mapt. Mapt gives you full access to all Packt books and video courses, as well as industry-leading tools to help you plan your personal development and advance your career.

Why subscribe?

- Fully searchable across every book published by Packt
- Copy and paste, print, and bookmark content
- On demand and accessible via a web browser

Customer Feedback

Thanks for purchasing this Packt book. At Packt, quality is at the heart of our editorial process. To help us improve, please leave us an honest review on this book's Amazon page at "`https://www.amazon.com/dp/1785885138`".

If you'd like to join our team of regular reviewers, you can e-mail us at `customerreviews@packtpub.com`. We award our regular reviewers with free eBooks and videos in exchange for their valuable feedback. Help us be relentless in improving our products!

Table of Contents

Preface

This book will cover the technical aspects of Apache Spark 2.0, one of the fastest growing open-source projects. In order to understand what Apache Spark is, we will quickly recap a the history of Big Data, and what has made Apache Spark popular. Irrespective of your expertise level, we suggest going through this introduction as it will help set the context of the book.

The Past

Before going into the present-day Spark, it might be worthwhile understanding what problems Spark intend to solve, and especially the data movement. Without knowing the background we will not be able to predict the future.

"You have to learn the past to predict the future."

Late 1990s: The world was a much simpler place to live, with proprietary databases being the sole choice of consumers. Data was growing at quite an amazing pace, and some of the biggest databases boasted of maintaining datasets in excess of a Terabyte.

Early 2000s: The dotcom bubble happened, meant companies started going online, and likes of Amazon and eBay leading the revolution. Some of the dotcom start-ups failed, while others succeeded. The commonality among the business models started was a razor-sharp focus on page views, and everything started getting focused on the number of users. A lot of marketing budget was spent on getting people online. This meant more customer behavior data in the form of weblogs. Since the defacto storage was an MPP database, and the value of such weblogs was unknown, more often than not these weblogs were stuffed into archive storage or deleted.

2002: In search for a better search engine, *Doug Cutting* and *Mike Cafarella* started work on an open source project called Nutch, the objective of which was to be a web scale crawler. Web-Scale was defined as billions of web pages and Doug and Mike were able to index hundreds of millions of web-pages, running on a handful of nodes and had a knack of falling down.

2004-2006: Google published a paper on the Google File System (GFS) (2003) and MapReduce (2004) demonstrating the backbone of their search engine being resilient to failures, and almost linearly scalable. Doug Cutting took particular interest in this development as he could see that GFS and MapReduce papers directly addressed Nutch's shortcomings. Doug Cutting added Map Reduce implementation to Nutch which ran on 20 nodes, and was much easier to program. Of course we are talking in comparative terms here.

2006-2008: Cutting went to work with Yahoo in 2006 who had lost the search crown to Google and were equally impressed by the GFS and MapReduce papers. The storage and processing parts of Nutch were spun out to form a separate project named Hadoop under AFS where as Nutch web crawler remained a separate project. Hadoop became a top-level Apache project in 2008. On February 19, 2008 Yahoo announced that its search index is run on a 10000 node Hadoop cluster (truly an amazing feat).

We haven't forget about the proprietary database vendors. the majority of them didn't expect Hadoop to change anything for them, as database vendors typically focused on relational data, which was smaller in volumes but higher in value. I was talking to a CTO of a major database vendor (will remain unnamed), and discussing this new and upcoming popular elephant (Hadoop of course! Thanks to Doug Cutting's son for choosing a sane name. I mean he could have chosen anything else, and you know how kids name things these days..). The CTO was quite adamant that the real value is in the relational data, which was the bread and butter of his company, and despite that fact that the relational data had huge volumes, it had less of a business value. This was more of a 80-20 rule for data, where from a size perspective unstructured data was 4 times the size of structured data (80-20), whereas the same structured data had 4 times the value of unstructured data. I would say that the relational database vendors massively underestimated the value of unstructured data back then.

Anyways, back to Hadoop: So, after the announcement by Yahoo, a lot of companies wanted to get a piece of the action. They realised something big was about to happen in the dataspace. Lots of interesting use cases started to appear in the Hadoop space, and the defacto compute engine on Hadoop, MapReduce wasn't able to meet all those expectations.

The MapReduce Conundrum: The original Hadoop comprised primarily HDFS and Map-Reduce as a compute engine. The original use case of web scale search meant that the architecture was primarily aimed at long-running batch jobs (typically single-pass jobs without iterations), like the original use case of indexing web pages. The core requirement of such a framework was scalability and fault-tolerance, as you don't want to restart a job that had been running for 3 days, having completed 95% of its work. Furthermore, the objective of MapReduce was to target acyclic data flows.

A typical MapReduce program is composed of a `Map()` operation and optionally a `Reduce()` operation, and any workload had to be converted to the MapReduce paradigm before you could get the benefit of Hadoop. Not only that majority of other open source projects on Hadoop also used MapReduce as a way to perform computation. For example: Hive and Pig Latin both generated MapReduce to operate on Big Data sets. The problem with the architecture of MapReduce was that the job output data from each step had to be store in a distributed system before the next step could begin. This meant that each iteration had to reload the data from the disk thus incurring a significant performance penalty. Furthermore, while typically design, for batch jobs, Hadoop has often been used to do exploratory analysis through SQL-like interfaces such as Pig and Hive. Each query incurs significant latency due to initial MapReduce job setup, and initial data read which often means increased wait times for the users.

Beginning of Spark: In June of 2011, *Matei Zaharia, Mosharaf Chowdhury, Michael J. Franklin, Scott Shenker* and *Ion Stoica* published a paper in which they proposed a framework that could outperform Hadoop 10 times in iterative machine learning jobs. The framework is now known as Spark. The paper aimed to solve two of the major inadequacies of the Hadoop/MR framework:

- Iterative jobs
- Interactive analysis

The idea that you can plug the gaps of map-reduce from an iterative and interactive analysis point of view, while maintaining its scalability and resilience meant that the platform could be used across a wide variety of use cases.

This created huge interest in Spark, particularly from communities of users who had become frustrated with the relatively slow response from MapReduce, particularly for interactive queries requests. Spark in 2015 became the most active open source project in Big Data, and had tons of new features of improvements during the course of the project. The community grew almost 300%, with attendances at Spark-Summit increasing from just 1,100 in 2014 to almost 4,000 in 2015. The number of meetup groups grew by a factor of 4, and the contributors to the project increased from just over a 100 in 2013 to 600 in 2015.

Spark is today the hottest technology for big data analytics. Numerous benchmarks have confirmed that it is the fastest engine out there. If you go to any Big data conference be it Strata + Hadoop World or Hadoop Summit, Spark is considered to be the technology for future.

Stack Overflow released the results of a 2016 developer survey (http://bit.ly/1MpdIlU) with responses from 56,033 engineers across 173 countries. Some of the facts related to Spark were pretty interesting. Spark was the leader in *Trending Tech* and the *Top-Paying Tech*.

Why are people so excited about Spark?

In addition to plugging MapReduce deficiencies, Spark provides three major things that make it really powerful:

- General engine with libraries for many data analysis tasks - includes built-in libraries for Streaming, SQL, machine learning and graph processing
- Access to diverse data sources, means it can connect to Hadoop, Cassandra, traditional SQL databases, and Cloud Storage including Amazon and OpenStack
- Last but not the least, Spark provides a simple unified API that means users have to learn just one API to get the benefit of the entire framework stack

We hope that this book gives you the foundation of understanding Spark as a framework, and helps you take the next step towards using it for your implementations.

What this book covers

Chapter 1, *Architecture and Installation*, will help you get started on the journey of learning Spark. This will walk you through key architectural components before helping you write your first Spark application.

Chapter 2, *Transformations and Actions with Spark RDDs*, will help you understand the basic constructs as Spark RDDs and help you understand the difference between transformations, actions, and lazy evaluation, and how you can share data.

Chapter 3, *ELT with Spark*, will help you with data loading, transformation, and saving it back to external storage systems.

Chapter 4, *Spark SQL*, will help you understand the intricacies of the DataFrame and Dataset API before a discussion of the under-the-hood power of the Catalyst optimizer and how it ensures that your client applications remain performant irrespective of your client AP.

Chapter 5, *Spark Streaming*, will help you understand the architecture of Spark Streaming, sliding window operations, caching, persistence, check-pointing, fault-tolerance before discussing structured streaming and how it revolutionizes Stream processing.

Chapter 6, *Machine Learning with Spark*, is where the rubber hits the road, and where you understand the basics of machine learning before looking at the various types of machine learning, and feature engineering utility functions, and finally looking at the algorithms provided by Spark MLlib API.

Chapter 7, *GraphX*, will help you understand the importance of Graph in today's world, before understanding terminology such vertex, edge, Motif etc. We will then look at some of the graph algorithms in GraphX and also talk about GraphFrames.

Chapter 8, *Operating in Clustered mode*, helps the user understand how Spark can be deployed as standalone, or with YARN or Mesos.

Chapter 9, *Building a Recommendation system*, will help the user understand the intricacies of a recommendation system before building one with an ALS model.

Chapter 10, *Customer Churn Predicting*, will help the user understand the importance of Churn prediction before using a random forest classifier to predict churn on a telecommunication dataset.

Appendix, *There's More with Spark*, is where we cover the topics around performance tuning, sizing your executors, and security before walking the user through setting up PySpark with Jupyter notebook.

What you need for this book

You will need Spark 2.0, which you can download from Apache Spark website. We have used few different configurations, but you can essentially run most of these examples inside a virtual machine with 4-8GB of RAM, and 10 GB of available disk space.

Who this book is for

This book is for people who have heard of Spark, and want to understand more. This is a beginner-level book for people who want to have some hands-on exercise with the fastest growing open source project. This book provides ample reading and links to exciting YouTube videos for additional exploration of the topics.

Conventions

In this book, you will find a number of text styles that distinguish between different kinds of information. Here are some examples of these styles and an explanation of their meaning.

Code words in text, database table names, folder names, filenames, file extensions, pathnames, dummy URLs, user input, and Twitter handles are shown as follows: "We can include other contexts through the use of the `include` directive."

A block of code is set as follows:

```
[default]
exten => s,1,Dial(Zap/1|30)
exten => s,2,Voicemail(u100)
exten => s,102,Voicemail(b100)
exten => i,1,Voicemail(s0)
```

When we wish to draw your attention to a particular part of a code block, the relevant lines or items are set in bold:

```
[default]
exten => s,1,Dial(Zap/1|30)
exten => s,2,Voicemail(u100)
exten => s,102,Voicemail(b100)
exten => i,1,Voicemail(s0)
```

Any command-line input or output is written as follows:

```
# cp /usr/src/asterisk-addons/configs/cdr_mysql.conf.sample
     /etc/asterisk/cdr_mysql.conf
```

New terms and **important words** are shown in bold. Words that you see on the screen, for example, in menus or dialog boxes, appear in the text like this: "Clicking the **Next** button moves you to the next screen."

Warnings or important notes appear in a box like this.

Tips and tricks appear like this.

Reader feedback

Feedback from our readers is always welcome. Let us know what you think about this book-what you liked or disliked. Reader feedback is important for us as it helps us develop titles that you will really get the most out of. To send us general feedback, simply e-mail `feedback@packtpub.com`, and mention the book's title in the subject of your message. If there is a topic that you have expertise in and you are interested in either writing or contributing to a book, see our author guide at `www.packtpub.com/authors`.

Customer support

Now that you are the proud owner of a Packt book, we have a number of things to help you to get the most from your purchase.

Downloading the example code

You can download the example code files for this book from your account at `http://www.packtpub.com`. If you purchased this book elsewhere, you can visit `http://www.packtpub.com/support` and register to have the files e-mailed directly to you.

You can download the code files by following these steps:

1. Log in or register to our website using your e-mail address and password.
2. Hover the mouse pointer on the **SUPPORT** tab at the top.
3. Click on **Code Downloads & Errata**.
4. Enter the name of the book in the **Search** box.
5. Select the book for which you're looking to download the code files.
6. Choose from the drop-down menu where you purchased this book from.
7. Click on **Code Download**.

Once the file is downloaded, please make sure that you unzip or extract the folder using the latest version of:

- WinRAR / 7-Zip for Windows
- Zipeg / iZip / UnRarX for Mac
- 7-Zip / PeaZip for Linux

The code bundle for the book is also hosted on GitHub at `https://github.com/PacktPubl ishing/Learning-Apache-Spark-2`. We also have other code bundles from our rich catalog of books and videos available at `https://github.com/PacktPublishing/`. Check them out!

Errata

Although we have taken every care to ensure the accuracy of our content, mistakes do happen. If you find a mistake in one of our books-maybe a mistake in the text or the code-we would be grateful if you could report this to us. By doing so, you can save other readers from frustration and help us improve subsequent versions of this book. If you find any errata, please report them by visiting `http://www.packtpub.com/submit-errata`, selecting your book, clicking on the **Errata Submission Form** link, and entering the details of your errata. Once your errata are verified, your submission will be accepted and the errata will be uploaded to our website or added to any list of existing errata under the Errata section of that title.

To view the previously submitted errata, go to `https://www.packtpub.com/books/conten t/support`and enter the name of the book in the search field. The required information will appear under the **Errata** section.

Piracy

Piracy of copyrighted material on the Internet is an ongoing problem across all media. At Packt, we take the protection of our copyright and licenses very seriously. If you come across any illegal copies of our works in any form on the Internet, please provide us with the location address or website name immediately so that we can pursue a remedy.

Please contact us at `copyright@packtpub.com` with a link to the suspected pirated material.

We appreciate your help in protecting our authors and our ability to bring you valuable content.

Questions

If you have a problem with any aspect of this book, you can contact us at `questions@packtpub.com`, and we will do our best to address the problem.

1
Architecture and Installation

This chapter intends to provide and describe the big-picture around Spark, which includes Spark architecture. You will be taken from the higher-level details of the framework to installing Spark and writing your very first program on Spark.

We'll cover the following core topics in this chapter. If you are already familiar with these topics please feel free to jump to the next chapter on Spark: **Resilient Distributed Datasets (RDDs)**:

Apache Spark architecture overview:

- Apache Spark deployment
- Installing Apache Spark
- Writing your first Spark program
- Submitting applications

Apache Spark architecture overview

Apache Spark is being an open source distributed data processing engine for clusters, which provides a unified programming model engine across different types data processing workloads and platforms.

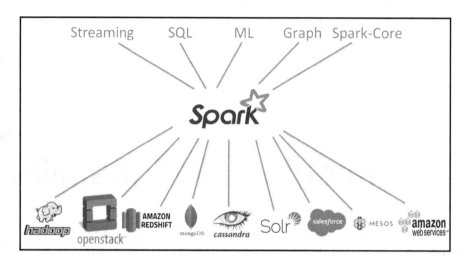

Figure 1.1: Apache Spark Unified Stack

At the core of the project is a set of APIs for **Streaming**, **SQL**, **Machine Learning** (**ML**), and **Graph**. Spark community supports the Spark project by providing connectors to various open source and proprietary data storage engines. Spark also has the ability to run on a variety of cluster managers like YARN and Mesos, in addition to the Standalone cluster manager which comes bundled with Spark for standalone installation. This is thus a marked difference from Hadoop eco-system where Hadoop provides a complete platform in terms of storage formats, compute engine, cluster manager, and so on. Spark has been designed with the single goal of being an optimized compute engine. This therefore allows you to run Spark on a variety of cluster managers including being run standalone, or being plugged into YARN and Mesos. Similarly, Spark does not have its own storage, but it can connect to a wide number of storage engines.

Currently Spark APIs are available in some of the most common languages including Scala, Java, Python, and R.

Let's start by going through various API's available in Spark.

Spark-core

At the heart of the Spark architecture is the core engine of Spark, commonly referred to as spark-core, which forms the foundation of this powerful architecture. Spark-core provides services such as managing the memory pool, scheduling of tasks on the cluster (Spark works as a **Massively Parallel Processing** (**MPP**) system when deployed in cluster mode), recovering failed jobs, and providing support to work with a wide variety of storage systems such as HDFS, S3, and so on.

> Spark-Core provides a full scheduling component for Standalone Scheduling: Code is available at: `https://github.com/apache/spark/tre e/master/core/src/main/scala/org/apache/spark/scheduler`

Spark-Core abstracts the users of the APIs from lower-level technicalities of working on a cluster. Spark-Core also provides the RDD APIs which are the basis of other higher-level APIs, and are the core programming elements on Spark. We'll talk about RDD, DataFrame and Dataset APIs later in this book.

> MPP systems generally use a large number of processors (on separate hardware or virtualized) to perform a set of operations in parallel. The objective of the MPP systems is to divide work into smaller task pieces and running them in parallel to increase in throughput time.

Spark SQL

Spark SQL is one of the most popular modules of Spark designed for structured and semi-structured data processing. Spark SQL allows users to query structured data inside Spark programs using SQL or the DataFrame and the Dataset API, which is usable in Java, Scala, Python, and R. Because of the fact that the DataFrame API provides a uniform way to access a variety of data sources, including Hive datasets, Avro, Parquet, ORC, JSON, and JDBC, users should be able to connect to any data source the same way, and join across these multiple sources together. The usage of Hive meta store by Spark SQL gives the user full compatibility with existing Hive data, queries, and UDFs. Users can seamlessly run their current Hive workload without modification on Spark.

Spark SQL can also be accessed through `spark-sql` shell, and existing business tools can connect via standard JDBC and ODBC interfaces.

Spark streaming

More than 50% of users consider **Spark Streaming** to be the most important component of Apache Spark. Spark Streaming is a module of Spark that enables processing of data arriving in passive or live streams of data. Passive streams can be from static files that you choose to stream to your Spark cluster. This can include all sorts of data ranging from web server logs, social-media activity (following a particular Twitter hashtag), sensor data from your car/phone/home, and so on. Spark-streaming provides a bunch of APIs that help you to create streaming applications in a way similar to how you would create a batch job, with minor tweaks.

As of Spark 2.0, the philosophy behind Spark Streaming is not to reason about streaming and building data application as in the case of a traditional data source. This means the data from sources is continuously appended to the existing tables, and all the operations are run on the new window. A single API lets the users create batch or streaming applications, with the only difference being that a table in batch applications is finite, while the table for a streaming job is considered to be infinite.

MLlib

MLlib is **Machine Learning Library** for Spark, if you remember from the preface, iterative algorithms are one of the key drivers behind the creation of Spark, and most machine learning algorithms perform iterative processing in one way or another.

 Machine learning is a type of **artificial intelligence** (**AI**) that provides computers with the ability to learn without being explicitly programmed. Machine learning focuses on the development of computer programs that can teach themselves to grow and change when exposed to new data.

Spark MLlib allows developers to use Spark API and build machine learning algorithms by tapping into a number of data sources including HDFS, HBase, Cassandra, and so on. Spark is super fast with iterative computing and it performs 100 times better than MapReduce. Spark MLlib contains a number of algorithms and utilities including, but not limited to, logistic regression, **Support Vector Machine** (**SVM**), classification and regression trees, random forest and gradient-boosted trees, recommendation via ALS, clustering via K-Means, **Principal Component Analysis** (**PCA**), and many others.

GraphX

GraphX is an API designed to manipulate graphs. The graphs can range from a graph of web pages linked to each other via hyperlinks to a social network graph on Twitter connected by followers or retweets, or a Facebook friends list.

> Graph theory is a study of graphs, which are mathematical structures used to model pairwise relations between objects. A graph is made up of vertices (nodes/points), which are connected by edges (arcs/lines).
>
> – Wikipedia.org

Spark provides a built-in library for graph manipulation, which therefore allows the developers to seamlessly work with both graphs and collections by combining ETL, discovery analysis, and iterative graph manipulation in a single workflow. The ability to combine transformations, machine learning, and graph computation in a single system at high speed makes Spark one of the most flexible and powerful frameworks out there. The ability of Spark to retain the speed of computation with the standard features of fault-tolerance makes it especially handy for big data problems. Spark GraphX has a number of built-in graph algorithms including **PageRank**, **Connected components**, **Label propagation**, **SVD++**, and **Triangle counter**.

Spark deployment

Apache Spark runs on both Windows and Unix-like systems (for example, Linux and Mac OS). If you are starting with Spark you can run it locally on a single machine. Spark requires Java 7+, Python 2.6+, and R 3.1+. If you would like to use Scala API (the language in which Spark was written), you need at least Scala version 2.10.x.

Spark can also run in a clustered mode, using which Spark can run both by itself, and on several existing cluster managers. You can deploy Spark on any of the following cluster managers, and the list is growing everyday due to active community support:

- Hadoop YARN
- Apache Mesos
- Standalone scheduler
- **Yet Another Resource Negotiator (YARN)** is one of the key features including a redesigned resource manager thus splitting out the scheduling and resource management capabilities from original Map Reduce in Hadoop .

- Apache Mesos is an open source cluster manager that was developed at the University of California, Berkeley. It provides efficient resource isolation and sharing across distributed applications, or frameworks.

Installing Apache Spark

As mentioned in the earlier pages, while Spark can be deployed on a cluster, you can also run it in local mode on a single machine.

In this chapter, we are going to download and install Apache Spark on a Linux machine and run it in local mode. Before we do anything we need to download Apache Spark from Apache's web page for the Spark project:

1. Use your recommended browser to navigate to
   http://spark.apache.org/downloads.html.
2. Choose a Spark release. You'll find all previous Spark releases listed here. We'll go with release 2.0.0 (at the time of writing, only the preview edition was available).
3. You can download Spark source code, which can be built for several versions of Hadoop, or download it for a specific Hadoop version. In this case, we are going to download one that has been pre-built for Hadoop 2.7 or later.
4. You can also choose to download directly or from among a number of different Mirrors. For the purpose of our exercise we'll use direct download and download it to our preferred location.

> If you are using Windows, please remember to use a pathname without any spaces.

5. The file that you have downloaded is a compressed TAR archive. You need to extract the archive.

> The TAR utility is generally used to unpack TAR files. If you don't have TAR, you might want to download that from the repository or use 7-ZIP, which is also one of my favorite utilities.

6. Once unpacked, you will see a number of directories/files. Here's what you would typically see when you list the contents of the unpacked directory:

> The `bin` folder contains a number of executable shell scripts such as `pypark`, `sparkR`, `spark-shell`, `spark-sql`, and `spark-submit`. All of these executables are used to interact with Spark, and we will be using most if not all of these.

7. If you see my particular download of spark you will find a folder called `yarn`. The example below is a Spark that was built for Hadoop version 2.7 which comes with YARN as a cluster manager.

```
spark@ubuntu:/spark/spark-2.0.0$ ls -la
total 112
drwxr-xr-x 12 spark spark  4096 May 17 18:40 .
drwxr-xr-x  3 spark root   4096 Jun 18 01:25 ..
drwxr-xr-x  2 spark spark  4096 May 17 18:40 bin
drwxr-xr-x  2 spark spark  4096 May 17 18:40 conf
drwxr-xr-x  4 spark spark  4096 May 17 18:40 data
drwxr-xr-x  4 spark spark  4096 May 17 18:40 examples
drwxr-xr-x  2 spark spark 12288 May 17 18:40 jars
-rw-r--r--  1 spark spark 17721 May 17 18:40 LICENSE
drwxr-xr-x  2 spark spark  4096 May 17 18:40 licenses
-rw-r--r--  1 spark spark 24737 May 17 18:40 NOTICE
drwxr-xr-x  6 spark spark  4096 May 17 18:40 python
drwxr-xr-x  3 spark spark  4096 May 17 18:40 R
-rw-r--r--  1 spark spark  3631 May 17 18:40 README.md
-rw-r--r--  1 spark spark   128 May 17 18:40 RELEASE
drwxr-xr-x  2 spark spark  4096 May 17 18:40 sbin
drwxr-xr-x  2 spark spark  4096 May 17 18:40 yarn
```

Figure 1.2: Spark folder contents

We'll start by running Spark shell, which is a very simple way to get started with Spark and learn the API. Spark shell is a Scala **Read-Evaluate-Print-Loop** (REPL), and one of the few REPLs available with Spark which also include Python and R.

You should change to the Spark download directory and run the Spark shell as follows:
`/bin/spark-shell`

```
spark@ubuntu:/spark/spark-2.0.05 ./bin/spark-shell
Using Spark's default log4j profile: org/apache/spark/log4j-defaults.properties
Setting default log level to "WARN".
To adjust logging level use sc.setLogLevel(newLevel).
16/06/18 04:33:50 WARN NativeCodeLoader: Unable to load native-hadoop library for your platform... using builtin-java classes where applica
ble
16/06/18 04:33:51 WARN Utils: Your hostname, ubuntu resolves to a loopback address: 127.0.1.1; using 192.168.193.143 instead (on interface
ens33)
16/06/18 04:33:51 WARN Utils: Set SPARK_LOCAL_IP if you need to bind to another address
16/06/18 04:33:56 WARN AbstractHandler: No Server set for org.spark_project.jetty.server.handler.ErrorHandler@29f38091
Spark context Web UI available at http://192.168.193.143:4040
Spark context available as 'sc' (master = local[*], app id = local-1466249636644).
Spark session available as 'spark'.
Welcome to


    ____              __
   / __/__  ___ _____/ /__
  _\ \/ _ \/ _ `/ __/  '_/
 /___/ .__/\_,_/_/ /_/\_\   version 2.0.0-preview
    /_/

Using Scala version 2.11.8 (OpenJDK 64-Bit Server VM, Java 1.8.0_91)
Type in expressions to have them evaluated.
Type :help for more information.

scala>
```

Figure 1.3: Starting Spark shell

We now have Spark running in standalone mode. We'll discuss the details of the deployment architecture a bit later in this chapter, but now let's kick start some basic Spark programming to appreciate the power and simplicity of the Spark framework.

Writing your first Spark program

As mentioned before, you can use Spark with Python, Scala, Java, and R. We have different executable shell scripts available in the `/spark/bin` directory and so far, we have just looked at Spark shell, which can be used to explore data using Scala. The following executables are available in the `spark/bin` directory. We'll use most of these during the course of this book:

- `beeline`
- `PySpark`
- `run-example`
- `spark-class`
- `sparkR`
- `spark-shell`
- `spark-sql`

- `spark-submit`

Whatever shell you use, based on your past experience or aptitude, you have to deal with one abstract that is your handle to the data available on the spark cluster, be it local or spread over thousands of machines. The abstraction we are referring to here is called **Resilient Distributed Datasets** (**RDD**), and is a fundamental unit of your data and computation in Spark. As the name indicates, among others, they have two key features:

- **They are resilient**: If the data in memory is lost, an RDD can be recreated
- **They are distributed**: You can Java objects or Python objects that are distributed across clusters

`Chapter 2`, *Transformations and Actions with Spark RDDs*, will walk through the intricacies of RDD while we will also discuss other higher-level APIs built on top of RDDs, such as Dataframes and machine learning pipelines.

Let's quickly demonstrate how you can explore a file on your local file system using Spark. Earlier in *Figure 1.2*, when we were exploring spark folder contents we saw a file called `README.md`, which contains an overview of Spark, the link to online documentation, and other assets available to the developers and analysts. We are going to read that file, and convert it into an RDD.

Scala shell examples

To enter Scala shell, please submit the following command:

```
./bin/spark-shell
```

Using the Scala shell, run the following code:

```
val textFile = sc.textFile("README.md") # Create an RDD called tTextFile
```

At the prompt you immediately get a confirmation on the type of variable created:

```
scala> val textFile= sc.textFile("README.md")
textFile: org.apache.spark.rdd.RDD[String] = README.md MapPartitionsRDD[3] at textFile at <console>:24
```

Figure 1.4: Creating a simple RDD

If you want to see the type of operations available on the RDD, at Command Prompt write the variable name `textFile` in this case, and press the *Tab* key. You'll see the following list of operations/actions available:

```
scala> textFile.take(7)
res16: Array[String] = Array(# Apache Spark, "", Spark is a fast and general cluster computing system for Big Data. It provides, high-level
  APIs in Scala, Java, Python, and R, and an optimized engine that, supports general computation graphs for data analysis. It also supports
a, rich set of higher-level tools including Spark SQL for SQL and DataFrames,, MLlib for machine learning, GraphX for graph processing,)
```

Figure 1.5: Operations on String RDDs

Since our objective is to do some basic exploratory analysis, we will look at some of the basic actions on this RDD.

 RDD's can have actions or transformations called upon them, but the result of each is different. Transformations result in new RDD's being created while actions result in the RDD to be evaluated, and return the values back to the client.

Let's look at the top seven lines from this RDD:

```
textFile.take(7) # Returns the top 7 lines from the file as an Array of
Strings
```

The result of this looks something like the following:

```
scala> textFile.
!=                 count               foreachPartitionAsync  mapPartitions           reduce             toLocalIterator
##                 countApprox         formatted              mapPartitionsWithIndex  repartition        toString
+                  countApproxDistinct getCheckpointFile      max                     sample             top
++                 countAsync          getClass               min                     saveAsObjectFile   treeAggregate
->                 countByValue        getNumPartitions       name                    saveAsTextFile     treeReduce
==                 countByValueApprox  getStorageLevel        ne                      setName            union
aggregate          dependencies        glom                   notify                  sortBy             unpersist
asInstanceOf       distinct            groupBy                notifyAll               sparkContext       wait
cache              ensuring            hashCode               partitioner             subtract           zip
canEqual           eq                  id                     partitions              synchronized       zipPartitions
cartesian          equals              intersection           persist                 take               zipWithIndex
checkpoint         filter              isCheckpointed         pipe                    takeAsync          zipWithUniqueId
coalesce           first               isEmpty                preferredLocations      takeOrdered        →
collect            flatMap             isInstanceOf           productArity            takeSample
collectAsync       fold                iterator               productElement          toDF
compute            foreach             keyBy                  productIterator         toDS
context            foreachAsync        localCheckpoint        productPrefix           toDebugString
copy               foreachPartition    map                    randomSplit             toJavaRDD
```

Figure 1.6: First seven lines from the file

Alternatively, let's look at the total number of lines in the file, another action available as a list of actions on a string RDD. Please note that each line from the file is considered a separate item in the RDD:

```
textFile.count() # Returns the total number of items
```

```
scala> textFile.count()
res17: Long = 97
```

Figure 1.7: Counting RDD elements

We've looked at some actions, so now let's try to look at some transformations available as a part of string RDD operations. As mentioned earlier, transformations are operations that return another RDD as a result.

Let's try to filter the data file, and find out the data lines with the keyword Apache:

```
val linesWithApache = textFile.filter(line => line.contains("Apache"))
```

This transformation will return another string RDD.

You can also chain multiple transformations and actions together. For example, the following will filter the text file on the lines that contain the word Apache, and then return the number of such lines in the resultant RDD:

```
textFile.filter(line => line.contains("Apache")).count()
```

```
scala> val linesWithApache=textFile.filter(line => line.contains("Apache"))
linesWithApache: org.apache.spark.rdd.RDD[String] = MapPartitionsRDD[6] at filter at <console>:26

scala> linesWithApache.first()
res20: String = # Apache Spark

scala> linesWithApache.count()
res21: Long = 2

scala> textFile.filter(line => line.contains("Apache")).count()
res22: Long = 2
```

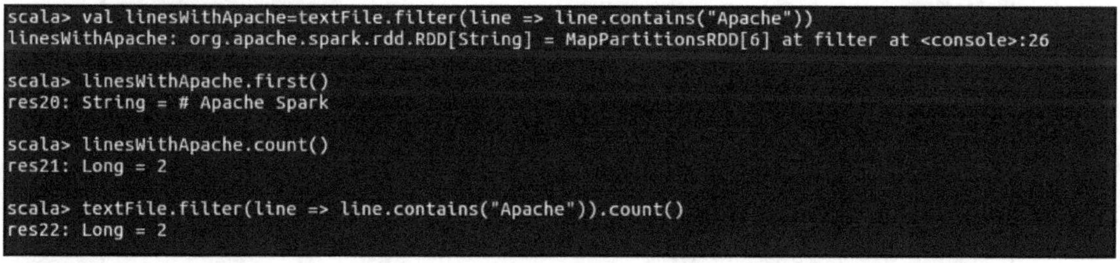

Figure 1.8: Transformations and actions

You can monitor the jobs that are running on this cluster from Spark UI, which is running by default at port 4040.

If you navigate your browser to `http://localhost:4040`, you should see the following Spark driver program UI:

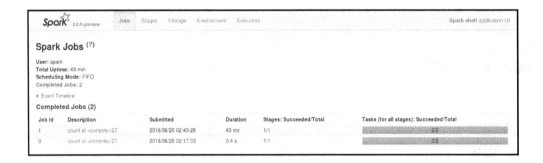

Figure 1.9: Spark driver program UI

Depending on how many jobs you have run, you will see a list of jobs based on their status. The UI gives you an overview of the type of job, its submission date/time, the amount of time it took, and the number of stages that it had to pass through. If you want to look at the details of the job, simply click the description of the job, which will take you to another web page that details all the completed stages. You might want to look at individual stages of the job. If you click through the individual stage, you can get detailed metrics about your job.

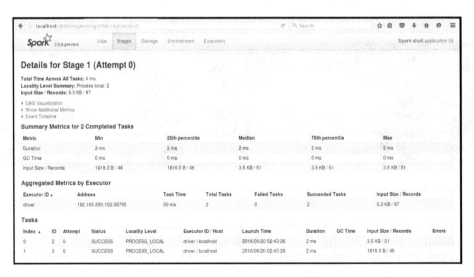

Figure 1.10: Summary metrics for the job

We'll go through **DAG Visualization, Event Timeline**, and other aspects of the UI in a lot more detail in later chapters, but the objective of showing this to you was to highlight how you can monitor your jobs during and after execution.

Before we go any further with examples, let's replay the same examples from a Python Shell for Python programmers.

Python shell examples

For those of you who are more comfortable with Python, rather than Scala, we will walk through the previous examples from the Python shell too.

To enter Python shell, please submit the following command:

```
./bin/pyspark
```

You'll see an output similar to the following:

```
spark@ubuntu:/spark/spark-2.0.0$ ./bin/pyspark
Python 2.7.11+ (default, Apr 17 2016, 14:00:29)
[GCC 5.3.1 20160413] on linux2
Type "help", "copyright", "credits" or "license" for more information.
Using Spark's default log4j profile: org/apache/spark/log4j-defaults.properties
Setting default log level to "WARN".
To adjust logging level use sc.setLogLevel(newLevel).
16/06/20 02:28:07 WARN NativeCodeLoader: Unable to load native-hadoop library for your platform... using builtin-java classes whe
re applicable
16/06/20 02:28:07 WARN Utils: Your hostname, ubuntu resolves to a loopback address: 127.0.1.1; using 192.168.200.102 instead (on
interface ens34)
16/06/20 02:28:07 WARN Utils: Set SPARK_LOCAL_IP if you need to bind to another address
16/06/20 02:28:08 WARN AbstractHandler: No Server set for org.spark_project.jetty.server.handler.ErrorHandler@59717f5c
16/06/20 02:28:08 WARN Utils: Service 'SparkUI' could not bind on port 4040. Attempting port 4041.
16/06/20 02:28:08 WARN AbstractHandler: No Server set for org.spark_project.jetty.server.handler.ErrorHandler@233459e5
Welcome to
      ____              __
     / __/__  ___ _____/ /__
    _\ \/ _ \/ _ `/ __/  '_/
   /__ / .__/\_,_/_/ /_/\_\   version 2.0.0-preview
      /_/

Using Python version 2.7.11+ (default, Apr 17 2016 14:00:29)
SparkSession available as 'spark'.
>>>
```

Figure 1.11: Spark Python shell

If you look closely at the output, you will see that the framework tried to start the Spark UI at port *4040*, but was unable to do so. It has instead started the UI at port *4041*. Can you guess why? The reason is because we already have port 4040 occupied, and Spark will continue trying ports after port 4040 until it finds one available to bind the UI to.

Let's do some basic data manipulation using Python at the Python shell. Once again we will read the README.md file:

```
textFile = sc.textFile("README.md") //Create and RDD called textFile by
reading the contents of README.md file
```

Let's read the top seven lines from the file:

```
textFile.take(7)
```

Let's look at the total number of lines in the file:

```
textFile.count()
```

You'll see output similar to the following:

```
>>> textFile = sc.textFile("README.md")
>>> textFile.take(7)
[u'# Apache Spark', u'', u'Spark is a fast and general cluster computing system for Big Data. It provides', u'high-level APIs in
Scala, Java, Python, and R, and an optimized engine that', u'supports general computation graphs for data analysis. It also suppo
rts a', u'rich set of higher-level tools including Spark SQL for SQL and DataFrames,', u'MLlib for machine learning, GraphX for g
raph processing,']
>>> textFile.count()
97
```

Figure 1.12: Exploratory data analysis with Python

As we demonstrated with Scala shell, we can also filter data using Python by applying transformations and chain transformations with actions.

Use the following code to apply transformation on the dataset. Remember, a transformation results in another RDD.

Here's a code to apply transformation, which is filtering the input dataset, and identifying lines that contain the word Apache:

```
linesWithApache = textFile.filter(lambda line: "Apache" in line) //Find
lines with Apache
```

Once we have obtained the filtered RDD, we can apply an action to it:

```
linesWithApache.count() //Count number of items
```

Let's chain the transformation and action together:

```
textFile.filter(lambda line: "Apache" in line).count() //Chain
transformation and action together
```

```
>>> linesWithApache = textFile.filter(lambda line: "Apache" in line)
>>> linesWithApache.count()
2
>>> textFile.filter(lambda line: "Apache" in line).count()
2
```

Figure 1.13: Chaining transformations and actions in Python

If you are unfamiliar with lambda functions in Python, please don't worry about it at this moment. The objective of this demonstration is to show you how easy it is to explore data with Spark. We'll cover this in much more detail in later chapters.

If you want to have a look at the driver program UI, you will find that the summary metrics are pretty much similar to what we saw when the execution was done using Scala shell.

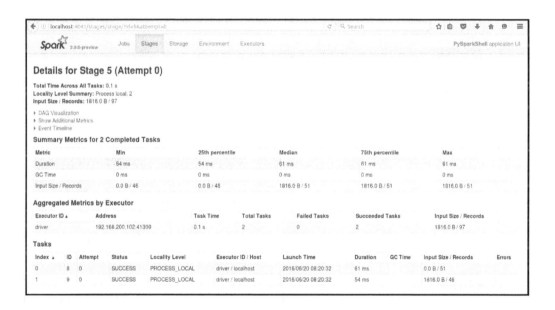

Figure 1.14: Spark UI demonstrating summary metrics.

We have now gone through some basic Spark programs, so it might be worth understanding a bit more about the Spark architecture. In the next section, we will dig deeper into Spark architecture before moving onto the next chapter where we will have a lot more code examples explaining the various concepts around RDDs.

Spark architecture

Let's have a look at Apache Spark architecture, including a high level overview and a brief description of some of the key software components.

High level overview

At the high level, Apache Spark application architecture consists of the following key software components and it is important to understand each one of them to get to grips with the intricacies of the framework:

- Driver program
- Master node
- Worker node
- Executor
- Tasks
- SparkContext
- SQL context
- Spark session

Here's an overview of how some of these software components fit together within the overall architecture:

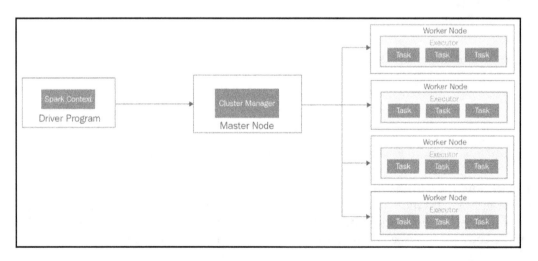

Figure 1.15: Apache Spark application architecture – Standalone mode

Driver program

Driver program is the main program of your Spark application. The machine where the Spark application process (the one that creates **SparkContext** and **Spark Session**) is running is called the **Driver node**, and the process is called the **Driver process**. The driver program communicates with the **Cluster Manager** to distribute tasks to the executors.

Cluster Manager

A cluster manager as the name indicates manages a cluster, and as discussed earlier Spark has the ability to work with a multitude of cluster managers including YARN, Mesos and a Standalone cluster manager. A standalone cluster manager consists of two long running daemons, one on the master node, and one on each of the worker nodes. We'll talk more about the cluster managers and deployment models in Chapter 8, *Operating in Clustered Mode*.

Worker

If you are familiar with Hadoop, a **Worker Node** is something similar to a slave node. Worker machines are the machines where the actual work is happening in terms of execution inside Spark executors. This process reports the available resources on the node to the master node. Typically each node in a Spark cluster except the master runs a worker process. We normally start one spark worker daemon per worker node, which then starts and monitors executors for the applications.

Executors

The master allocates the resources and uses the workers running across the cluster to create **Executors** for the driver. The driver can then use these executors to run its tasks. Executors are only launched when a job execution starts on a worker node. Each application has its own executor processes, which can stay up for the duration of the application and run tasks in multiple threads. This also leads to the side effect of application isolation and non-sharing of data between multiple applications. Executors are responsible for running tasks and keeping the data in memory or disk storage across them.

Tasks

A task is a unit of work that will be sent to one executor. Specifically speaking, it is a command sent from the driver program to an executor by serializing your Function object. The executor deserializes the command (as it is part of your JAR that has already been loaded) and executes it on a partition.

A partition is a logical chunk of data distributed across a Spark cluster. In most cases Spark would be reading data out of a distributed storage, and would partition the data in order to parallelize the processing across the cluster. For example, if you are reading data from HDFS, a partition would be created for each HDFS partition. Partitions are important because Spark will run one task for each partition. This therefore implies that the number of partitions are important. Spark therefore attempts to set the number of partitions automatically unless you specify the number of partitions manually e.g. `sc.parallelize (data,numPartitions)`.

SparkContext

SparkContext is the entry point of the Spark session. It is your connection to the Spark cluster and can be used to create RDDs, accumulators, and broadcast variables on that cluster. It is preferable to have one `SparkContext` active per JVM, and hence you should call `stop()` on the active `SparkContext` before you create a new one. You might have noticed previously that in the local mode, whenever we start a Python or Scala shell we have a `SparkContext` object created automatically and the variable `sc` refers to the `SparkContext` object. We did not need to create the `SparkContext`, but instead started using it to create RDDs from text files.

Spark Session

Spark session is the entry point to programming with Spark with the dataset and DataFrame API.

Apache Spark cluster manager types

As discussed previously, Apache Spark currently supports three Cluster managers:

- Standalone cluster manager
- ApacheMesos
- Hadoop YARN

We'll look at setting these up in much more detail in Chapter 8, *Operating in Clustered Mode*, which talks about the operation in a clustered mode.

Building standalone applications with Apache Spark

Until now we have used Spark for exploratory analysis, using Scala and Python shells. Spark can also be used in standalone applications that can run in Java, Scala, Python, or R. As we saw earlier, Spark shell and PySpark provide you with a SparkContext. However, when you are using an application, you need to initialize your own SparkContext. Once you have a SparkContext reference, the remaining API remains exactly the same as for interactive query analysis. After all, it's the same object, just a different context in which it is running.

The exact method of using Spark with your application differs based on your preference of language. All Spark artifacts are hosted in Maven central. You can add a Maven dependency with the following coordinates:

```
groupId: org.apache.spark
artifactId: spark_core_2.10
version: 1.6.1
```

You can use Maven to build the project or alternatively use Scale/Eclipse IDE to add a Maven dependency to your project.

 Apache Maven is a build automation tool used primarily for Java projects. The word maven means *"accumulator of knowledge"* in Yiddish. Maven addresses the two core aspects of building software: first, it describes how the software is built and second, it describes its dependencies.

You can configure your IDE's to work with Spark. While many of the Spark developers use SBT or Maven on the command line, the most common IDE being used is IntelliJ IDEA. Community edition is free, and after that you can install JetBrains Scala Plugin. You can find detailed instructions on setting up either **IntelliJIDEA** or Eclipse to build Spark at http://bit.ly/28RDPFy.

Submitting applications

The spark submit script in Spark's `bin` directory, being the most commonly used method to submit Spark applications to a Spark cluster, can be used to launch applications on all supported cluster types. You will need to package all dependent projects with your application to enable Spark to distribute that across the cluster. You would need to create an assembly JAR (aka uber/fat JAR) file containing all of your code and relevant dependencies.

A spark application with its dependencies can be launched using the bin/spark-submit script. This script takes care of setting up the classpath and its dependencies, and it supports all the cluster-managers and deploy modes supported by Spark.

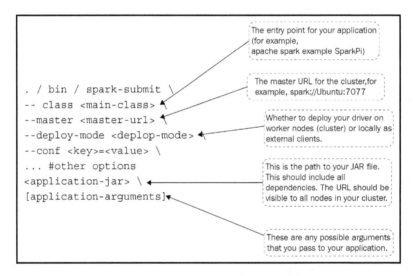

Figure 1.16: Spark submission template

For Python applications:

- Instead of `<application-jar>`, simply pass in your `.py` file.
- Add Python `.zip`, `.egg`, and `.py` files to the search path with − `.py` files.

Deployment strategies

- **Client mode:** This is commonly used when your application is located near to your cluster. In this mode, the driver application is launched as a part of the spark-submit process, which acts as a client to the cluster. The input and output of the application is passed on to the console. The mode is suitable when your gateway machine is physically collocated with your worker machines, and is used in applications such as Spark shell that involve REPL. This is the default mode.
- **Cluster mode:** This is useful when your application is submitted from a machine far from the worker machines (for example, locally on your laptop) to minimize network latency between the drivers and the executors. Currently only YARN supports cluster mode for Python applications. The following table shows that the combination of cluster managers, deployment managers, and usage are not supported in *Spark 2.0.0*:

Cluster Manager	Deployment Mode	Application Type	Support
MESOS	Cluster	R	Not Supported
Standalone	Cluster	Python	Not Supported
Standalone	Cluster	R	Not Supported
Local	Cluster	–	Incompatible
–	Cluster	Spark-Shell	Not applicable
–	Cluster	Sql-Shell	Not Applicable
–	Cluster	Thrift Server	Not Applicable

Running Spark examples

Spark comes with packaged examples for Java, Python, Scala, and R. We'll demonstrate how you can run a program provided in the examples directory.

As we only have a local installation, we'll run the Spark PI example locally on 4 cores. The examples are available at the Apache Spark GitHub page http://bit.ly/28S1hDY. We've taken an excerpt out of the example to explain how SparkContext is initialized:

```
val conf = new SparkConf().setAppName("Spark Pi")
val spark = new SparkContext(conf)
```

The example comes packaged with Spark binaries. The code can be downloaded from GitHub too. Looking closely at the code you will realize that we instantiate our own `SparkContext` object from a `SparkConf` object. The application name `Spark PI` will appear in the Spark UI as a running application during the execution, and will help you track the status of your job. Remember, this is in stark contrast to the spark-shell where a `SparkContext` is automatically instantiated and passed as a reference.

Let's run this example with Spark submit script:

```
spark@ubuntu:/spark/spark-2.0.0-preview$ ./bin/spark-submit \
> --class org.apache.spark.examples.SparkPi \
> --master local[4] \
> examples/target/original-spark-examples_2.11-2.0.0-preview.jar \
> 100
Using Spark's default log4j profile: org/apache/spark/log4j-defaults.properties
16/06/25 03:13:45 INFO SparkContext: Running Spark version 2.0.0-preview
16/06/25 03:13:45 WARN NativeCodeLoader: Unable to load native-hadoop library for your platform... using builtin-java classes where applicable
16/06/25 03:13:45 WARN Utils: Your hostname, ubuntu resolves to a loopback address: 127.0.1.1; using 192.168.193.143 instead (on interface ens33)
16/06/25 03:13:45 WARN Utils: Set SPARK_LOCAL_IP if you need to bind to another address
16/06/25 03:13:45 INFO SecurityManager: Changing view acls to: spark
16/06/25 03:13:45 INFO SecurityManager: Changing modify acls to: spark
16/06/25 03:13:45 INFO SecurityManager: Changing view acls groups to:
16/06/25 03:13:45 INFO SecurityManager: Changing modify acls groups to:
16/06/25 03:13:45 INFO SecurityManager: SecurityManager: authentication disabled; ui acls disabled; users  with view permissions: Set(spark); groups wi
th view permissions: Set(); users  with modify permissions: Set(spark); groups with modify permissions: Set()
16/06/25 03:13:45 INFO Utils: Successfully started service 'sparkDriver' on port 41598.
```

The log of the script spans over multiple pages, so we will skip over the intermediate manipulation step and go to the part where the output is printed. Remember in this case we are running `Spark Pi`, which prints out a value of `Pi`. Here's the second part of the log:

```
16/06/25 03:13:59 INFO TaskSetManager: Finished task 96.0 in stage 0.0 (TID 96) in 74 ms on localhost (99/100)
16/06/25 03:13:59 INFO TaskSetManager: Finished task 97.0 in stage 0.0 (TID 97) in 74 ms on localhost (100/100)
16/06/25 03:13:59 INFO TaskSchedulerImpl: Removed TaskSet 0.0, whose tasks have all completed, from pool
16/06/25 03:13:59 INFO DAGScheduler: ResultStage 0 (reduce at SparkPi.scala:36) finished in 11.871 s
16/06/25 03:13:59 INFO DAGScheduler: Job 0 finished: reduce at SparkPi.scala:36, took 12.146851 s
Pi is roughly 3.1422268
16/06/25 03:13:59 INFO SparkUI: Stopped Spark web UI at http://192.168.193.143:4040
16/06/25 03:13:59 INFO MapOutputTrackerMasterEndpoint: MapOutputTrackerMasterEndpoint stopped!
16/06/25 03:13:59 INFO MemoryStore: MemoryStore cleared
16/06/25 03:13:59 INFO BlockManager: BlockManager stopped
16/06/25 03:13:59 INFO BlockManagerMaster: BlockManagerMaster stopped
16/06/25 03:13:59 INFO OutputCommitCoordinator$OutputCommitCoordinatorEndpoint: OutputCommitCoordinator stopped!
16/06/25 03:13:59 INFO SparkContext: Successfully stopped SparkContext
16/06/25 03:13:59 INFO ShutdownHookManager: Shutdown hook called
16/06/25 03:13:59 INFO ShutdownHookManager: Deleting directory /tmp/spark-eecbd1a3-e94e-4144-bbae-c239262723dd
```

Figure 1.17: Running Spark Pi example

At the moment we have seen an example in Scala. If we see the example for this in Python, you will realize that we will just need to pass in the Python source code. We do not have to pass in any JAR files, as we are not referencing any other code. Similar to the Scala example, we have to instantiate the `SparkContext` directly, which is unlike how `PySpark` shell automatically provides you with a reference to the context object:

```
sc = SparkContext(appName="PythonPi")
```

Running the `Spark Pi` example is a bit different to the Scala example:

```
spark@ubuntu:/spark/spark-2.0.0-preview$ ./bin/spark-submit examples/src/main/python/pi.py
Using Spark's default log4j profile: org/apache/spark/log4j-defaults.properties
16/06/25 03:44:22 INFO SparkContext: Running Spark version 2.0.0-preview
16/06/25 03:44:23 WARN NativeCodeLoader: Unable to load native-hadoop library for your platform... using builtin-java classes where applicable
16/06/25 03:44:23 WARN Utils: Your hostname, ubuntu resolves to a loopback address: 127.0.1.1; using 192.168.193.143 instead (on interface ens33)
16/06/25 03:44:23 WARN Utils: Set SPARK_LOCAL_IP if you need to bind to another address
16/06/25 03:44:23 INFO SecurityManager: Changing view acls to: spark
16/06/25 03:44:23 INFO SecurityManager: Changing modify acls to: spark
16/06/25 03:44:23 INFO SecurityManager: Changing view acls groups to:
16/06/25 03:44:23 INFO SecurityManager: Changing modify acls groups to:
```

Similar to the `PySpark` example, the log of the `SparkPi` program in spark-shell spans multiple pages. We'll just move directly to the part where the value of `Pi` is printed in the log:

```
16/06/25 03:44:25 INFO TaskSetManager: Finished task 0.0 in stage 0.0 (TID 0) in 750 ms on localhost (1/2)
16/06/25 03:44:25 INFO TaskSetManager: Finished task 1.0 in stage 0.0 (TID 1) in 710 ms on localhost (2/2)
16/06/25 03:44:25 INFO TaskSchedulerImpl: Removed TaskSet 0.0, whose tasks have all completed, from pool
16/06/25 03:44:25 INFO DAGScheduler: ResultStage 0 (reduce at /spark/spark-2.0.0-preview/examples/src/main/python/pi.py:39) finished in 0.793 s
16/06/25 03:44:25 INFO DAGScheduler: Job 0 finished: reduce at /spark/spark-2.0.0-preview/examples/src/main/python/pi.py:39, took 1.112120 s
Pi is roughly 3.141800
16/06/25 03:44:26 INFO SparkUI: Stopped Spark web UI at http://192.168.193.143:4040
16/06/25 03:44:26 INFO MapOutputTrackerMasterEndpoint: MapOutputTrackerMasterEndpoint stopped!
16/06/25 03:44:26 INFO MemoryStore: MemoryStore cleared
16/06/25 03:44:26 INFO BlockManager: BlockManager stopped
16/06/25 03:44:26 INFO BlockManagerMaster: BlockManagerMaster stopped
16/06/25 03:44:26 INFO OutputCommitCoordinator$OutputCommitCoordinatorEndpoint: OutputCommitCoordinator stopped!
16/06/25 03:44:26 INFO SparkContext: Successfully stopped SparkContext
```

Figure 1.18: Running Spark Pi Python example

Building your own programs

We have tested pre-compiled programs but, as discussed earlier in this chapter, you can create your own programs and use `sbt` or `Maven` to package the application together and run using spark-submit script. In the later chapters in this book, we will use both the REPL environments and spark-submit for various code examples. For a complete code example, we'll build a Recommendation system in `Chapter 9`, *Building a Recommendation System,* and predict customer churn in a `telco` environment in `Chapter 10`, *Customer Churn Prediction.* Both of these examples (though fictional) will help you understand the overall life cycle of a machine learning application.

Brain teasers

Port 4041 instead of 4040 for Spark shell.

As we already had a Scala shell running, which had created a Spark UI at port 4040, the Python shell had to bind the UI to a different port, which in this case was 4041.

References

- https://en.wikipedia.org/wiki/Apache_Mesos
- https://aws.amazon.com/ec2/
- http://spark.apache.org/docs/2.0.0-preview/quick-start.html
- http://spark.apache.org/docs/2.0.0-preview/cluster-overview.html
- http://spark.apache.org/docs/2.0.0-preview/submitting-applications.html
- https://en.wikipedia.org/wiki/Apache_Maven
- http://cdn2.hubspot.net/hubfs/438089/DataBricks_Surveys_-_Content/2016_Spark_Survey/2016_Spark_Infographic.pdf

Summary

In this chapter, we have gone through a Spark architecture overview, written our first Spark program, looked at the software components of Spark, and ran a Spark application. This provides a solid foundation to move to the next chapter where we will discuss Spark RDDs, which is one of the most important constructs of Apache Spark.

2
Transformations and Actions with Spark RDDs

Now that we have had a basic overview of the architecture of Spark and key software components, we will cover Spark RDD's in this chapter. During the course of this chapter, we'll walk through the following topics:

- How to construct RDDs
- Operations on RDDs, such as transformations and actions
- Passing functions to Spark (Scala, Java, and Python)
- Transformations such as map, filter, flatMap, and sample
- Set operations such as distinct, intersection, and union
- Actions such as reduce, collect, count, take, and first
- PairRDDs
- Shared and broadcast variables

Let's get cracking!

What is an RDD?

What's in a name might be true for a rose, but perhaps not for **Resilient Distributed Datasets** (**RDD**) which, in essence, describes what an RDD is.

They are basically datasets, which are distributed across a cluster (remember the Spark framework is inherently based on an MPP architecture), and provide resilience (automatic failover) by nature.

Before we go into any further detail, let's try to understand this a little bit, and again we are trying to be as abstract as possible. Let us assume that you have a sensor data from aircraft sensors and you want to analyze the data irrespective of its size and locality. For example, an Airbus A350 has roughly 6000 sensors across the entire plane and generates 2.5 TB data per day, while the newer model expected to launch in 2020 will generate roughly 7.5 TB per day. From a data engineering point of view, it might be important to understand the data pipeline, but from an analyst and a data scientist point of view, the major concern is to analyze the data irrespective of the size and number of nodes across which it has been stored. This is where the neatness of the RDD concept comes into play, where the sensor data can be encapsulated as an RDD concept, and any transformation/action that you perform on the RDD applies across the entire dataset. Six month's worth of dataset for an A350 would be approximately 450 TBs of data, and would need to sit across multiple machines.

For the sake of discussion, we assume that you are working on a cluster of four worker machines. Your data would be partitioned across the workers as follows:

	NODE1	NODE2	NODE3	NODE4
RDD1	RDD 1 Partition 1	RDD 1 Partition 2		RDD 1 Partition 3
RDD2		RDD 2 Partition 1		RDD 2 Partition 2
RDD3	RDD 3 Partition 1		RDD 3 Partition 2	
RDD4	RDD 4 Partition 1	RDD 4 Partition 2	RDD 4 Partition 3	RDD 4 Partition 4

Figure 2.1: RDD split across a cluster

The figure basically explains that an RDD is a distributed collection of the data, and the framework distributes the data across the cluster. Data distribution across a set of machines brings its own set of nuisances including recovering from node failures. RDD's are resilient as they can be recomputed from the RDD lineage graph, which is basically a graph of e entire parent RDDs of the RDD. In addition to resilience, distribution, and representing a data set, an RDD has various other distinguishing qualities:

- **In Memory**: An RDD is a memory-resident collection of objects. We'll look at options where an RDD can be stored in memory, on disk, or both. However, the execution speed of Spark stems from the fact that the data is in memory, and is not fetched from disk for each operation.
- **Partitioned**: A partition is a division of a logical dataset or constituent elements into independent parts. Partitioning is a defacto performance optimization technique in distributed systems to achieve minimal network traffic, a killer for high performance workloads. The objective of partitioning in key-value oriented data is to collocate a similar range of keys and in effect, minimize shuffling. Data inside RDD is split into partitions and across various nodes of the cluster. We'll discuss this in more detail later in this chapter.
- **Typed**: Data in an RDD is strongly typed. When you create an RDD, all the elements are typed depending on the data type.
- **Lazy evaluation**: The transformations in Spark are lazy, which means data inside RDD is not available until you perform an action. You can, however, make the data available at any time using a `count()` action on the RDD. We'll discuss this later and the benefits associated with it.
- **Immutable**: An RDD once created cannot be changed. It can, however, be transformed into a new RDD by performing a set of transformations on it.
- **Parallel**: An RDD is operated on in parallel. Since the data is spread across a cluster in various partitions, each partition is operated on in parallel.
- **Cacheable**: Since RDD's are lazily evaluated, any action on an RDD will cause the RDD to revaluate all transformations that led to the creation of the RDD. This is generally not a desirable behavior on large datasets, and hence Spark allows the option to cache the data on memory or disk. We'll discuss caching later in this chapter.

A typical Spark program flow with an RDD includes:

1. Creation of an RDD from a data source.
2. A set of transformations, for example, `filter`, `map`, `join`, and so on.
3. Persisting the RDD to avoid re-execution.

4. Calling actions on the RDD to start performing parallel operations across the cluster.

This is depicted in the following figure:

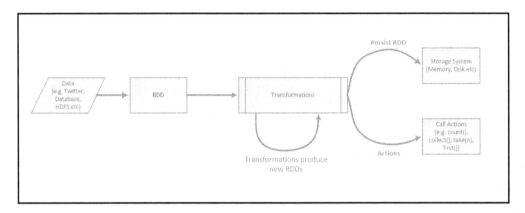

Figure 2.2: Typical Spark RDD flow

Let's quickly look at the various ways by which you can create an RDD.

Constructing RDDs

There are two major ways of creating an RDD:

- Parallelizing an existing collection in your driver program.
- Creating an RDD by referencing an external data source, for example, Filesystem, HDFS, HBase, or any data source capable of providing a Hadoop Input format.

Parallelizing existing collections

Parallelizing collections are created by calling the `parallelize()` method on `SparkContext` within your driver program. The `parallelize()` method asks Spark to create a new RDD based on the dataset provided. Once the local collection/dataset is converted into an RDD, it can be operated on in parallel. `Parallelize()` is often used for prototyping and not often used in production environments due to the need of the data set being available on a single machine. Let's look at examples of Parallelizing a collection in Scala, Python, and Java:

```
scala> val namesList = sc.parallelize(List("rob","james","adrian","greg","paul","jochen"))
namesList: org.apache.spark.rdd.RDD[String] = ParallelCollectionRDD[4] at parallelize at <console>:24

scala> namesList.count()
res8: Long = 6
```

Figure 2.3: Parallelizing a collection of names in Scala

Parallelizing a collection in Python is quite similar to Scala, as you can see in the following example:

```
>>> namesList = sc.parallelize(["rob","james","adrian","greg","paul","jochen"])
>>> namesList
ParallelCollectionRDD[2] at parallelize at PythonRDD.scala:475
>>> namesList.count()
6
```

Figure 2.4: Parallelizing a collection of names in Python

It is an similar case with Java:

```
textFile = sc.textFile("README.md") //Create and RDD called textFile by
reading the contents of README.md file.
```

The `parallelize` method has many variations including the option to specify a range of numbers. For example:

```
scala> val daysInYear=sc.parallelize(1 to 365)
daysInYear: org.apache.spark.rdd.RDD[Int] = ParallelCollectionRDD[6] at parallelize at <console>:24

scala> daysInYear.count()
res11: Long = 365
```

Figure 2.5: Parallelizing a range of integers in Scala

In Python however, you need to use the `range()` method .The ending value is exclusive, and hence you can see that unlike the Scala example, the ending value is `366` rather than `365`:

```
>>> daysInYear=sc.parallelize(range(1,366))
>>> daysInYear.count()
365
```

Figure 2.6: Parallelizing a range of integers in Python

In Python you can also use the `xrange()` function, which works similar to range, but is much faster, as it is essentially a sequence object that evaluates lazily compared to `range()`, which creates a list in the memory.

Now that an RDD is created, it can be operated in Parallel. You can optimize this further by passing in a second argument to the `parallelize()` method indicating the number of partitions the data needs to be sliced into. Spark will run a task for each partition of the cluster:

```
scala> val daysInYear=sc.parallelize(1 to 365,4)
daysInYear: org.apache.spark.rdd.RDD[Int] = ParallelCollectionRDD[8] at parallelize at <console>:24

scala> daysInYear.getNumPartitions
res15: Int = 4
```

Figure 2.7: Parallelizing a range of integers in Scala sliced into four partitions

The Python Syntax looks quite similar to that of Scala. For example, if you would like to parallelize a range of integers sliced over 4 partitions, you can use the following example:

```
>>> daysInYear=sc.parallelize(range(1,366),4)
>>> daysInYear
ParallelCollectionRDD[12] at parallelize at PythonRDD.scala:475
>>> daysInYear.getNumPartitions()
4
```

Figure 2.8: Parallelizing a range of integers in Python sliced into four partitions

Referencing external data source

You have created a Spark RDD using the `parallelize` method which, as we discussed is primarily used for prototyping. For production use, Spark can load data from any storage source supported by Hadoop ranging from a text file on your local file system, to data available on HDFS, HBase, or Amazon S3.

As we saw in the previous example, you can load a text file from the local filesystem using the `textFile` method. The other available methods are:

- `hadoopFile()`: Create an RDD from a Hadoop file with an arbitrary input format
- `objectFile()`: Load an RDD saved as `SequenceFile` containing serialized objects, with `NullWritable` keys and `BytesWritable` values that contain a serialized partition
- `sequenceFile()`: Create an RDD from the Hadoop sequence file with a given key and value types
- `textFile()`: A method that we have already seen, which reads a `textFile` from either HDFS or a local file system and returns as an RDD of strings

> You might want to visit Spark context's API documentation (`http://bit.ly/SparkContextScalaAPI`) to look at the details of these methods as some are overloaded and allow you to pass certain arguments to load a variety of the file types.

Once an RDD is created you can operate on the RDD by applying transformations or actions, which will operate on the RDD in parallel.

> When reading a file from a local file system, make sure that the path exists on all the worker nodes. You might want to use a network-mounted shared file system as well.

Spark's `textFile()` method provides a number of different useful features most notably, the ability to scan a directory, working with compressed files and using wildcard characters. People who are working with production systems and need to work with machine logs will appreciate the usefulness of this feature.

For example, in your `Spark` folder you have two `.md` files, and while we have already loaded `README.md` previously, let's use wildcard characters to read all the `.md` files, and try other options:

```
scala> val dataFiles = sc.textFile("*.md")
dataFiles: org.apache.spark.rdd.RDD[String] = *.md MapPartitionsRDD[7] at textFile at <console>:24

scala> dataFiles.count()
res4: Long = 115

scala> val readmeFile = sc.textFile("README.md")
readmeFile: org.apache.spark.rdd.RDD[String] = README.md MapPartitionsRDD[9] at textFile at <console>:24

scala> readmeFile.count()
res5: Long = 99

scala> val contributions = sc.textFile("CONT*.md")
contributions: org.apache.spark.rdd.RDD[String] = CONT*.md MapPartitionsRDD[11] at textFile at <console>:24

scala> contributions.count()
res6: Long = 16
```

Figure 2.9: Different uses of the textFile() method in Scala

Loading a text file in Python is quite similar with a familiar syntax. You will still call the `textFile()` method in the Spark context and then use the RDD for other operations, such as transformations and actions:

```
Welcome to
      ____              __
     / __/__  ___ _____/ /__
    _\ \/ _ \/ _ `/ __/  '_/
   /__ / .__/\_,_/_/ /_/\_\   version 2.0.0
      /_/

Using Python version 2.7.11+ (default, Apr 17 2016 14:00:29)
SparkSession available as 'spark'.
>>> dataFiles = sc.textFile("*.md")
>>> dataFiles.count()
115
>>> readmeFile = sc.textFile("RE*ME.md")
>>> readmeFile.count()
99
>>> contributions = sc.textFile("CONT*.md")
>>> contributions.count()
16
```

Figure 2.10: Different uses of the textFile() method in Python

Similarly, for Java the relevant code examples would be as follows:

```
//To read all the md files in the directory
JavaRDD<String> dataFiles = sc.textFile("*.md");

//To read the README.md file
JavaRDD<String> readmeFile = sc.textFile("README.md");
```

```
//To read all CONTRIBUTIONS.md file
JavaRDD<String> contributions = sc.textFile("CONT*.md");
```

So far we have only worked with the local file system. How difficult would it be to read the file from a file system such as HDFS or S3? Let's have a quick look at the various options made available to us via Spark.

 I expect most of the audience to be already familiar with HDFS and Hadoop already, and how to load the data onto Hadoop. If you still haven't started your journey to Hadoop, you might want to take a look at the following Hadoop quick start guide to get you started: `http://bit.ly/HadoopQuickstart`.

We now have some data loaded onto HDFS. The data is available in the `/spark/sample/telcom` directory. These are sample **Call Detail Records** (**CDRs**) created to serve the purpose of this exercise. You will find the sample data on this book's GitHub page:

```
//Load the data onto your Hadoop cluster
Hadoop fs -copyFromLocal /spark/data/ /spark/sample/telecom/

//Accessing the HDFS data from Scala-Shell
val dataFile =
sc.textFile("hdfs://yournamenode:8020/spark/sample/telecom/2016*.csv")

//Accessing the HDFS data from Python Shell
dataFile =
sc.textFile("hdfs://yournamenode:8020/spark/sample/telecom/2016*.csv")
```

You can access Amazon S3 in a very similar way.

Now that we have looked at the RDD creation process, let us quickly look at the types of operations that can be performed on an RDD.

Operations on RDD

Two major operation types can be performed on an RDD. They are called:

- Transformations
- Actions

Transformations

Transformations are operations that create a new dataset, as RDDs are immutable. They are used to transform data from one to another, which could result in amplification of the data, reduction of the data, or a totally different shape altogether. These operations do not return any value back to the driver program, and hence are lazily evaluated, which is one of the main benefits of Spark.

An example of a transformation would be a `map` function that will pass through each element of the RDD and return a totally new RDD representing the results of application of the function on the original dataset.

Actions

Actions are operations that return a value to the driver program. As previously discussed, all transformations in Spark are lazy, which essentially means that Spark remembers all the transformations carried out on an RDD, and applies them in the most optimal fashion when an action is called. For example, you might have a 1 TB dataset, which you pass through a set of `map` functions by applying various transformations. Finally, you apply the reduce action on the dataset. Apache Spark will return only a final dataset, which might be few MBs rather than the entire 1 TB dataset of mapped intermediate result.

You should, however, remember to persist intermediate results; otherwise Spark will recompute the entire RDD graph each time an Action is called. The `persist()` method on an RDD should help you avoid recomputation and saving intermediate results. We'll look at this in more detail later.

Let's illustrate the work of transformations and actions by a simple example. In this specific example, we'll be using `flatmap()` transformations and a count action. We'll use the `README.md` file from the local filesystem as an example. We'll give a line-by-line explanation of the Scala example, and then provide code for Python and Java. As always, you must try this example with your own piece of text and investigate the results:

```
//Loading the README.md file
val dataFile = sc.textFile("README.md")
```

Now that the data has been loaded, we'll need to run a transformation. Since we know that each line of the text is loaded as a separate element, we'll need to run a `flatMap` transformation and separate out individual words as separate elements, for which we'll use the `split` function and use space as a delimiter:

```
//Separate out a list of words from individual RDD elements
val words = dataFile.flatMap(line => line.split(" "))
```

Remember that until this point, while you seem to have applied a transformation function, nothing has been executed and all the transformations have been added to the logical plan. Also note that the transformation function returns a new RDD. We can then call the `count()` action on the words RDD, to perform the computation, which then results in fetching of data from the file to create an RDD, before applying the transformation function specified. You might note that we have actually passed a function to Spark, which is an area that is covered in the *Passing Functions to Spark* section later in this chapter. Now that we have another RDD of RDDs, we can call `count()` on the RDD to get the total number of elements within the RDD:

```
//Separate out a list of words from individual RDD elements
words.count()
```

Upon calling the `count()` action the RDD is evaluated, and the results are sent back to the driver program. This is very neat and especially useful during big data applications.

If you are Python savvy, you may want to run the following code in `PySpark`. You should note that lambda functions are passed to the Spark framework:

```
//Loading data file, applying transformations and action
dataFile = sc.textFile("README.md")
words = dataFile.flatMap(lambda line: line.split(" "))
words.count()
```

Programming the same functionality in Java is also quite straightforward and will look pretty similar to the program in Scala:

```
JavaRDD<String> lines = sc.textFile("README.md");
JavaRDD<String> words = lines.map(line -> line.split(" "));
int wordCount = words.count();
```

This might look like a simple program, but behind the scenes it is taking the `line.split(" ")` function and applying it to all the partitions in the cluster in parallel. The framework provides this simplicity and does all the background work of coordination to schedule it across with the cluster, and get the results back.

Passing functions to Spark (Scala)

As you have seen in the previous example, passing functions is a critical functionality provided by Spark. From a user's point of view you would pass the function in your driver program, and Spark would figure out the location of the data partitions across the cluster memory, running it in parallel. The exact syntax of passing functions differs by the programming language. Since Spark has been written in Scala, we'll discuss Scala first.

In Scala, the recommended ways to pass functions to the Spark framework are as follows:

- Anonymous functions
- Static singleton methods

Anonymous functions

Anonymous functions are used for short pieces of code. They are also referred to as lambda expressions, and are a cool and elegant feature of the programming language. The reason they are called **anonymous functions** is because you can give any name to the input argument and the result would be the same.

For example, the following code examples would produce the same output:

```scala
val words = dataFile.map(line => line.split(" "))
val words = dataFile.map(anyline => anyline.split(" "))
val words = dataFile.map(_.split(" "))
```

```
scala> val dataFile = sc.textFile("README.md")
dataFile: org.apache.spark.rdd.RDD[String] = README.md MapPartitionsRDD[1] at textFile at <console>:24

scala> val words = dataFile.flatMap(line => line.split(" "))
words: org.apache.spark.rdd.RDD[String] = MapPartitionsRDD[2] at flatMap at <console>:26

scala> val totalWords = words.count()
totalWords: Long = 540
```

Figure 2.11: Passing anonymous functions to Spark in Scala

Static singleton functions

While anonymous functions are really helpful for short snippets of code, they are not very helpful when you want to request the framework for a complex data manipulation. Static singleton functions come to the rescue with their own nuances, which we will discuss in this section.

In software engineering, the **Singleton pattern** is a design pattern that restricts instantiation of a class to one object. This is useful when exactly one object is needed to coordinate actions across the system.

Static methods belong to the class and not an instance of it. They usually take input from the parameters, perform actions on it, and return the result.

```
scala> val dataFile = sc.textFile("README.md")
dataFile: org.apache.spark.rdd.RDD[String] = README.md MapPartitionsRDD[13] at textFile at <console>:24

scala> object UtilFunctions{ def mySplit(s: String): Array[String] = {s.split(" ")} }
defined object UtilFunctions

scala> dataFile.flatMap(UtilFunctions.mySplit(_)).count()
res15: Long = 540
```

Figure 2.12: Passing static singleton functions to Spark in Scala

Static singleton is the preferred way to pass functions, as technically you can create a class and call a method in the class instance. For example:

```
class UtilFunctions{
    def split(inputParam: String): Array[String] = {inputParam.split(" ")}
    def operate(rdd: RDD[String]): RDD[String] ={rdd.map(split)}
}
```

You can send a method in a class, but that has performance implications as the entire object would be sent along the method.

Passing functions to Spark (Java)

In Java, to create a function you will have to implement the interfaces available in the `org.apache.spark.api.java` function package. There are two popular ways to create such functions:

- Implement the interface in your own class, and pass the instance to Spark.
- Starting Java 8, you can use **Lambda** expressions to pass off the functions to the Spark framework.

Let's implement the preceding word count examples in Java:

```java
@SuppressWarnings("serial")
JavaRDD<Integer> numWordsPerLine = distFile.map(new Function<String,Integer>(){
        public Integer call(String s) {
            return s.split(" ").length;
        }
    }
);

@SuppressWarnings("serial")
int totalWords = numWordsPerLine.reduce(new Function2<Integer, Integer, Integer>() {
        public Integer call(Integer len1, Integer len2) throws Exception{
        {
                return len1 + len2;
        }
    }
}
);

System.out.println("Total number of Words: "+totalWords);
```

Figure 2.13: Code example of Java implementation of word count (inline functions)

If you belong to a group of programmers who feel that writing inline functions makes the code complex and unreadable (a lot of people do agree to that assertion), you may want to create separate functions and call them as follows:

```java
@SuppressWarnings("serial")
class GetNumWords implements Function<String,Integer>{
    public Integer call(String s) { return s.split(" ").length; }
}

@SuppressWarnings("serial")
class SumWords implements Function2<Integer, Integer, Integer>{
    public Integer call(Integer len1, Integer len2){ return len1 +len2; }
}

public void totalWords(JavaSparkContext sc, String fileName) {

    JavaRDD<String> distFile =  sc.textFile(fileName, 4);
    JavaRDD<Integer> numWords = distFile.map(new GetNumWords());
    int totalWords = numWords.reduce(new SumWords());
    System.out.println("Total number of Words: "+totalWords);

}
```

Figure 2.14: Code example of Java implementation of word count

Passing functions to Spark (Python)

Python provides a simple way to pass functions to Spark. The Spark programming guide available at spark.apache.org suggests there are three recommended ways to do this:

- Lambda expressions is the ideal way for short functions that can be written inside a single expression
- Local defs inside the function calling into Spark for longer code
- Top-level functions in a module

While we have already looked at the lambda functions in some of the previous examples, let's look at local definitions of the functions. We can encapsulate our business logic which is splitting of words, and counting into two separate functions as shown below.

```python
def splitter(lineOfText):
    words = lineOfText.split(" ")
    return len(words)
def aggregate(numWordsLine1, numWordsLineNext):
    totalWords = numWordsLine1 + numWordsLineNext
    return totalWords
```

Let's see the working code example:

```
>>> dataFile = sc.textFile("README.md")
>>> dataFile.count()
99
>>> def splitter(lineOfText):
...     words = lineOfText.split(" ")
...     return len(words)
...
>>> def aggregate(numWordsLine1, numWordsLineNext):
...     totalWords = numWordsLine1 + numWordsLineNext
...     return totalWords
...
>>> wordsPerLine = dataFile.map(splitter)
>>> totalWords = wordsPerLine.reduce(aggregate)
>>> totalWords
540
```

Figure 2.15: Code example of Python word count (local definition of functions)

Here's another way to implement this by defining the functions as a part of a UtilFunctions class, and referencing them within your map and reduce functions:

```
>>> dataFile = sc.textFile("README.md")
>>> class UtilFunctions():
...     def splitter(self,lineOfText):
...         words = lineOfText.split(" ")
...         return len(words)
...     def aggregate(self,numWordsLine1, numWordsLineNext):
...         totalWords = numWordsLine1 + numWordsLineNext
...         return totalWords
...
>>> uf = UtilFunctions()
>>> wordsPerLine = dataFile.map(uf.splitter)
>>> wordsPerLine.count()
99
>>> totalWords = wordsPerLine.reduce(aggregate)
>>> totalWords
540
```

Figure 2.16: Code example of Python word count (Utility class)

You may want to be a bit cheeky here and try to add a countWords() to the UtilFunctions, so that it takes an RDD as input, and returns the total number of words. This method has potential performance implications as the whole object will need to be sent to the cluster. Let's see how this can be implemented and the results in the following screenshot:

```
>>> dataFile = sc.textFile("README.md")
>>> class UtilFunctions():
...        def splitter(self,lineOfText):
...             words = lineOfText.split(" ")
...             return len(words)
...        def aggregate(self,numWordsLine1, numWordsLineNext):
...             totalWords = numWordsLine1 + numWordsLineNext
...             return totalWords
...        def countWords(self, rdd):
...             return rdd.map(self.splitter).reduce(aggregate)
...
>>> uf = UtilFunctions()
>>> uf.countWords(dataFile)
540
```

Figure 2.17: Code example of Python word count (Utility class – 2)

This can be avoided by making a copy of the referenced data field in a local object, rather than accessing it externally.

Now that we have had a look at how to pass functions to Spark, and have already looked at some of the transformations and actions in the previous examples, including `map`, `flatMap`, and `reduce`, let's look at the most common transformations and actions used in Spark. The list is not exhaustive, and you can find more examples in the Apache Spark documentation in the programming guide section (`http://bit.ly/SparkProgrammingGuide`). If you would like to get a comprehensive list of all the available functions, you might want to check the following API docs:

	RDD	PairRDD
Scala	http://bit.ly/2bfyoTo	http://bit.ly/2bfzgah
Python	http://bit.ly/2bfyURl	N/A
Java	http://bit.ly/2bfyRov	http://bit.ly/2bfyOsH
R	http://bit.ly/2bfyrOZ	N/A

Table 2.1 – RDD and PairRDD API references

Transformations

We've used few transformation functions in the examples in this chapter, but I would like to share with you a list of the most commonly used transformation functions in Apache Spark. You can find a complete list of functions in the official documentation `http://bit.ly/RDDT ransformations`.

Most Common Transformations	
`map(func)`	coalesce(numPartitions)
`filter(func)`	repartition(numPartitions)
`flatMap(func)`	repartitionAndSortWithinPartitions(partitioner)
`mapPartitions(func)`	join(otherDataset, [numTasks])
`mapPartitionsWithIndex(func)`	cogroup(otherDataset, [numTasks])
`sample(withReplacement, fraction, seed)`	cartesian(otherDataset)

Map(func)

The `map` transformation is the most commonly used and the simplest of transformations on an RDD. The `map` transformation applies the function passed in the arguments to each of the elements of the source RDD. In the previous examples, we have seen the usage of `map()` transformation where we have passed the `split()` function to the input RDD.

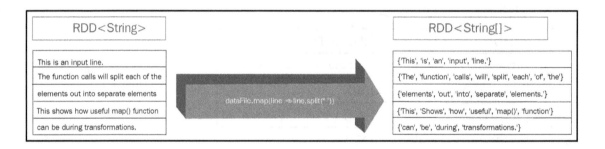

Figure 2.18: Operation of a map() function

We'll not give examples of `map()` functions as we have already seen plenty of examples of `map` functions previously.

Let's have a look at the `filter()` transformation which is one of the most widely used transformation functions, especially during log analysis.

Filter(func)

Filter, as the name implies, filters the input RDD, and creates a new dataset that satisfies the predicate passed as arguments.

Example 2.1: Scala filtering example:

```
val dataFile = sc.textFile("README.md")
val linesWithApache = dataFile.filter(line => line.contains("Apache"))
```

Example 2.2: Python filtering example:

```
dataFile = sc.textFile("README.md")
linesWithApache = dataFile.filter(lambda line: "Apache" in line)
```

Example 2.3: Java filtering example:

```
JavaRDD<String> dataFile = sc.textFile("README.md")
JavaRDD<String> linesWithApache = dataFile.filter(line ->
line.contains("Apache"));
```

flatMap(func)

The `flatMap()` transformation is similar to `map`, but it offers a bit more flexibility. From the perspective of similarity to a `map` function, it operates on all the elements of the RDD, but the flexibility stems from its ability to handle functions that return a sequence rather than a single item. As you saw in the preceding examples, we had used `flatMap()` to flatten the result of the `split("")` function, which returns a flattened structure rather than an RDD of string arrays.

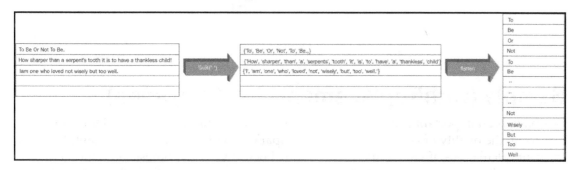

Figure 2.19: Operational details of the flatMap() transformation

Let's look at the `flatMap` example in Scala.

The following example demonstrates how you can flatten a list (in this case movies) using `flatmap()` in Scala.

Example 2.4: The `flatmap()` example in Scala:

```
val favMovies = sc.parallelize(List("Pulp Fiction","Requiem for a dream","A
clockwork Orange"));
favMovies.flatMap(movieTitle=>movieTitle.split(" ")).collect()
```

The following `flatmap()` example in Python achieves a similar objective as *Example 2.4*. Python syntax in this example looks quite similar to that of Scala.

Example 2.5: The `flatmap()` example in Python:

```
movies = sc.parallelize(["Pulp Fiction","Requiem for a dream","A clockwork
Orange"])
movies.flatMap(lambda movieTitle: movieTitle.split(" ")).collect()
```

If you are a Java fan, you can use the following code example to implement the flattening of a movie list in Java. This example in Java is a bit long-winded, but it essentially produces the same results.

Example 2.6: The `flatmap()` example in Java:

```
JavaRDD<String> movies = sc.parallelize
(Arrays.asList("Pulp Fiction","Requiem for a dream",
  "A clockwork Orange")
);
JavaRDD<String> movieName = movies.flatMap(
      new FlatMapFunction<String,String>(){
        public Iterator<String> call(String movie){
          return Arrays.asList(movie.split(" ")).iterator();
        }
      }
);
```

Sample (withReplacement, fraction, seed)

Sampling is an important component of any data analysis and it can have a significant impact on the quality of your results/findings. Spark provides an easy way to sample RDD's for your calculations, if you would prefer to quickly test your hypothesis on a subset of data before running it on a full dataset. We'll discuss more about sampling during the machine learning chapter, but here is a quick overview of the parameters that are passed onto the method:

- `withReplacement`: Is a Boolean (True/False), and it indicates if elements can be sampled multiple times (replaced when sampled out). Sampling with replacement means that the two sample values are independent. In practical terms this means that, if we draw two samples with replacement, what we get on the first one doesn't affect what we get on the second draw, and hence the covariance between the two samples is zero.

  If we are sampling without replacement, the two samples aren't independent. Practically, this means what we got on the first draw affects what we get on the second one and hence the covariance between the two isn't zero.

- `fraction`: Fraction indicates the expected size of the sample as a fraction of the RDD's size. The fraction must be between *0* and *1*. For example, if you want to draw a 5% sample, you can choose *0.05* as a fraction.
- `seed`: The `seed` used for the random number generator.

Let's look at the sampling example in Scala.

Example 2.7: The `sample()` example in Scala:

```
val data = sc.parallelize(
List(1,2,3,4,5,6,7,8,9,10,11,12,13,14,15,16,17,18,19,20));
data.sample(true,0.1,12345).collect()
```

The sampling example in Python looks similar to the one in Scala.

Example 2.8: The `sample()` example in Python:

```
data = sc.parallelize(
[1,2,3,4,5,6,7,8,9,10,11,12,13,14,15,16,17,18,19,20])
data.sample(1,0.1,12345).collect()
```

In Java, our sampling example returns an RDD of integers.

Example 2.9: The `sample()` example in Java:

```
JavaRDD<Integer> nums = sc.parallelize(Arrays.asList(
1,2,3,4,5,6,7,8,9,10,11,12,13,14,15,16,17,18,19,20));
nums.sample(true,0.1,12345).collect();
```

Set operations in Spark

For those of you who are from the database world and have now ventured into the world of big data, you're probably looking at how you can possibly apply set operations on Spark datasets. You might have realized that an RDD can be a representation of any sort of data, but it does not necessarily represent a set based data. The typical set operations in a database world include the following operations, and we'll see how some of these apply to Spark. However, it is important to remember that while Spark offers some of the ways to mimic these operations, spark doesn't allow you to apply conditions to these operations, which is common in SQL operations:

- **Distinct:** Distinct operation provides you a non-duplicated set of data from the dataset
- **Intersection**: The intersection operations returns only those elements that are available in both datasets
- **Union**: A union operation returns the elements from both datasets
- **Subtract**: A subtract operation returns the elements from one dataset by taking away all the matching elements from the second dataset
- **Cartesian**: A Cartesian product of both datasets

Distinct()

During data management and analytics, working on a distinct non-duplicated set of data is often critical. Spark offers the ability to extract distinct values from a dataset using the available transformation operations. Let's look at the ways you can collect distinct elements in Scala, Python, and Java.

Example 2.10: Distinct in Scala:

```
val movieList = sc.parallelize(List("A Nous Liberte","Airplane","The
Apartment","The Apartment"))
moviesList.distinct().collect()
```

Example 2.11: Distinct in Python:

```
movieList = sc.parallelize(["A Nous Liberte","Airplane","The
Apartment","The Apartment"])
movieList.distinct().collect()
```

Example 2.12: Distinct in Java:

```
JavaRDD<String> movieList = sc.parallelize(Arrays.asList("A Nous
Liberte","Airplane","The Apartment","The Apartment"));
movieList.distinct().collect();
```

Intersection()

Intersection is similar to an inner join operation with the caveat that it doesn't allow joining criteria. Intersection looks at elements from both RDDs and returns the elements that are available across both data sets. For example, you might have candidates based on skillset:

```
java_skills = "Tom Mahoney","Alicia Whitekar","Paul Jones","Rodney Marsh"
db_skills = "James Kent", "Paul Jones", Tom Mahoney", "Adam Waugh"
java_and_db_skills = java_skills.intersection(db_skills)
```

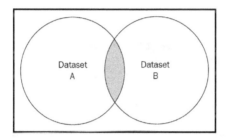

Figure 2.20: Intersection operation

Let's look at examples of `intersection` of two datasets in Scala, Python, and Java.

Example 2.13: Intersection in Scala:

```
val java_skills=sc.parallelize(List("Tom Mahoney","Alicia Whitekar","Paul
Jones","Rodney Marsh"))
val db_skills= sc.parallelize(List("James Kent","Paul Jones","Tom
Mahoney","Adam Waugh"))
java_skills.intersection(db_skills).collect()
```

Example 2.14: Intersection in Python:

```
java_skills= sc.parallelize(["Tom Mahoney","Alicia Whitekar","Paul
Jones","Rodney Marsh"])
db_skills= sc.parallelize(["James Kent","Paul Jones","Tom Mahoney","Adam
Waugh"])
java_skills.intersection(db_skills).collect()
```

Example 2.15: Intersection in Java:

```
JavaRDD<String> javaSkills= sc.parallelize(Arrays.asList("Tom
Mahoney","Alicia Whitekar","Paul Jones","Rodney Marsh"));
JavaRDD<String> dbSkills= sc.parallelize(Arrays.asList("James Kent","Paul
Jones","Tom Mahoney","Adam Waugh"));
javaSkills.intersection(dbSkills).collect();
```

Union()

Union is basically an aggregation of both the datasets. If few data elements are available across both datasets, they will be duplicated. If we look at the data from the previous examples, you have people like Tom Mahoney and Paul Jones having both the Java and DB skills. A union of the two datasets will result in a two entries of them. We'll only look at a Scala example in this case.

Example 2.16: Union in Scala:

```
val java_skills=sc.parallelize(List("Tom Mahoney","Alicia Whitekar","Paul
Jones","Rodney Marsh"))
val db_skills= sc.parallelize(List("James Kent","Paul Jones","Tom
Mahoney","Adam Waugh"))
java_skills.union(db_skills).collect()
//The Result shown would be like:
Tom Mahoney, Alicia Whitekar, Paul Jones, Rodney Marsh, James Kent, Paul
Jones, Tom Mahoney, Adam Waugh.
```

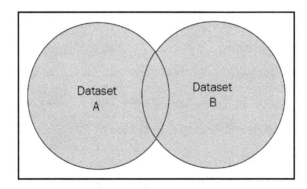

Figure 2.21: Union operation

Subtract()

Subtraction as the name indicates, removes the elements of one dataset from the other. Subtraction is very useful in ETL operations to identify new data arriving on successive days, and making sure you identify the new data items before doing the integration. Let's take a quick look at the Scala example, and view the results of the operation.

Example 2.17: The `subtract()` in Scala:

```
val java_skills=sc.parallelize(List("Tom Mahoney","Alicia Whitekar","Paul
Jones","Rodney Marsh"))
val db_skills= sc.parallelize(List("James Kent","Paul Jones","Tom
Mahoney","Adam Waugh"))
java_skills.subtract(db_skills).collect()
```

Results: `Alicia Whitekar, Rodney Marsh.`

Cartesian()

Cartesian simulates the cross-join from an SQL system, and basically gives you all the possible combinations between the elements of the two datasets. For example, you might have 12 months of the year, and a total of five years, and you wanted to look at all the possible dates where you need to perform a particular operation. Here's how you would generate the data using the `cartesian()` transformation in spark:

```
scala> val months = sc.parallelize(List("Jan","Feb","Mar","Apr","Jun","Jul","Aug","Sep","Oct","Nov","Dec"))
months: org.apache.spark.rdd.RDD[String] = ParallelCollectionRDD[9] at parallelize at <console>:24

scala> val years = sc.parallelize(List(2010,2011,2012,2013,2014))
years: org.apache.spark.rdd.RDD[Int] = ParallelCollectionRDD[10] at parallelize at <console>:24

scala> val cartesianProduct = years.cartesian(months)
cartesianProduct: org.apache.spark.rdd.RDD[(Int, String)] = CartesianRDD[11] at cartesian at <console>:28

scala> cartesianProduct.count()
res2: Long = 55

scala> cartesianProduct.take(5)
res3: Array[(Int, String)] = Array((2010,Jan), (2010,Feb), (2010,Mar), (2010,Apr), (2010,Jun))
```

Figure 2.22: Cartesian product in Scala

For brevity, we are not going to give the examples for Python and Java here, but you can find them at this book's GitHub page.

Actions

As discussed previously, Actions are what makes Spark perform the actual computation from the graph that the framework has been building in the background while you were busy performing transformations on it. While there is a long list of actions offered by Spark, we'll list the most common actions offered by Spark and take you through some of the most common ones:

`reduce(func)`	`takeOrdered(n, [ordering])`
`collect()`	`saveAsTextFile(path)`
`count()`	`saveAsSequenceFile(path) *`
`first()`	`saveAsObjectFile(path)  *`
`take(n)`	`foreach(func)`
`takeSample(withReplacement,num, [seed])`	

The methods `saveAsSequenceFile()` and `saveAsObjectFil()` are only available in Java and Scala.

We have already seen `reduce()`, `collect()`, and `count()` in the previous examples, so we'll be quickly going through their semantics, but will not provide examples for the sake of brevity.

Reduce(func)

As the name implies, reduce performs aggregation on the input dataset, which is often the result of a `map` function call. You can pass a function to the `reduce` action, which should be commutative and associative for it to be run in parallel.

The word commutative comes from commute or move around, so the **commutative property** is the one that refers to moving stuff around. For addition, the rule is $a + b = b + a$; in numbers, this means $2 + 3 = 3 + 2$. For multiplication, the rule is $ab = ba$; in numbers, this means $2{\times}3 = 3{\times}2$.

The word associative comes from associate or group; the **associative property** is the rule that refers to grouping. For addition, the rule is $a + (b + c) = (a + b) + c$; in numbers, this means $2 + (3 + 4) = (2 + 3) + 4$. For multiplication, the rule is $a(bc) = (ab)c$; in numbers, this means $2(3{\times}4) = (2{\times}3)4$.

In the earlier examples, we have seen how to count words from the output of a `FlatMap` function.

Collect()

Collect will return the contents of the RDD upon which it is called, back to the driver program. Typically this is a subset of the input data that you have transformed and filtered by applying Spark's list of transformations, for example, `Map()` and `Filter()`. There are a few caveats with `collect()`, which you should know before calling:

- Typically used during unit testing. In production you would use the `SaveAsXXXFile` methods to store the results for downstream processes to take over.
- The entire contents of the RDD will be sent back to the driver program, meaning that it should be able to fit in memory on a single machine. Don't call `collect()` on large datasets otherwise you may see crashed clients.
- Since an RDD is partitioned across multiple `nodes()`, a `collect()` call will not return an ordered result.

We have seen the examples of `collect()` in previous examples, so we will be skipping code examples for this.

Count()

As seen in earlier examples, `count()` will return the total number of elements in the RDD. For example, in our case of loading a file from a filesystem, the `count()` function returned the total number of lines in the file. Count is often used during unit testing, but being an action it is a heavy operation, since it will re-evaluate the RDD graph before returning a count. If there is a dataset where you frequently need to check the row count, it might be worth caching it (we'll look at `cache ()` a bit later).

The Spark framework provides a few variations of the `count` function:

- `countByValue()`: Returns a count of each unique value in the RDD as a map of *(value, count)* pairs
- `CountByValueApprox()`: An Approximate version of `CountByValue()` – This returns a potentially incomplete result with error bounds
- `CountByKey()`: Only available for RDD of type `(K,V)`. Returns a map of *(key, number)* pairs with the count for each key

Take(n)

Take is a very useful function if you want to have a peek at the resultant dataset. This function will fetch the first *n* number of elements from the RDD. Since an RDD has typically more than one partitions, `Take(n)` will scan one partition and use the results from the partition to estimate the number of additional partitions it needs to scan to satisfy the desired request of n output rows. The function is quite efficient during unit testing and debugging of Spark programs.

`Take(n)` has a few variations in Spark:

- `takeSample (withReplacement, num, [seed])`: As the name indicates, it is very similar to `take()`, but it returns a fixed-size sampled subset of the RDD in an array. Special care is to be taken when using this method, as you should only use it if you expect the resulting array to be small. All the data returned is loaded to the driver's memory.
- `takeOrdered (n, [ordering])`: This returns the first n elements from the RDD as defined by the implicit `Ordering[T]`. Similar to the `takeSample()` method this method returns the data in an array, which is loaded into the driver's memory.

Example 2.18: `takeOrdered()` in Scala:

```
sc.parallelize(Seq(10, 4, 2, 12, 3)).takeOrdered(1)
// returns Array(2)

sc.parallelize(Seq(2, 3, 4, 5, 6)).takeOrdered(2)
// returns Array(2, 3)
```

First()

First is essentially `Take(1)`, and it is implemented in a similar way within Spark. Basically, this will return the first element from the RDD.

SaveAsXXFile()

In a data integration application, saving of the data to files occurs after you have performed a major operation, which could be a transformation or a machine learning model. Spark provides three handy `SaveAsXXXFile()` functions, with each having similar syntax, but slightly different implications. The three methods are as follows:

- `saveAsTextFile(path)`: `SaveAsTextFile()` allows saving the RDD as a text file on the local system, HDFS, or any other Hadoop supported filesystem. The input element can be of any type; however, Spark will call the `toString()` on each element to convert it to text before saving it to a file. We'll see the example of this in our chapter covering ETL with Spark.
- `saveAsSequenceFile(path)` *: This method is only available in Java and Scala, and it writes the RDD out as a Hadoop `SequenceFile` to the path provided in the arguments. The path can refer to a local filesystem, HDFS, or any other Hadoop supported file system.
- `saveAsObjectFile(path)` *: This method is again available with Java and Scala only. The elements within the RDD are written to the path provided in the arguments. The object can then be reloaded using Spark Context's `objectFile()` method.

 `saveAsSequenceFile()` and `saveAsObjectFile()` are available in Java and Scala only.

foreach(func)

So we have seen a map function, which basically applies the function to each element within the RDD, and returns an output that is another RDD. Consider a scenario where you want to apply an operation on each element of the RDD, without returning a result back to the driver program. In these special scenarios, you can use the foreach(func) to initiate a computation without returning a result back to the driver program. The typical cases where you would use this is:

- Updating an accumulator (see the *Shared variables* section)
- Interacting with external systems, for example, storing to a database

While we will look at the accumulators in the later section on *Shared variables*, for the moment, just understand that accumulators are variables that are used for aggregating information across executors. We've been playing with the README.md text file and have done some basic word counting, but the business wants to understand the average length of words in the file. Now, if you don't have a background that covers the MPP platform you might feel that calculating average is just a simple operation. The fact that Spark is a distributed system means that each of the executors would be operating independently of each other, and in order to have a global aggregation, you need to have a globally defined variable that all the executors can update after looking at the length of each word. This is where accumulator would come to the rescue. Furthermore, we would also need to add the total for each word, which is where we would need a foreach() operation. Let's dive straight into an example in Python to demonstrate the foreach() usage:

```
>>> def updateTotals(currWord, numWords, numLetters):
...     numWords += 1
...     numLetters += len(currWord)
...
>>> totalWordsInDocument = sc.accumulator(0)
>>> totalLettersInWords = sc.accumulator(0.0)
>>> allWords = sc.textFile("README.md").flatMap(lambda lineOfText: lineOfText.split())
>>> allWords.foreach(lambda currWord: updateTotals(currWord, totalWordsInDocument, totalLettersInWords))
>>> print "Average word Length in the File : ", totalLettersInWords.value/totalWordsInDocument.value
Average word Length in the File :  6.96610169492
```

Figure 2.23: The foreach() usage, to find average word length in Python

PairRDDs

So far we have seen basic RDD where elements have been words, numbers, or lines of text. We'll now discuss **PairRDD**, which are essentially datasets of key/value pairs. People who have been using MapReduce will be familiar with the concept of key/value pairs and their benefits during aggregation, joining, sorting, counting, and other ETL operations. The beauty of having key value pairs is that you can operate on data belonging to a particular key in parallel, which includes operations such as aggregation or joining. The simplest example could be retail store sales with `StoreId` as the key, and the sales amount as the value. This helps you perform advanced analytics on `StoreId`, which can be used to operate the data in parallel.

Creating PairRDDs

The first step in understanding PairRDDs is to understand how they are created. As we have seen previously, it is not necessary that we have the data available in key/value form upon ingestion and hence there is a need to transform the data using traditional RDD transformation functions into a PairRDD.

Converting a data set into key/value pairs requires careful consideration. The most important of those considerations include answering the following key questions:

- What should be the key?

- What should be the value?

The answer to this lies in the business problem that you are trying to solve. For example, if you had a text file with `StoreId` (1000 different stores) and sales per month (000's of dollars), the key would be the `StoreId`, and the value would be the sales. We are going to work through a comma-separated file, which has the `StoreId` and the relevant sales values per month. The file `storesales.csv` is available for you to be downloaded from the book's website.

Let's look at the structure of the file, before we make any decisions on a future course of action:

```
spark@ubuntu:~/sampledata$ head storesales.csv
744,5477
479,2902
218,6762
14,6623
146,6108
489,7148
787,6039
430,7507
122,3358
944,8580
```

Figure 2.24: File structure of storesales.csv

The structure of the file indicates that we have a three digit `StoreID`, followed by a comma and the value of store sales. Our objective is to calculate the total store sales per store, to understand how each store is doing. As discussed earlier, the first thing is to convert this into a PairRDD, which can be done using a `map` (Python and Scala) and `MapToPair` (Java) function. Let's have a quick look at the examples in Scala, Python, and Java:

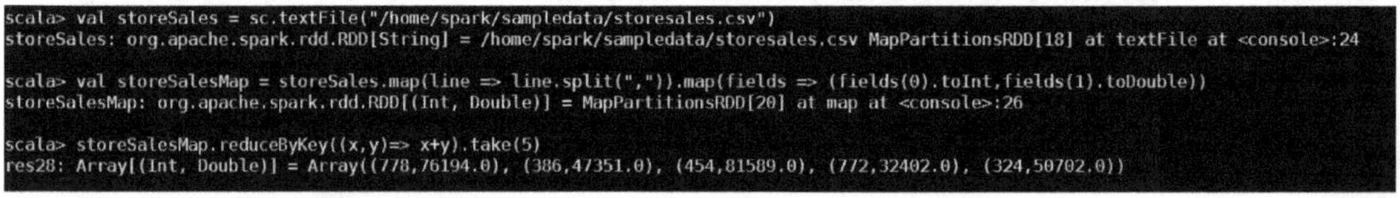

```
scala> val storeSales = sc.textFile("/home/spark/sampledata/storesales.csv")
storeSales: org.apache.spark.rdd.RDD[String] = /home/spark/sampledata/storesales.csv MapPartitionsRDD[18] at textFile at <console>:24

scala> val storeSalesMap = storeSales.map(line => line.split(",")).map(fields => (fields(0).toInt,fields(1).toDouble))
storeSalesMap: org.apache.spark.rdd.RDD[(Int, Double)] = MapPartitionsRDD[20] at map at <console>:26

scala> storeSalesMap.reduceByKey((x,y)=> x+y).take(5)
res28: Array[(Int, Double)] = Array((778,76194.0), (386,47351.0), (454,81589.0), (772,32402.0), (324,50702.0))
```

Figure 2.25: Total sales per store using PairRDDs (Scala)

The code in Python looks similar as we can use a `map` function to transform it to a `PairRDD`:

```
>>> storeSales = sc.textFile("/home/spark/sampledata/storesales.csv")
>>> storeSalesMap = storeSales.map(lambda line:line.split(",")).map(lambda fields:  (fields[0],float(fields[1])))
>>> storeSalesMap.reduceByKey(lambda x,y: x+y).take(5)
[(u'344', 48484.0), (u'346', 49901.0), (u'340', 36650.0), (u'342', 69896.0), (u'810', 52940.0)]
```

Figure 2.26: Total sales per store using PairRDDs (Python)

In Java however, we have to use the `mapToPair()` function to transform it into a PairRDD:

```
JavaRDD<String> dataFile = sc.textFile("c:/spark/sampledata/storesales.csv");
JavaPairRDD<Integer, Integer> lines = dataFile.mapToPair(new PairFunction<String,Integer, Integer>() {
    public Tuple2<Integer, Integer> call(String input) throws Exception{
        String[] tokens = input.split(",");
        return new Tuple2<Integer, Integer>
                    ( new Integer(tokens[0]), new Integer(tokens[1])
                    );

    }
});

System.out.println("Top 5 rows "+lines.reduceByKey((x,y)-> x+y).take(5));
```

Figure 2.27: Total sales per store using PairRDDs (Java)

PairRDD transformations

Spark not only provides the construct of PairRDDs, but it also provides special transformations that are only applicable to PairRDDs in addition to the ones available to the standard RDDs. As the name PairRDD indicates, a pair of two elements *(a,b)* makes up an element; hence, you would see that the operations are applicable to pairs/tuples.

> Tuples are data structures consisting of multiple parts. In relational databases, it refers to an ordered set of data that constitutes a record.

The hint on which operations are designated to be used for PairRDDs can be taken from the fact that operations would either have a word key or value in them indicating that they should be used for PairRDDs:

Key	Value
reduceByKey(func)	flatMapValues(func)
groupByKey()	mapValues(func)
combineByKey()	values()
keys()	
sortByKey()	

We'll run the examples with sales data from regions within the United Kingdom using the following sample input data:

```
{(London, 23.4),(Manchester,19.8),(Leeds,14.7),(London,26.6)}
```

reduceByKey(func)

We have already seen examples of reduceByKey(func) where it combines values for the same key, in our case, store sales based on the storeid(key). The function that has to be passed as an argument has to be an associative function, which applies to the source RDD and creates a new RDD with the resulting values. Since the data from various keys can be on various executors, this function might require the shuffling of data. The following examples demonstrate reduceByKey() with Scala, Python, and Java:

```
scala> val storeSales = sc.parallelize(Array(("London",23.4),("Manchester",19.8),("Leeds",14.7),("London",26.6)))
storeSales: org.apache.spark.rdd.RDD[(String, Double)] = ParallelCollectionRDD[22] at parallelize at <console>:24

scala> storeSales.reduceByKey((accum,sales) => (accum+sales)).collect()
res29: Array[(String, Double)] = Array((Manchester,19.8), (London,50.0), (Leeds,14.7))
```

Figure 2.28: Reduce by key (scala)

The code in Python looks very similar to Scala:

```
>>> storeSales = sc.parallelize([("London",23.4),("Manchester",19.8),("Leeds",14.7),("London",26.6)])
>>> storeSales.reduceByKey(lambda accum,sales: accum + sales).collect()
[('London', 50.0), ('Leeds', 14.7), ('Manchester', 19.8)]
```

Figure 2.29: Reduce by key (Python)

As seen in previous examples, the code in Java looks a bit long winded where you have to create a list of Tuple2 objects before running the reduceByKey action:

```
List<Tuple2<String,Float>> pairsData = new ArrayList();
pairsData.add(new Tuple2("London",23.4));
pairsData.add(new Tuple2("Manchester",19.8));
pairsData.add(new Tuple2("Leeds",14.7));
pairsData.add(new Tuple2("London",26.6));

JavaPairRDD<String,Float> storeSales = sc.parallelizePairs(pairsData);
JavaPairRDD<String,Float> totalStoreSales = storeSales.reduceByKey( (accum, sales) -> accum + sales);
System.out.println("Sales Per Store : "+totalStoreSales);
```

Figure 2.30: Reduce by key (Java)

GroupByKey(func)

As the name indicates, it groups the values based on the same key. For brevity's sake, we will leave the readers to play around with the dataset that you had loaded for `reduceByKey()`, and apply the `groupByKey()` to see the result.

reduceByKey vs. groupByKey – Performance Implications

`reduceByKey()` and `groupByKey()` can be used for similar results, but their execution is plan is different and can have a huge impact on your performance. Behind the scenes both of them use `combineByKey` with different combine/merge implementations which is the key differentiator. `groupByKey()` operation may be very expensive especially if you are grouping in order to perform an aggregation (such as a sum or average) over each key. In such a scenario, using `aggregateByKey` or `reduceByKey()` will provide much better performance. Key differences are:

- `reduceByKey()`: Offers a Map side combine, which means the amount of data shuffled will be lesser than the `groupByKey()`.
- `groupByKey()`: Must be able to hold all key-value pairs for any key in memory. If a key has too many values (quite common with a popular e.g. stock trades), it can potentially result in an `OutOfMemoryError`. `groupByKey()` calls the `combineByKey()` with the `mapSideCombine` parameter as false, which results in exaggerated shuffling, thus impact performance.
- In summary you should avoid `groupbyKey()`. For example, in the following scala example, the same aggregation which is being attempted by `groupByKey()` can be attempted with `reduceByKey()`.

Example 2.19: `groupByKey()` and `reduceByKey()` in Scala:

```
#Input Data
val storeSales = sc.parallelize(Array(("London",
23.4),("Manchester",19.8),("Leeds",14.7),("London",26.6)))

#GroupByKey
storeSales.groupByKey().map(location=>(location._1,location._2.sum)).collec
t()

#SampleResult
#res2: Array[(String, Double)] = Array((Manchester,19.8), (London,50.0),
(Leeds,14.7))
```

```
#ReduceByKey
storeSales.reduceByKey(_+_).collect()

#Sample Result
#res1: Array[(String, Double)] = Array((Manchester,19.8), (London,50.0),
(Leeds,14.7))
```

CombineByKey(func)

To better understand `combinebykey()`, you'll need to understand the combiner functionality from Hadoop MapReduce. Combiner is basically a map side reduce function, to reduce the amount of data shuffled. `combineByKey()` takes three different arguments:

- `CreateCombiner`: This is the first argument of the `combineByKey()` function: As the name indicates, it is used to create the combiner that will be used later. This is called for the first time when a key is found for a partition.
- `MergeValue`: This is called when the key already has an accumulator.
- `MergeCombiner`: This is called when more than one partition has an accumulator for the same key.

Let us consider the example of a dataset, with the following data:

```
("k1",10),("k2",5),("k1",6),("k3",4),("k2",1),("k3",4)
```

For simplicity's sake we have kept the data to three keys, (k1, k2, k3) with at least two values each. Our objective is to calculate the average value for each key. Let's see the Python example first, as it is probably the simplest one:

```
>>>
>>>
>>> sampleData = sc.parallelize([("k1",10),("k2",5),("k1",6),("k3",4),("k2",1),("k3",4)])
>>> sumCount =  sampleData.combineByKey(
...     lambda val: (val,1),
...     lambda valcntpair, val: (valcntpair[0] + val, valcntpair[1] +1),
...         lambda valcntpair,valcntpairnxt: ((valcntpair[0] + valcntpairnxt[0]), (valcntpair[1]+valcntpairnxt[1])))
>>> sumCount.take(3)
[('k3', (8, 2)), ('k1', (16, 2)), ('k2', (6, 2))]
>>> avgByKey = sumCount.map(lambda (label, (valuesum,count)): (label, valuesum/count))
>>> avgByKey.take(3)
[('k3', 4), ('k1', 8), ('k2', 3)]
```

Figure 2.31: CombineByKey (Python)

In the first step we parallelize the data across the cluster. Now let's go through each step of the `combineByKey()` and see what it does to explain the semantics of the operation:

- `lambda val: (val,1):` As mentioned previously, this is the creation of a combiner, which will be called for each partition of the key. This will take the value data item from the *(key, value)* pair in the input dataset, and convert it to another pair, which will be `(value,1)`. So, for example, when it comes across `("k1",10)`, it will pick the value `10` and convert it to `10,1` pair. This is basically the initialization of the combiner. Whenever it comes across a new key partition, it will repeat the same process. The magic is hidden in the name of the operation, which is `combineByKey`.

- `lambda valcntpair, val: (valcntpair[0] + val, valcntpair[1] +1):` This step is the merge value step, which means that this will come into play whenever we come across another key within the partition. When that happens (another key is found), it uses the `valcntpair`, (short for value-count pair) that we created in the create combiner process, and merges the new value and count with the existing one. In our case, the logic was very simple, which is to add the value to the existing aggregated value, and increment the counter by `1` to indicate that we have found another key.

- `lambda valcntpair,valcntpairnxt: ((valcntpair[0] + valcntpairnxt[0]), (valcntpair[1]+valcntpairnxt[1])):` This step as mentioned previously, is the merge combiner step, which basically means that you might have multiple combiners across multiple partitions. Essentially, this is the global summation of all the occurrences of the values and their counts. The end result should be the total value and final count.

For those of you who prefer Scala, here's the same example in Scala:

Example 2.20: `combineBeKey()` example in Scala:

```
val sampleData =
sc.parallelize(Array(("k1",10),("k2",5),("k1",6),("k3",4),("k2",1),("k3",4)
))
val sumCount = sampleData.combineByKey(value => (value,1),
(valcntpair: (Int,Int), value) => (valcntpair._1 + value, valcntpair._2+1),
(valcntpair: (Int,Int), valcntpairnxt: (Int,Int)) => ((valcntpair._1 +
valcntpairnxt._1),(valcntpair._2 + valcntpairnxt._2)))

sumCount.take(3)

val avgByKey = sumCount.map{case (label,value) => (label,
value._1/value._2)}
avgByKey.take(3)
```

We have now looked at the implementation of Average across a set of key value pairs. We have provided a very good dataset earlier in this chapter in the storesales.csv file. As an exercise, can you implement the average sales per store in your favorite programming language?

There is nothing better than going through the examples with your own dataset to grasp a better understanding of the subject.

Transformations on two PairRDDs

So far the transformations that we have seen are the ones on a single PairRDD. However, it is important to look at two of the transformations that apply on more than one PairRDD, as in real-life scenarios you would be working with multiple datasets, which can be facts or dimensions and join them based on their key-values to get a final dataset.

The major two PairRDD transformations are similar to the pseudo set operations that we saw earlier. We have three join operations (join, leftOuterJoin, rightOutJoin) in addition to a subtraction and a cogrouping operation:

Join	**Returns an RDD containing all pair elements with matching keys from both RDDs.**
leftOuterJoin	Performs a left outer join.
rightOuterJoin	Performs a right outer join/.
coGroup	Groups data from both RDDs that share the same key.

Actions available on PairRDDs

Similar to actions available to the standard RDDs, PairRDDs also offer some actions that look essentially the same as the actions we discussed earlier, but generally accept a key as a parameter:

CountByKey()	**This is similar to the** count() **action, but it returns a count based on keys.**
CollectAsMap()	Returns the key-value pairs in this RDD to the master as a map.
Lookup(Key)	Lookup() as the name implies returns the elements for the specific key.

Shared variables

Spark being an MPP environment generally does not provide a shared state as the code is executed in parallel on a remote cluster node. Separate copies of data and variables are generally used during the map() or reduce() phases, and providing an ability to have a read-write shared variable across multiple executing tasks would be grossly inefficient. Spark, however, provides two types of shared variables:

- Broadcast variables – Read-only variables cached on each machine
- Accumulators – Variables that can be added through associative and commutative property

Broadcast variables

Largescale data movement is often a major factor in negatively affecting performance in MPP environments and hence every care is taken to reduce data movement while working on a clustered environment. One of the ways to reduce data movement is to cache frequently accessed data objects on the machines, which is essentially what Spark's broadcast variables are about – keep read-only variables cached on each machine rather than shipping a copy of it with its tasks. This is often required when you need to have the same copy of a small data set (typically a dimension table) accessible to every node in the cluster. Spark will distribute the data to the worker nodes using a very efficient algorithm:

- Broadcast variables are set by the calling program/driver program and will be retrieved by the workers across the cluster
- Since the objective is to share the data across the cluster, they are read-only after they have been set
- The value of a broadcast variable is retrieved and stored only on the first read

A very common example is processing weblogs, where the weblogs contain only the pageId, whereas the page titles are stored in a lookup table. During the analysis of the weblogs you might want to join the page Id from the weblog to the one in the lookup table to identify what particular page was being browsed, which page gets the most hits, which page loses the most customers, and so on. This can be done using the web page lookup table being broadcasted across the cluster. For an example of Broadcast variables, please visit Appendix, *There's More with Spark*.

Accumulators

Accumulators are variables that support associative and commutative properties, which are essential for parallel computations. They are often required to implement counters and are natively supported by Spark for numeric types. Accumulators are different from broadcast variables because:

- They are not read-only
- Executors across the cluster can add to the value of the accumulator variables
- The driver program can access the value of the accumulator variables
- For an example on Accumulators, please visit `Appendix`, *There's More with Spark*.

References

- `https://spark.apache.org/docs/latest/programming-guide.html`
- `http://www.purplemath.com/modules/numbprop.htm`

Summary

In this chapter, we have gone through the concept of creating an RDD, to manipulating data within the RDD. We've looked at the transformations and actions available to an RDD, and walked you through various code examples to explain the differences between transformations and actions. Finally, we moved on to the advanced topics of PairRDD, where we demonstrated the creation of a Pair RDD along with some advanced transformations on the RDD.

We are now ready to explain the ETL process and the types of external storage systems that Spark can read/write data from including external filesystems, Apache Hadoop HDFS, Apache Hive, Amazon S3, and so on. We'll also look at some of the connectors to the most popular databases and how to optimally load data from storage systems, and store it back.

However, before moving on to the next chapter, have a break as you definitely deserve it!

3
ETL with Spark

So we have gone through the architecture of Spark, and have had some detailed level discussions around RDDs. By the end of `Chapter 2`, *Transformations and Actions with Spark RDDs*, we had focused on PairRDDs and some of the transformations.

This chapter focuses on doing ETL with Apache Spark. We'll cover the following topics, which hopefully will help you with taking the next step on Apache Spark:

- Understanding the ETL process
- Commonly supported file formats
- Commonly supported filesystems
- Working with NoSQL databases

Let's get started!

What is ETL?

ELT stands for **Extraction**, **Transformation**, and **Loading**. The term has been around for decades and it represents an industry standard representing the data movement and transformation process to build data pipelines to deliver BI and Analytics. ETL processes are widely used on the data migration and master data management initiatives. Since the focus of our book is on Spark, we'll lightly touch upon the subject of ETL, but will not go into more detail.

Exaction

Extraction is the first part of the ETL process representing the extraction of data from source systems. This is often one of the most important parts of the ETL process, and it sets the stage for further downstream processing. There are a few major things to consider during an extraction process:

- The source system type (RDBMS, NoSQL, FlatFiles, Twitter/Facebook streams)
- The file formats (CSV, JSON, XML, Parquet, Sequence, Object files)
- The frequency of the extract (Daily, Hourly, Every second)
- The size of the extract

Loading

Once the data is extracted, the next logical step is to load the data into the relevant framework for processing. The objective of loading the data into the relevant framework/tool before transformation is to allow the transformations to happen on the system that is more relevant and **performant** for such a processing. For example, if you extract data from a system for which Spark does not have a connector, say **Ingres** database and save it as a text file. Now you may need to do a few transformations before the data is usable. You have two options here: either do the transformations on the file that you have extracted, or first load the data into a framework such as Spark for processing. The benefit of the latter approach is that MPP frameworks like Spark will be much more performant than doing the same processing on the filesystem.

Transformation

Once the data is available inside the framework, you can then apply the relevant transformations. Since the core abstraction within Spark is an RDD, we have already seen the transformations available to RDDs.

Spark provides connectors to certain systems, which essentially combines the process of extraction and loading into a single activity, as it streams the data directly from the source system to Spark. In many cases, since we have a huge variety of source systems available, Spark will not provide you with such connectors, which means you will have to extract the data using the tools made available by the particular system or third-party tools.

How is Spark being used?

Matei Zaharia is the creator of Apache Spark project and co-founder of DataBricks, the company which was formed by the creators of Apache Spark. Matei in his keynote at the Spark summit in Europe during fall of 2015 mentioned some key metrics on how Spark is being used in various runtime environments. The numbers were a bit surprising to me, as I had thought Spark on YARN would have higher numbers than what was presented. Here are the key figures:

- Spark in Standalone mode – 48%
- Spark on YARN – 40%
- Spark on MESOS – 11%

As we can see from the numbers, almost 90% of Apache Spark installations are in standalone mode or on YARN. When Spark is being configured on YARN, we can make an assumption that the organization has chosen Hadoop as their data operating system, and are planning to move their data onto Hadoop, which means our primary source of data ingest might be Hive, HDFS, HBase, or other No SQL systems.

When Apache Spark is installed in standalone mode, the possibility of primary sources increases, but the data on HDFS still remains a huge possibility as it is entirely likely that the customer has a Hadoop installation, but wishes to keep Spark separate as a discovery platform.

Spark can work with a variety of sources. Let's look at the most common sources that we come across:

- File Formats
- File Systems
- Structured Data sources / Databases
- Key/Value Stores

Commonly Supported File Formats

We've already seen the ease with which you can manipulate text files using Spark with the `textFile()` method on `SparkContext`. However, you'll be pleased to know that Apache Spark supports a large number of other formats, which are increasing with every release of Spark. With Apache Spark release 2.0, the following file formats are supported out of the box:

- TextFiles (already covered)
- JSON files
- CSV Files
- Sequence Files
- Object Files

Text Files

We've already seen various examples in Chapter 1, *Architecture and Installation* and Chapter 2, *Transformations and Actions with Spark RDDs* on how to read text files using the `textFile()` function. Each line in the text file is assumed to be a new record. We've also seen examples of `wholeTextFiles()`, which return a PairRDD, with the key being the identifier of the file. This is very useful in ETL jobs, where you might want to process data differently based on the key, or even pass that on to downstream processing.

An important part of the ETL process is to save the data after processing for applications sitting on top of the platform to benefit from. The `saveAsTextFile(pathToFile)` method comes in really handy. It is important to note that this path passed on to the method is basically a directory name, and output from multiple nodes would be saved to this particular directory.

Example 3.1: `saveAsTextFile()` with Scala:

```
//To read all README.md file
val dataFile = sc.textFile("README.md")

//Split line to words, and flatten the result of each split
val words = dataFile.flatMap(line => line.split(" "))
//Save to textFile
words.saveAsTextFile("/tmp/scalawords/")
```

```
spark@ubuntu:~$ ls -ltr /tmp/scalawords
total 8
-rw-r--r-- 1 spark spark 1915 Sep  6 22:20 part-00000
-rw-r--r-- 1 spark spark 1913 Sep  6 22:20 part-00001
-rw-r--r-- 1 spark spark    0 Sep  6 22:20 _SUCCESS
spark@ubuntu:~$ head /tmp/scalawords/part-00000
#
Apache
Spark

Spark
is
a
fast
and
general
```

Figure 3.1: Scala saveAsTextFile() output of multiple files

Example 3.2: `saveAsTextFile()` with Python:

```
//To read all README.md file
dataFile = sc.textFile("README.md")

//Split line to words, and flatten the result of each split
words = dataFile.flatMap(lambda line: line.split(" "))
//Save as TextFile
words.saveAsTextFile("/tmp/pythonwords/")
```

Example 3.3: `saveAsTextFile()` with Java:

```
//To read all README.md file
JavaRDD<String> dataFile = sc.textFile(fileName);
//Split line to words, and flatten the result of each split
JavaRDD<String> words = dataFile.flatMap(line -> Arrays.asList(line.split("
")).iterator());
//Save as TextFile
words.saveAsTextFile(outputFile);
```

CSV and TSV Files

CSV is a common data exchange format that is widely supported by consumer, business, and scientific applications. One of its most common uses is to move data between applications and platforms and in many cases it is considered a defacto standard for ETL applications. In addition to that, lots of publicly available data is in CSV format.

Beginning with Spark 2.0, CSV is now a native data source based on Databrick's **Spark-CSV** module (`http://bit.ly/2cAXCyr`). It is important to understand that CSV typically represents a structured dataset, which has a particular number of columns in the file separated by commas. Before we go a bit further, we need to understand that up until now we have used RDD API, which looks at the data from an unstructured data perspective. The Spark framework does not know the contents of your RDD and considers it an object that can be persisted, transferred over the network, or be manipulated using an Iterator. This obviously means it limits the framework's ability to perform advanced optimization (such as compression, and so on). However, applying structure means by definition, we will limit the ability to our expressiveness. But, what do we need to do with our data generally? The typical computations are reading data, joining data, filtering data, counting data, and aggregating data, which means we can apply a wide variety of computations even if we have a more structured API.

DataFrames are an immutable distributed collection of data organized into named columns. If you are from a database background, consider it similar to a database table. If you are from a Python/R background, you will find yourself at home with DataFrames in Spark; however, the framework offers much richer optimizations. The objective of DataFrames is to take away the complexity of RDDs, and make Spark available to a much wider audience.

Spark unifies the DataFrames and Datasets in 2.0 (which were separate until 1.6), which gives you both syntax and analysis errors at compile time, which is more like typed RDDs. Dataset API is a typed-safe object, which can be operated with compiled lambda functions. We'll look at DataFrames and Datasets more in Chapter 5, *Spark Streaming* but the reason to introduce them right now is because we would like to use the simpler way of reading a CSV files, which uses a `SparkSession` and returns a DataFrame rather than an RDD.

We'll be loading a public data set on house prices in the UK, published by the land registry. You can download the dataset from the following link (`http://bit.ly/2cb258h`).

Example 3.4: Reading a CSV with Scala:

```
val pricePaidDS =
spark.read.format("csv").option("header","false").load("/home/spark/sampled
ata/pp-monthly-update-new-version.csv")
```

You can still go back to your old way of working by converting the dataSet to an RDD using the `toJavaRDD()` operation.

Example 3.5: Reading a CSV with Python:

```
pricePaidDS = spark.read.csv("/home/spark/sampledata/pp-monthly-update-new-
version.csv",header=False)
```

Example 3.6: Reading a CSV with Java:

```
SparkSession spark = SparkSession.builder()
.master("local")
.appName("SparkCSVExample")
.config("spark.some.config.option", "some-value")
.getOrCreate();
Dataset<Row> pricePaidDS = spark.read().csv(fileName);
JavaRDD<Row> pricePaidRDD = pricePaidDS.toJavaRDD();
```

Writing CSV files

Writing CSV files is quite similar to reading, although you have to use `spark.write()` to save the data back and choose `csv` as an output format. It is important to realize that Spark will write multi-part output files, which you may need to concatenate together.

Example 3.7: Writing a CSV with Scala:

```
pricePaidDS.write.format("csv").save("/home/spark/sampledata/price_paid_out
put")
```

Tab Separated Files

Tab Separated Files (TSV) are also commonly used for storing structured data and can act as an alternative to CSV format, which often has difficulties because of the wide use of literal commas in textual data and hence the need to provide escape commas. Spark lets you read TSV files in an equally efficient way. Remember the `tsv` is similar to `csv`, but the only difference is the change in delimiter from a comma to a tab.

We have a sample file `test.tsv`, which is a tab-delimited file created to demonstrate the code that you need to use for loading a `tsv` file.

Example 3.8: Reading a TSV with Scala:

```
val testDS =
spark.read.format("csv").option("delimiter","t").load("/home/spark
/sampledata/test.tsv")
```

Example 3.9: Reading a TSV with Python:

```
testDS = spark.read.csv("/home/spark/sampledata/test.tsv",sep="t")
```

Example 3.10: Reading a TSV with Java:

```
SparkSession spark = SparkSession.builder()
.master("local")
.appName("SparkCSVExample")
.config("spark.some.config.option", "some-value")
.getOrCreate();
Dataset<Row> pricePaidDS = spark.read().option("sep","t").csv(fileName);
```

As you can see, you would just need to specify the delimiter `sep` and pass in the `t` parameter to specify that you are reading a TSV file.

JSON files

JSON is short for JavaScript object notation, and it is an open standard format that uses plain text to transmit data objects consisting of attribute-value pairs. It is the most common data format for asynchronous browser/sever communication and is essentially a replacement of XML (Extensible Markup Language). JSON is a language-independent data format. It derives from JavaScript, but as of 2016, code to generate and parse JSON-format data is available in many programming languages.

JSON is a semi-structured data format and like CSV, a number of public data sets are available in JSON format. In fact, the most popular public data is Twitter feed, which is available in JSON format too. Let's demonstrate this using a simple example of a multi-structured text in JSON format.

Here's a screenshot of the JSON file `products.json` also available from the book's accompanying website.

```
{"prodname":"iPhone", "model":"4s", "price":490}
{"prodname":"Samsung", "model":"Galaxy Note 7", "desc":"Catches fire while charging"}
{"prodname":"iPhone", "model":"7s", "description":"nothing changed"}
```

Figure 3.2: products.json file

Loading a JSON file is similar to loading a CSV file in Scala. Let's look at an example where the file is converted into a DataFrame and then available for all data-frame related operations:

```
scala> val products = spark.read.json("/home/spark/sampledata/json/products.json")
products: org.apache.spark.sql.DataFrame = [desc: string, description: string ... 3 more fields]

scala> products.show()
+--------------------+----------------+------------+-----+--------+
|                desc|     description|       model|price|prodname|
+--------------------+----------------+------------+-----+--------+
|                null|            null|          4s|  490|  iPhone|
|Catches fire whil...|            null|Galaxy Note 7| null| Samsung|
|                null|nothing changed|          7s| null|  iPhone|
+--------------------+----------------+------------+-----+--------+
```

Figure 3.3: Loading a JSON file in Scala

Python also offers a very similar method to read JSON files:

```
>>> products = spark.read.json("/home/spark/sampledata/json/products.json")
>>> products.show()
+--------------------+----------------+------------+-----+--------+
|                desc|     description|       model|price|prodname|
+--------------------+----------------+------------+-----+--------+
|                null|            null|          4s|  490|  iPhone|
|Catches fire whil...|            null|Galaxy Note 7| null| Samsung|
|                null|nothing changed|          7s| null|  iPhone|
+--------------------+----------------+------------+-----+--------+

>>> products.groupBy("prodname").count().show()
+--------+-----+
|prodname|count|
+--------+-----+
|  iPhone|    2|
| Samsung|    1|
+--------+-----+
```

Figure 3.4: Loading a JSON file in Python

Reading a JSON file using java:

```
/*
 * Reading a JSON
 */
Dataset<Row> products = spark.read().json("/home/spark/sampledata/json/products.json");
products.show();
```

Figure 3.5: Loading a JSON file in Java

So we have covered standard text files, CSV, TSV, and JSON files. However, we have been working with local file systems. We did explain how to work with Hadoop in the first chapter, and how to read files off HDFS. When we talk about Hadoop, which has become a ubiquitous data platform, we need to look at popular Hadoop formats including sequence, object, and parquet files.

Sequence files

Sequence files are flat files consisting of binary key/value pairs. Sequence files are one of the most popular Hadoop formats, and if you are using Apache Spark with Hadoop, there is a high likelihood that your data is already in the form of sequence files. A sequence file consists of a header followed by one or more records. A sync marker is used to allow a reader to synchronize to a record boundary from any position in the file. The internal format of a record depends on whether compression is enabled, and if it is, whether you have chosen record compression or block compression. By default, no compression is enabled on the file.

To optimally read data from Hadoop, seeking to a particular point in the file always comes in handy. Sequence files have two ways to seek to a given position in the file:

- Seek() method: Positions the reader to a given point in the file. If the position is not a record boundary, the reader would fail when the next() method is called, so you do need to be synchronized with the record boundaries.
- Sync() method: The second way to find a record boundary, is using sync points. You can call sync with any position in the stream, not necessarily a record boundary and the reader will connect to the next sync point to continue reading.

Due to the popularity of Sequence files, Apache Spark framework supports sequence files. You can use the seqeuenceFile(Key, Value) method to load sequence files. The key and value types should be subclasses of Hadoop's writable interface. For example, you may have a key that stores time stamps represented by a LongWritable and the value would be text, which represents the log text being logged. Spark does allow you to specify native types for common Writables; for example, sequenceFile[Long, String] will automatically read LongWritable and text.

Let's create a sequence file, save it to disk, and load it into an RDD.

Example 3.11: Saving an RDD as a sequence file using Scala:

```
val data =
sc.parallelize(List(("MyKey1","MyValue1"),("MyKey2","MyValue2"),("MyKey3","
MyValue3")))data.saveAsSequenceFile("/home/spark/sampledata/seq-example")
```

```
spark@ubuntu:~/sampledata$ ls -ll /home/spark/sampledata/seq-example/
total 8
-rw-r--r-- 1 spark spark 102 Sep 13 06:20 part-00000
-rw-r--r-- 1 spark spark 126 Sep 13 06:20 part-00001
-rw-r--r-- 1 spark spark   0 Sep 13 06:20 _SUCCESS
spark@ubuntu:~/sampledata$ cat /home/spark/sampledata/seq-example/part-00000
SEQorg.apache.hadoop.io.Textorg.apache.hadoop.io.Text    <TB V  c MyKeyMyValue1spark@ubuntu:~/sampledata$
```

Figure 3.6: RDD saved as sequence file-Scala example

As you can see, the file contents are of binary type. We can use SparkContext's sequence file method to load the sequence file:

```
scala> data.count()
res1: Long = 3

scala> import org.apache.hadoop.io.Text
import org.apache.hadoop.io.Text

scala> val data = sc.sequenceFile("/home/spark/sampledata/seq-example",classOf[Text],classOf[Text])
data: org.apache.spark.rdd.RDD[(org.apache.hadoop.io.Text, org.apache.hadoop.io.Text)] = /home/spark/sampledata/seq-example HadoopRDD[1] at sequenceFile
at <console>:26

scala> data.count()
res2: Long = 3
```

Figure 3.7: Loading a sequence file – Scala example

Python offers the ability to save data as a sequence file, and load it back as an RDD.

Example 3.12: Saving an RDD as a sequence file using Python:

```
data =
sc.parallelize([("MyKey1","MyValue1"),("MyKey2","MyValue2"),("MyKey3","MyVa
lue3")])data.collect()      [('MyKey1', 'MyValue1'), ('MyKey2', 'MyValue2'),
('MyKey3', 'MyValue3')]data.saveAsSequenceFile("/home/spark/sampledata/seq-
py-example")
```

```
spark@ubuntu:~/sampledata$ ls -ll /home/spark/sampledata/seq-py-example/
total 8
-rw-r--r-- 1 spark spark 102 Sep 13 06:41 part-00000
-rw-r--r-- 1 spark spark 126 Sep 13 06:41 part-00001
-rw-r--r-- 1 spark spark   0 Sep 13 06:41 _SUCCESS
spark@ubuntu:~/sampledata$ cat /home/spark/sampledata/seq-py-example/part-00000
SEQorg.apache.hadoop.io.Textorg.apache.hadoop.io.Text  & P  LE   MyKeyMyValue1spark@ubuntu:~/sampledata$
```

Figure 3.8: Contents of a sequence file saved via PySpark

Similar to Scala, the `SparkContext` in python allows you to load the sequence file from the filesystem:

```
>>> data = sc.sequenceFile("/home/spark/sampledata/seq-py-example")
>>> data.count()
3
>>> data.collect()
[(u'MyKey2', u'MyValue2'), (u'MyKey3', u'MyValue3'), (u'MyKey1', u'MyValue1')]
```

Figure 3.9: Loading a sequence file in Python

Saving a sequence file in Java is a bit more convoluted as the API does not provide the support to save a sequence file directly. You would instead need to use the `saveAsHadoopFile()` to save it. However, you can still use the `SparkContext` to retrieve a sequence file using the `sequenceFile()` method.

Object files

Apache Spark allows you to read object files. This is achieved using the `objectFile()` method.

```
objectFile[T] (path:String, minPartitions:
    Int=defaultMinPartitions)(implicit arg0:ClassTag[T]):RDD[T]
```

This method is simple enough to save and retrieve arbitrary objects; however, the default Java Serialization makes it slow. Please visit `Appendix`, *There's More with Spark*, to understand how you can override the default serializer with **Kyro**, and the associated benefits. Apache Spark provides methods such as `objectFile()` with the `SparkContext` object to retrieve a sequence file containing serialized objects, and the RDD interface also provides the `saveAsObjectFile()` method to save the RDD as an object file.

Commonly supported file systems

Until now we have mostly focused on the functional aspects of Spark and hence tried to move away from the discussion of filesystems supported by Spark. You might have seen a couple of examples around HDFS, but the primary focus has been local file systems. However, in production environments, it will be extremely rare that you will be working on a local filesystem and chances are that you will be working with distributed file systems such as HDFS and Amazon S3.

Working with HDFS

Hadoop Distributed File System (**HDFS**) is a distributed, scalable, and portable filesystem written in Java for the Hadoop framework. HDFS provides the ability to store large amounts of data across commodity hardware and companies are already storing massive amounts of data on HDFS by moving it off their traditional database systems and creating data lakes on Hadoop. Spark allows you to read data from HDFS in a very similar way that you would read from a typical filesystem, with the only difference being pointing towards the `NameNode` and the HDFS port.

If you are running Spark on YARN inside a Hadoop cluster, you might not even need to mention the details of `NameNode` and HDFS, as the path that you will pass will default to HDFS.

Most of the methods that we have seen previously can be used with HDFS. The path to be specified for HDFS is as follows:

```
hdfs://master:port/filepath
```

As an example, we have the following settings for our Hadoop cluster:

```
NameNode Node: hadoopmaster.packtpub.comHDFS Port: 8020File Location:
/spark/samples/productsales.csv
```

The path that you need to specify would be as follows:

```
hdfs://hadoopmaster.packtpub.com:8020/spark/samples/productsales.csv
```

Working with Amazon S3

S3 stands for **Simple Storage Service**, an online storage service provided by Amazon Web Services. As of 2013, Amazon S3 was reported to store more than 2 trillion objects. The core principles of S3 include scalability, high-availability, low-latency, and low-pricing. Notable users of S3 include Netflix, Reddit, Dropbox, Mojang (creators of Minecraft), Tumblr, and Pinterest.

S3 provides amazing speed when your cluster is inside Amazon EC2, but the performance can be a nightmare if you are accessing large amounts of data over public Internet. Accessing S3 data is relatively straightforward as you need a path starting with `s3n://` to be passed to Spark's file input methods.

However, before reading from S3, you do need to either set the `AWS_ACCESS_KEY_ID` and `AWS_SECRET_ACCESS_KEY` environment variables, or pass them as a part of your path:

- Configuring the parameters:

```
sc.hadoopConfiguration.set("fs.s3n.awsAccessKeyId", "myaccessKeyID")
sc.hadoopConfiguration.set("fs.s3n.awsSecretAccessKey",
"mySecretAccessKey")
val data = sc.textFile("s3n://bucket/fileLocation")
```

- Passing the Access Key Id and Secret Key:

```
val data = sc.textFile("s3n://MyAccessKeyID:MySecretKey@svr/fileloc")
```

Having looked at the most common file systems, let's focus our attention on Spark's ability to interact with common databases and structured sources. We've already highlighted Spark's ability to fetch data from CSV and TSV files and loading them to DataFrames. However, it is about time we discuss Spark's ability to interact with databases, which will be covered in much more detail in `Chapter 4`, *Spark SQL*.

Structured Data sources and Databases

Spark works with a variety of structured data sources including, but not limited to, the following:

1. **Parquet Files**: Apache Parquet is a columnar storage format. More details about the structure of Parquet and how spark makes use of it is available in the Spark SQL chapter.
2. **Hive tables**.
3. **JDBC**: Spark allows the use of JDBC to connect to a wide variety of databases. Of course the data access via JDBC is relatively slow compared to native database utilities.

We'll cover most of the structured sources in `Chapter 4`, *Spark SQL* later in this book.

Working with NoSQL Databases

A `NoSQL` (originally referring to *non SQL*, *non relational* or *not only SQL*) database provides a mechanism for storage (`https://en.wikipedia.org/wiki/Computer_data_storage`) and retrieval (`https://en.wikipedia.org/wiki/Data_retrieval`) of data which is modeled in means other than the tabular relations used in Relational databases (`https://en.wikipedia.org/wiki/Relational_database`). NoSQL is a relatively new approach to data management and has been quite popular. The core challenges addressed by No SQL include scalability and performance issues for big data problems. It is important to understand that No SQL databases can often be accessed through SQL, but generally provide API level access to their data structures, which can be exceedingly fast. In addition to that the data might be organized in key/value pairs rather than standard database tables and columns.

The most popular No SQL databases include:

- **Cassandra**
- **HBase**
- **MongoDB**
- **Solr**

Let's look at how you can interact with some of these NoSQL systems, and we will start with Cassandra, which is the most popular among these.

Working with Cassandra

Apache Cassandra is a free and open source database management system designed to handle large amounts of data across many commodity servers, providing high availability with no single point of failure. In 2012, University of Toronto researchers studying NoSQL (`https://en.wikipedia.org/wiki/NoSQL`) systems concluded that – "*In terms of scalability, there is a clear winner throughout our experiments. Cassandra achieves the highest throughput for the maximum number of nodes in all experiments*" although "*this comes at the price of high write and read latencies*".

DataStax, Inc. is a software company that develops and provides commercial support for an enterprise edition of the Cassandra database. In order to set up Spark to work with Cassandra you will need to use the open source Spark Cassandra connector available on GitHub (`http://bit.ly/1Rlsuw0`). Once you have set up Spark and Cassandra, you are good to work with Cassandra tables.

Obtaining a Cassandra table as an RDD

You can load Cassandra table objects into Spark as RDDs and operate on them as a normal RDD. You would need to load implicit functions before you proceed with your usual RDD operations. Please do remember to load the relevant JAR files to your JAR files folder in Spark:

```
import com.datastax.spark.connector._sc.cassandraTable("keyspace
name","table name")
```

As you can see, you are not providing any types to the `cassandraTable` operation. This will result in `CassandraRDD[CassandraRow]` objects. If you don't want to map your Cassandra rows to `CassandraRow` class types, you can use your own desired Tuple types as follows:

```
sc.cassandraTable[(String,Int)]("key","value").select("word","count").toArr
aysc.cassandraTable[(Int,String)]("key","value").select("count","word").toA
rray
```

You can alternatively define a case class with properties named as the Cassandra columns:

```
case class WordCounts(word: String, count:
Int)sc.cassandraTable[WordCount].select("count","word").toArray
```

Saving data to Cassandra

Once you have the connector configured, you can also save any RDD to Cassandra. Similar to the concept of providing mapping while reading data from Cassandra, you can provide mapping while saving data to Cassandra. If no mapping is provided, you must ensure that the RDD object class a tuple, or have the property names corresponding to Cassandra column names. Saving data to Cassandra is quite straightforward, as you have to essentially call a `saveToCassandra` method with a keyspace name, table name, and optionally a list of columns.

You can save a collection of tuples to Cassandra as follows:

```
val reviews = sc.parallelize(List(("Saving Private
Ryan",9992),("Schindler's
List",1092)))reviews.saveToCassandra("movies","reviews",
SomeColumns("movieTitle","numReviews"))
```

For more complex mappings, you can define a case class to save the RDD back to Cassandra:

```
case class Review (movieTitle: String, numReviews: Long) reviews =
sc.parallelize(List(Review("Saving Private Ryan",9992), Review("Schindler's
list",1092)))reviews.saveToCassandra("movies","reviews",SomeColumns("moveie
Title","numReviews"))
```

Hopefully this gives you an introduction of working with Cassandra tables. For more details you can visit the GitHub page (`http://bit.ly/2capip3`) or look at the datastax website, which has abundant information around integration of Cassandra and Spark.

Working with HBase

HSBC is an open source, non-relational, distributed database modeled after **Google BigTable** and it is written in Java. It is developed as a part of the ASF Hadoop project and it runs on top of HDFS providing BigTable like capabilities for Hadoop. It provides a fault-tolerant way of storing large quantities of sparse data.

HBase features compression, in-memory operation, and Bloom filters on a per-column basis. HBase is serving several data-driven websites including Facebook's messaging platform. The most notable enterprises using HBase include Adobe, AirBnb, Amadeus IT Group, Imagur, LinkedIn, NetFlix, Sears, and Yahoo.

Accessing HBase is made easy using the HBase Spark module, thanks to the great work by the community and most notably Cloudera's Ted Malaska in his famous blog post announcing the integration work (`http://bit.ly/2cv9xMt`). The excerpts of the code have been taken from the Apache/HBase GitHub page. You may refer to `http://bit.ly/2cSCXD 1`, for full examples.

The basic architecture is to get an HBase connection object on every spark executor. The Spark on HBase project from Cloudera provides Spark HBase integration at an RDD level.

Bulk Delete example

This is a relatively simple bulk delete example where we use the `hbaseBulkDelete()` method to delete relevant data.

```
val hbaseCtx = new HBaseContext(sc,
config)rdd.hbaseBulkDelete(hbaseCtx,TableName.valueOf(tableName),putRecord
=> new Delete(putRecord), 4)
```

Map Partition Example

This is a relatively simple map partitions example.

```
val hbaseCtx = new HBaseContext(sc, config)val getRdd =
rdd.hbaseMapPartitions(hbaseCtx, (it, conn) => {val table =
conn.getTable(TableName.valueOf(tableName))...})
```

As we have discussed previously, RDD's can sometimes be complex for some users and a lot of users prefer DataFrame-based APIs, which provide built-in query plan optimization.

Hotonworks in their blog post in June 2016 announced a DataFrame-based HBase connector (`http://bit.ly/2cSCXD1`) leveraging the Spark Catalyst engine for query optimization. The objective of the Spark-HBase connector was to enable users to perform complex data analysis using Data Frames on an HBase key/value store.

At the time of writing, the connector was hosted in Hortonworks Repo and was in the process of being migrated to HBase Trunk.

Working with MongoDB

MongoDB (from humongous) is a NoSQL, scalable, high-performance, open source, document-oriented database built for speed providing rich document-based queries for easy readability. Instead of storing data in tables and rows, as you would in a traditional relational database, MongoDB allows you to store JSON-like documents in dynamic schemas. MongoDB increases productivity, as modeling data as documents is simpler and allows schemas to evolve rapidly without duplication. MongoDB scales by adding more servers thus adding capacity based on requirements.

Some of the key users of MongoDB include SAP, Mcafee, Foursquare, eBay, Adobe, and LinkedIn.

MongoDB Spark connector (`http://bit.ly/2cDtRZG`) was released on Sep 6, 2016 and provides integration between MongoDB and Apache Spark. The connector allows you to use all Spark libraries with MongoDB datasets. The MongoDB spark-connector website (`http://bit.ly/2cO98Y9`) provides detailed examples on accessing MongoDB from Spark, and we'll list some of them for the benefit of the readers.

Connection to MongoDB

Connection to MongoDB happens automatically when an RDD action performs a read/write to MongoDB. However, to enable the MongoDB connector specific functions and implicits for SparkConext and **Resilient Distributed Dataset (RDD)**, you need to import the relevant objects:

```
import com.mongodb.spark._
```

Writing to MongoDB

To write an RDD to MongoDB, you can use the save method on MongoSpark, which is a helper object that allows easy creation of RDDs, DataFrames, and Datasets. The MongoSpark object uses `SparkConf` for the configuration, and requires SparkSession to be set either explicitly or via the SparkContext object:

```
MongoSpark.save(myRDD) //Uses SparkConf for Configuration
```

You can also use the RDD implicit helper method, `saveToMongoDB()`, to write the data to MongoDB:

```
myRDD.saveToMongoDB()//Uses SparkConf for Configuration
```

Loading data from MongoDB

You can use the `MongoSpark.load()` method to create an RDD representing a collection. You can either pass the configuration when you start Spark-Shell, or optionally create a `ReadConfig` object, which will provide various read configuration settings. For more detailed examples, you should visit the spark-connector page (`http://bit.ly/2cO98Y9`) or the GitHub page for the mongo-spark connector (`http://bit.ly/2cZHNTC`).

Working with Apache Solr

Apache Solr is an open source search platform built upon a Java library called **Lucene**. Solr is a popular search platform for websites because it can index and search multiple sites and return recommendations for related content based on the search query's taxonomy.

The **Spark-Solr** project (`http://bit.ly/1Ub12GU`) provides tools for reading data from Solr as a Spark RDD and indexing objects.

Importing the JAR File via Spark-shell

Before starting you will need to import the JAR file via Spark-shell:

```
cd $SPARK_HOME./bin/spark-shell --packages "com.lucidworks.spark:spark-
solr:2.1.0"or./bin/spark-shell --jars spark-solr-2.0.1.jar
```

Once you have imported the JAR file you can connect to your `SolrCloud` instance via DataFrame API or via an RDD.

Connecting to Solr via DataFrame API

```
val options = Map(  "collection" -> "{solr_collection_name}",  "zkhost" ->
"{zk_connect_string}")val df =
sqlContext.read.format("solr").options(options).load
```

Connecting to Solr via RDD

```
import com.lucidworks.spark.rdd.SolrRDD  val solrRDD = new SolrRDD(zkHost,
collectionName, sc)
```

There are a couple of good examples of using Spark with Solr including Indexing and Querying Twitter data (`http://bit.ly/2cvPjSV`) and Analyzing NYC yellow taxi csv data (`http://bit.ly/2d56EUI`) on the project's GitHub page.

References

The following valuable references have been used during the chapter, and will aid you in exploring further. Each of the integrations that we have discussed are generally a topic of their own and an entire chapter can be written on them. It would be worthwhile to look deeper into the following reference articles.

1. `http://prod.publicdata.landregistry.gov.uk.s3-website-eu-west-1.amazon aws.com/pp-monthly-update-new-version.csv`

2. `http://www.purplemath.com/modules/numbprop.htm`

3. `https://en.wikipedia.org/wiki/JSON`

4. `http://data.consumerfinance.gov/api/views.json`

5. `https://databricks.com/blog/2015/02/17/introducing-dataframes-in-spark -for-large-scale-data-science.html`

6. `https://en.wikipedia.org/wiki/Apache_Cassandra`

7. `https://www.youtube.com/watch?v=_gFgU3phogQ&feature=youtu.be`

8. https://docs.datastax.com/en/datastax_enterprise/4.5/datastax_enterprise/spark/sparkSave.html

9. http://blog.cloudera.com/blog/2015/08/apache-spark-comes-to-apache-hbase-with-hbase-spark-module/

10. https://en.wikipedia.org/wiki/Couchbase_Server

11. https://docs.mongodb.com/spark-connector/getting-started/

Summary

In this chapter, we have covered the basics of ELT, and Spark's ability to interact with a variety of sources including standard text, CSV, TSV, and JSON files. We moved on to look at accessing filesystems including local filesystems, HDFS, and S3. Finally, we spent some time on helping you understand access to a variety of NoSQL databases and the connectors available. As you can see, we have covered a few of the popular systems, but the massive open-source ecosystem around Spark means there are new connectors coming almost on a monthly basis. It is highly recommended to look closely at the project's GitHub page for the latest developments.

We'll now move on to the next chapter, where we are going to focus on Spark SQL, DataFrames, and Datasets. The next chapter is important as it builds on what we have covered already and helps us understand how Spark 2.0 abstracts developers from the relatively complex concept of RDD's by expanding on the already introduced concept of DataFrames and DataSets.

4
Spark SQL

We've had a roller coaster ride so far. In the last chapter, we looked at performing ELT with Spark, and most importantly, loading and saving data from and to various data sources. We've looked at structured data streams and NoSQL databases, and during all that time we have tried to keep our attention on using RDDs to work with such data sources. We had slightly touched upon DataFrame and DataSet API, but refrained from going into too much detail around these topics, as we wanted to cover it in full detail in this chapter.

If you have a database background and are still trying to come to terms with RDD API, this is the chapter you'll love the most, as it essentially explains how you can use SQL to exploit the capabilities of the Spark framework.

In this chapter we will be covering the following key topics:

- DataFrame API
- DataSet API
- Catalyst Optimizer
- Spark Session
- Manipulating Spark DataFrames
- Working with Hive, Parquet files, and other databases

Let's get cracking!

What is Spark SQL?

SQL has been the defacto language for business analysts for over two decades now. With the evolution and rise of big data came a new way of building business applications – APIs. However, people writing Map-Reduce soon realized that while Map-Reduce is an extremely powerful paradigm, it has limited reach due to the complex programming paradigm, and was akin to sidelining the business analysts who would previously use SQL to solve their business problems. The business analysts are people who have deep business knowledge, but limited knowledge around building applications through APIs and hence it was a huge ask to have them code their business problems in the new and shiny frameworks that promised a lot. This led the open source community to develop projects such as Hive and Impala, which made working with big data easier.

Similarly in the case of Spark, while RDDs are the most powerful APIs, they are perhaps too low level for business users. Spark SQL comes to the rescue of people who would like to use Spark, but perhaps prefer to stay away from RDDs and concentrate on solving their business problems.

SQL as most of us know stands for structured query language, thus emphasizing its power around structured data. Spark SQL is thus a module that can be used primarily for structured data processing. Imagine an optimizer who has to work with data without knowing what it is working with, and trying to figure that out during the computation compared to being provided with information up front on the type of data and computation being performed. Spark SQL provides this additional information to the optimizer, which helps it provide additional optimizations. It is important to understand that Spark SQL will use the same computation engine for all APIs, thus ensuring similar computational performance irrespective of the API chosen to specify the computation.

There are multiple ways to interact with Spark SQL including SQL and the DataSet API. The results of running SQL are a Dataset or a DataFrame, and hence it is important to understand what a Dataset and DataFrame is.

What is DataFrame API?

I believe before looking at what a DataFrame API is, we should probably review what an RDD is and identify what could possibly be improved on the RDD interface. RDD has been the user facing API in Apache Spark since its inception and as discussed earlier can represent unstructured data, is compile-time safe, has dependencies, is evaluated lazily, and represents a distributed collection of data across a Spark cluster. RDDs can have partitions, which can be aided by locality info, thus aiding Spark scheduler to allow the computation to be performed on the machines where the data is already available to reduce the costly network overload.

However from a programming perspective, the computation itself is less transparent, as Spark doesn't know what you are doing, for example, join/filters, and so on. They express the *how* of a solution better than the *what* of a solution. The data itself is opaque to the optimizer, which means Spark gets an object either in Scala, Java, or Python and the only thing Spark as a Framework can do is to take a Serializer and convert it to bytes limiting the ability to look at individual columns, special compression, and so on. This limits your and the optimizer's ability to perform optimization on the data. Another issue with Spark RDD API is that they are slow on non-JVM languages such as Python. In other words, it is very easy to build inefficient transformations, for example, reduce followed by a filter rather than vice-versa.

A DataFrame API is similar to RDD because it represents an immutable distributed collection of data like an RDD. The core objective behind DataFrame API was to get the developers to express what they want to accomplish rather than how they want to accomplish and leave the low-level optimization to the Spark framework. Another objective of DataFrame was to expand the usage of Spark to a wider audience beyond data engineers who can code in Java and/or Scala. DataFrame allows the imposition of structure onto a distributed collection of data to allow higher-level abstractions and provide a domain specific API to manipulate your distributed data. The characteristic of DataFrame in Spark is that it has schema, which means it is something that can be viewed as a column having a name and a type. Once you have a DataFrame, you can manipulate it with SQL.

What is DataSet API?

Spark announced Dataset API in Spark 1.6, an extension of DataFrame API representing a strongly-typed immutable collection of objects mapped to a relational schema. Dataset API was developed to take advantage of the Catalyst optimiser by exposing expressions and data fields to the query planner. Dataset brings the compile-type safety, which means you can check your production applications for errors before they are run, an issue that constantly comes up with DataFrame API.

One of the major benefits of DataSet API was a reduction in the amount of memory being used, as Spark framework understood the structure of the data in the dataset and hence created an optimal layout in the memory space when caching datasets. Tests have shown that DataSet API can utilize 4.5x lesser memory space compared to the same data representation with an RDD.

Figure 4.1 shows analysis errors shown by Spark with various APIs for a distributed job with SQL at one end of the spectrum and Datasets at the other end of the spectrum:

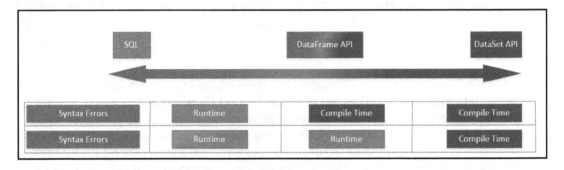

Figure 4.1: Analysis errors shown by Spark with various APIs

What's new in Spark 2.0?

For some of you who have stayed closed to the announcements of Spark 2.0, you might have heard of the fact that DataFrame API has now been merged with the Dataset API, which means developers now have to learn fewer concepts to learn and work with a single high-level, type-safe API called a Dataset.

The Dataset API takes on two distinct characteristics:

- A strongly typed API
- An untyped API

A DataFrame in Apache Spark 2.0 is just a dataset of generic row objects, which are especially useful in cases when you do not know the fields ahead of time; if you don't know the class that is eventually going to wrap this data, you will want to stay with a generic object that can later be cast into any other class (as soon as you figure out what that is). If you want to switch to a particular class, you can request Spark SQL to enforce types on the previously generated generic row objects using the as method of the DataFrame.

Let us consider a simple example of loading a Product available as a JSON document and enforcing a class object on top of that:

```
val df = spark.read.json("products.json")
case class Product(ProductId:Int, ProductName: String, ProductCategory:
String)ls -1
val ds:DataSet[Product] = df.as[Product]
```

A dataset by contrast is a collection of strongly-typed JVM objects, dictated by a case class that you define in Scala or a class in Java. The following table indicates a list of typed and un-typed APIs:

Language	Dataset [Typed]	DataFrame [Untyped]
Scala	Dataset[T]	Dataset[Row]
Java	Dataset[T]	** No Untyped APIs
Python	** No Typed APIs	DataFrame
R	** No Typed APIs	DataFrame

As we are aware Python and R do not provide a compile time type-safety; hence, you will only find untyped APIs, namely DataFrames, for those two languages.

Having said all that, what it means to use one language over the other, and weather you get a better performance by using Scala versus Python are in discussions that have been happening in Spark circles since the availability of multiple APIs. You would be pleased to know that DataFrames, Datasets, and SQL share the same optimization/execution pipeline under the covers. The following figure originally presented at the Spark Summit by *Michael Armbrust* essentially covers how the Catalyst optimizer works under the hood to promise similar performance irrespective of what API you use to describe your computation. We'll look into the details of the Catalyst optimizer in a bit more detail later in this chapter.

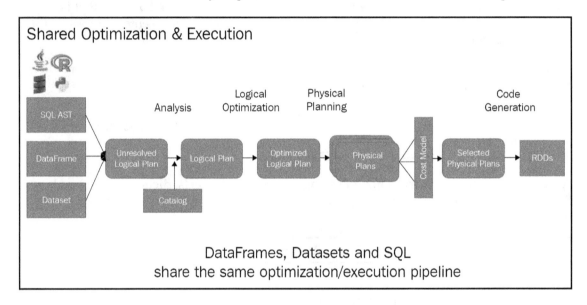

Figure 4.2: Shared optimization and execution

It is important to note, that irrespective of the API or language being used the first step is the construction of a logical query plan. For example, it might be filtering data or a join condition and the actual optimization pipeline is agnostic of the location of the query, hence resulting in a similar performance across all APIs.

Under the hood – catalyst optimizer

We have mentioned catalyst optimizer a couple of times in this book and perhaps it's time to explain what makes catalyst optimizer so powerful. Before going into Catalyst optimizer I want to get the users (especially with database backgrounds) to think for a moment on how they have used their platforms. For example, you might know that in the SQL world you specify what you want, and not how you want it, which basically means that you are concerned about the business logic and not the technical implementation of how your programs will execute in the cluster. This essentially means that you have little control over how to optimize the query outside of creating statistics and indexes on specific columns and tables. However, if you have been with us since the first chapter of this book, you will have seen that the RDD API is extremely powerful, which means that two programs that achieve the same objective can massively differ in their execution plans. Let us consider two scenarios, where you have two tables, namely products and sales transactions, and you want to get the total count of sales transactions for the product ID # 3500, which is *Women's Shoes size 7.*

Here's how you would write it in SQL language:

```
Select Count (*)
From (
    Select Transactions.TransactionId
    From Transactions Join Products
    Where
        Transactions.ProductId = Products.ProductId
        And Product.ProductId = 3500)
```

The preceding solution seems simple enough and would be a simple implementation in most databases with varying performance based on the number of rows, underlying database, and the types of indexes that you have created. The only optimization that you would perhaps do in the preceding query is to have the database administrator create indexes on the `ProductId` and `TransactionId` columns and additionally create statistics on the table.

Now let's implement the solution as an RDD in Spark. They are implemented by engineers with different skillsets who approach the problem slightly differently.

Solution 1

Let's look at the first solution.

```
val transCount = transactions.cartesian(products).filter{
    case (TransProdId, ProdProdId) => TransProdId ==
```

```
    ProdProdId
  }
  .filter{case(TransProdId, ProdProdId) => ProdProdId = 3500
  }
  .map{
    case (TransProdId,ProdProdId) => TransProdId
  }.count
  Println(transCount)
```

Solution 2

Let's now look at the second solution.

```
val filteredProducts = products.filter(prodProdId = 3500)
val preparedTransactions = Transactions.map(TransProdId => (TransProdId,
TransProdId))
val preparedProducts = filteredProducts.map(prodProdId => (prodProdId,
prodProdId))
val transCount = preparedTransactions.join(preparedProducts).map {
case (transProdId, _) => transProdId}.count
Println(transCount)
```

We ran this test in our local cluster with 200,000 transactions and over 10,000 products. *Solution 2*, which ran in 0.5 seconds, was 300 times faster than *Solution 1*, which took almost 150 seconds. If you look at the code, you'll see *Solution 2* does a lot more prep work and avoids the expensive Cartesian join operation. While you would expect this skill from data engineers building data pipelines on a daily basis, you cannot expect this engineering focus from data analysts who would want to focus on the analysis and let somebody else take care of this optimization detail. While using RDD API's your functions are black-boxes with opaque computation and data types, thus giving you, the developer, great power over how the programs execute across a cluster. As we know, with great power comes great responsibility, and thus RDD API mandates the developers to write efficient programs for different kinds of workloads. This is not easy for a variety of workloads and you would probably prefer to focus on solving the business problem rather than the execution flow of your code across a cluster.

Spark comes to your rescue to take the pain of the optimization away from analysts to let them focus on the business problems while you optimize the code behind the scenes to find the most efficient way to run it across the cluster. You will need to use one of the high-level programming interfaces such as SQL, DataFrames, or Dataset and describe the data operations needed for your business problems, such as filter and join. Spark Catalyst optimizer will find the best possible way to execute the program.

Let's have a quick look at how the Catalyst Optimizer works.

Catalyst has an internal representation of a user's program called a query plan. The high-level programming interface is a public API of the executing query plan. Once we have the initial version of the query plan, Catalyst will apply different transformations to convert the query plan to the optimized query plan. Using Spark's SQL code generation mechanism, the optimized query plan will get converted into a DAG of RDDs ready for execution. At its core, Catalyst defines user programs as a tree, and transforms one tree into another tree.

In Catalyst, there are two types of plans:

- **Logical Plan**: Defines computation on a dataset without defining how to conduct the execution. This is a high level representation of the user's intended compute to be run on the Spark platform. Every logical plan defines a list of attributes and constraints as requested by the user's program, but it stops short of defining how the actual execution will take place within Spark.
- **Physical Plan**: A physical plan is generated from a logical plan, and as the name implies, it is much more tangible in terms of what computation to perform on the platform and the specifics of how to actually execute. An example of logical to physical conversion is a `join` operation in logical terms being converted to a *sort-merge* join in the physical terms. It is important to note that Spark will generate multiple physical plans and choose the best one with the lowest cost.

In catalyst there are two major types of transformations:

- A tree to another tree of the same kind, for example:

    a. Expression => Expression

    b. Logical plan => Logical Plan

    c. Physical Plan => Physical Plan

- A tree to a tree of a different kind, for example,

    Logical Tree => Physical Tree

On a high level, the following figure depicts how Catalyst optimizes a user's query plans:

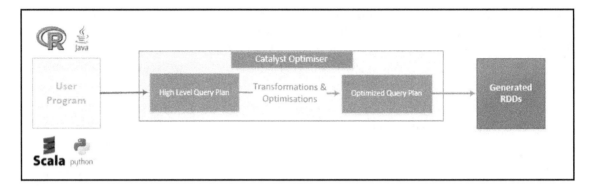

Figure 4.3: High level working of Catalyst Optimiser

This conversion of a logical to a physical plan is quite complex as it uses strategies to find the best execution plan. The optimization of a plan includes various rules, for example:

1. If you are using predicates, Spark will try to push the predicate down to the datastore and pull only relevant information to optimize the performance.
2. If you are using constant values in expressions, they are evaluated at completion time rather than at runtime for each row.
3. If you are using only a specific subset of columns rather than an entire list of columns from a table, Spark will try to fetch only the relevant columns that are being used. This means if you are using a columnar, store your performance will be even more optimal for such cases.

Catalyst is a top-class optimization engine and you will appreciate the depth of the engine once you start understanding the internal details. The conversion from an unresolved query plan to an optimized query plan involves a number of steps under the hood, which can be seen in the following figure:

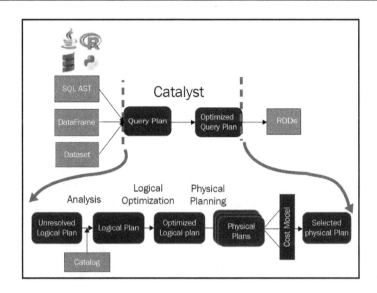

Figure 4.4: Inner details of transformation from unresolved to a selected physical plan

It is for this reason that a user can specify their computation in any of the specified APIs (Java, Scala, Python, or R), and Spark will find the optimum execution plan for this. If you would like to learn more about this, I would highly recommend *Yin Huai*'s talk during Spark Summit in June 2016 (`http://bit.ly/DeepDiveIntoCatalyst`). You should also look at specific code on GitHub.

Now that you have had a quick walk through Catalyst optimizer, it might be worthwhile understanding how other components of the Spark framework interact with the Catalyst optimiser.

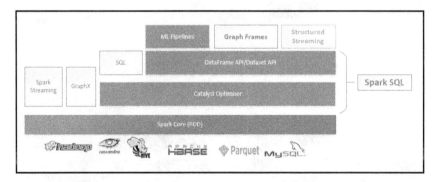

Figure 4.5: Catalyst as the engine behind ML Pipelines, GraphFrames, and Structured Streaming

ML Pipelines, Structured streaming, and GraphFrames making use of DataFrame/Dataset APIs all benefit from Catalyst optimiser.

The Sparksession

In computer science a session is a semi-permanent interactive information interchange between two communicating devices or between a computer and a user. `SparkSession` is something similar, which provides a time bounded interaction between a user and the Spark framework and allows you to program with DataFrames and Datasets. We have used `SparkContext` in the previous chapters while working with RDDs, but Spark Session should be your go-to starting point when starting to work with Data Frames or Datasets.

Creating a SparkSession

In Scala, Java, and Python you will use the Builder pattern to create a `SparkSession`. It is important to understand that when you are using `spark-shell` or `pyspark`, Spark session will already be available as a spark object:

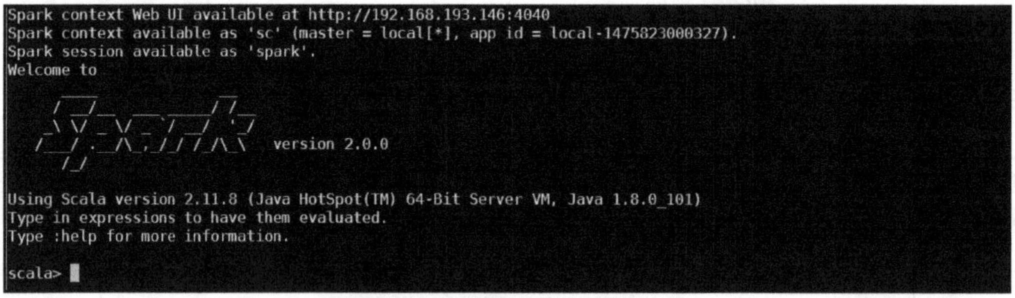

Figure 4.6: Spark session in Scala shell

The following image shows SparkSession in an Python shell:

Figure 4.7: SparkSession in Python shell

Example 4.1: Scala – Programmatically creating a Spark Session:

```
import org.apache.spark.sql.SparkSession
val spark = SparkSession.builder().appName("Spark SQL basic
example").config("spark.some.config.option", "some-value").getOrCreate()
```

Example 4.2: Java – Programmatically creating a Spark Session:

```
import org.apache.spark.sql.SparkSession;
SparkSession spark = SparkSession
  .builder()
  .appName("Java Spark SQL basic example")
  .config("spark.some.config.option", "some-value")
  .getOrCreate();
```

Example 4.3: Python – Programmatically creating a Spark Session:

```
from pyspark.sql import SparkSession
spark = SparkSession \
  .builder \
  .appName("Python Spark SQL basic example") \
  .config("spark.some.config.option", "some-value") \
  .getOrCreate()
```

Example 4.4: R – Programmatically creating a SparkSession:

```
sparkR.session(appName = "MyApp", sparkConfig =
list(spark.some.config.option = "some-value"))
```

Prior to Spark 2.0, you needed `HiveContext` to work with Hive. Spark 2.0 provides full built-in Hive support, which gives you the ability to write `HiveQL`, access Hive UDFs, and the ability to read/write from Hive tables. To enable Hive support, you have to use the `enableHiveSupport()` option while building the Spark session via the API.

Creating a DataFrame

With Spark session object, applications can create DataFrames from an existing RDD, a Hive table, or a number of data sources we mentioned earlier in `Chapter 3`, *ELT with Spark*. We have looked at creating DataFrames in our previous chapter especially from TextFiles and JSON documents. We are going to use a **Call Detail Records** (**CDR**) dataset for some basic data manipulation with DataFrames. The dataset is available from this book's website if you want to use the same dataset for your practice.

A sample of the data set looks like the following screenshot:

```
{"OriginatingNum": 797308107, "TerminatingNum": 797131221, "Origin": "London", "Dest": "Birmingham","DateTime": "02/11/2016 01:51:41", "CallCharge": 549}
{"OriginatingNum": 777121117, "TerminatingNum": 777440332, "Origin": "Manchester","Dest": "London", "DateTime": "05/02/2016 01:26:54", "CallCharge": 2645}
{"OriginatingNum": 797009202, "TerminatingNum": 784243404, "Origin": "Victoria", "Dest": "Manchester","DateTime": "01/12/2016 21:12:54","CallCharge": 1233}
{ "OriginatingNum": 777557705, "TerminatingNum": 796420467, "Origin": "Twickenham", "Dest": "Victoria", "DateTime": "07/11/2016 01:07:34", "CallCharge": 2651}
{"OriginatingNum": 765434022, "TerminatingNum": 799086250, "Origin": "Leeds", "Dest": "Scotland", "DateTime": "02/11/2016 22:22:26", "CallCharge": 3162}
{"OriginatingNum": 779716002, "TerminatingNum": 795127353, "Origin": "Bradford", "Dest": "Virginia Water", "DateTime": "05/01/2016 20:12:35", "CallCharge": 2246}
{"OriginatingNum": 775490102, "TerminatingNum": 775019605, "Origin": "Yorkshire", "Dest": "Ascot", "DateTime": "04/12/2016 23:53:52", "CallCharge": 571}
```

Figure 4.8: Sample CDRs data set

Manipulating a DataFrame

We are going to perform the following actions on this data set:

1. Load the dataset as a DataFrame.
2. Print the top 20 records from the data frame.
3. Display Schema.
4. Count total number of calls originating from London.
5. Count total revenue with calls originating from revenue and terminating in Manchester.
6. Register the dataset as a table to be operated on using SQL.

Scala DataFrame manipulation – examples

Let us look at Scala examples of DataFrame manipulation.

1. The following example shows how to load a dataset as a DataFrame and showing top 20 records using scala.

```
val df=spark.read.json("/home/spark/sampledata/json/cdrs.json")
```

Executing the previous code will give the output as seen in *Figure 4.9:*

```
scala> val df=spark.read.json("/home/spark/sampledata/json/cdrs.json")
df: org.apache.spark.sql.DataFrame = [CallCharge: bigint, DateTime: string ... 4 more fields]

scala> df.show()
+----------+-------------------+-------------+--------------+--------------+--------------+
|CallCharge|           DateTime|         Dest|        Origin|OriginatingNum|TerminatingNum|
+----------+-------------------+-------------+--------------+--------------+--------------+
|       549|02/11/2016 01:51:41|   Birmingham|        London|     797308107|     797131221|
|      2645|05/02/2016 01:26:54|       London|    Manchester|     777121117|     777440392|
|      1233|01/12/2016 21:12:54|   Manchester|      Victoria|     797009202|     784243404|
|      2651|07/11/2016 01:07:34|     Victoria|    Twickenham|     777557705|     798420467|
|      3162|02/11/2016 22:22:26|     Scotland|         Leeds|     785434022|     779086250|
|      2246|05/01/2016 20:12:35|Virginia Water|     Bradford|     779716202|     795137353|
|       571|04/12/2016 23:53:52|        Ascot|     Yorkshire|     775490102|     775019605|
|      3291|06/11/2016 20:31:49|     Bracknell|    Birmingham|     787581376|     797043387|
|      2270|03/12/2016 12:15:17|      Bradford|     Coventary|     789231956|     787649491|
|      3420|06/02/2016 20:57:44|     Yorkshire|         Wales|     785969980|     789993090|
|      3084|02/01/2016 02:44:27|    Birmingham|      Scotland|     797662091|     777765510|
|      3037|09/01/2016 00:48:43|        Marlow|Virginia Water|     784036802|     798095485|
|      3011|08/11/2016 20:19:19|    Sunningdale|        Ascot|     785160169|     797922170|
|      1018|05/01/2016 11:24:28|         Lords|     Bracknell|     789519210|     774080821|
|       771|02/12/2016 02:07:09|          Oval|        Marlow|     775617249|     786549418|
|      3585|07/11/2016 03:43:23|     Coventary|    Sunningdale|     797932062|     788292522|
|       908|06/01/2016 23:08:06|         Wales|         Lords|     777561966|     788455450|
|        95|04/12/2016 24:17:54|      Scotland|          Oval|     777508024|     789954417|
|      2754|03/11/2016 00:45:24|    Birmingham|    Birmingham|     777087537|     778710691|
|      1327|03/01/2016 03:11:03|     Coventary|        London|     774688108|     797626213|
+----------+-------------------+-------------+--------------+--------------+--------------+
only showing top 20 rows
```

Figure 4.9: Loading DataFrame and viewing the data set

2. Printing a schema of a JSON document:

```
scala> df.printSchema()
root
 |-- CallCharge: long (nullable = true)
 |-- DateTime: string (nullable = true)
 |-- Dest: string (nullable = true)
 |-- Origin: string (nullable = true)
 |-- OriginatingNum: long (nullable = true)
 |-- TerminatingNum: long (nullable = true)
```

Figure 4.10: Printing a schema of a JSON document

3. Filtering all calls originating from London:

```
scala> df.filter("Origin = 'London'").show()
+----------+-------------------+----------+------+--------------+--------------+
|CallCharge|           DateTime|      Dest|Origin|OriginatingNum|TerminatingNum|
+----------+-------------------+----------+------+--------------+--------------+
|       549|02/11/2016 01:51:41|Birmingham|London|     797308107|     797131221|
|      1327|03/01/2016 03:11:03| Coventary|London|     774688108|     797626213|
|      2940|04/01/2016 01:19:28|Manchester|London|     775584064|     795017614|
|      1780|03/11/2016 01:41:37|      Oval|London|     794018876|     776154503|
|       420|08/02/2016 14:47:38| Bracknell|London|     779461846|     776103392|
+----------+-------------------+----------+------+--------------+--------------+
```

Figure 4.11: Filtering all calls originating from London

4. Filtering calls originating from London and Terminating at Manchester:

```
scala> df.filter("Origin = 'London'").filter("Dest = 'Manchester'").show()
+----------+-------------------+----------+------+-------------+-------------+
|CallCharge|           DateTime|      Dest|Origin|OriginatingNum|TerminatingNum|
+----------+-------------------+----------+------+-------------+-------------+
|      2940|04/01/2016 01:19:28|Manchester|London|    775584064|    795017614|
+----------+-------------------+----------+------+-------------+-------------+
```

Figure 4.12: Filtering all calls originating from London and Terminating at Manchester

5. Finding out the average revenue earned from such calls:

```
scala> df.filter("Origin = 'London'").filter("Dest = 'Manchester'").agg(sum("CallCharge")).show()
+---------------+
|sum(CallCharge)|
+---------------+
|           2940|
+---------------+
```

Figure 4.13: Average revenue earned from calls between London and Manchester

6. Registering DataFrame as a table and querying the dataset.
   We can alternatively register the DataFrame as a table using
   `CreateOrReplaceTempView()` on the dataframe and then executing an SQL
   query. If you are familiar with SQL, you'll find the SQL capability of great use.
   Don't forget that your original data was in a JSON format, which could
   potentially be billions of rows, now available for you to query as a database table:

   ```
   Dataframe.createOrReplaceTempView("<TableName>")
   sparkSession.sql("Select <projectionList> from <RegisteredTable>")
   ```

```
scala> spark.sql("select Dest, count(*) as callCnt from calldetails group by Dest Order by callCnt Desc").show()
+-------------+-------+
|         Dest|callCnt|
+-------------+-------+
|   Birmingham|     10|
|        Ascot|      8|
|    Coventary|      8|
|        Wales|      8|
|    Bracknell|      8|
|     Scotland|      8|
|    Yorkshire|      7|
|Virginia Water|     7|
|     Bradford|      7|
|       Marlow|      4|
|        Lords|      4|
|         Oval|      4|
|  Sunningdale|      4|
|     Victoria|      3|
|   Manchester|      3|
|        Leeds|      3|
|       London|      3|
|    Twickenham|     1|
+-------------+-------+
```

Figure 4.14: Top called destinations

Python DataFrame manipulation – examples

You can try these examples in your PySpark shell:

1. Load the dataset as a DataFrame:

   ```
   df = spark.read.json("/home/spark/sampledata/json/cdrs.json")
   ```

2. Print the top 20 records from the data frame:

   ```
   df.show(20)
   ```

3. Display Schema:

   ```
   df.printSchema()
   ```

4. Count and view the total number of calls originating from London:

   ```
   df.filter("Origin = 'London'").count()
   df.filter("Origin = 'London'").show()
   ```

5. Count total revenue with calls originating from revenue and terminating in Manchester:

```
df.filter("Origin = 'London'").filter("Dest = 'Manchester'").show()
df.filter("Origin = 'London'").filter("Dest =
  'Manchester'").agg({"CallCharge":"sum"}).show()
```

6. Register the dataset as a table to be operated on using SQL:

```
df.createOrReplaceTempView("calldetails")
spark.sql("select Dest, count(*) as callCnt from calldetails
group by Dest Order by callCnt Desc").show()
```

R DataFrame manipulation – examples

The following examples can be tried in an R shell:

1. Load the dataset as a DataFrame:

```
df <- read.json("/home/spark/sampledata/json/cdrs.json")
```

2. Print the top 20 records from the data frame:

```
head(df,20)
```

3. Display Schema:

```
printSchema(df)
```

4. Count the total number of calls originating from London:

```
head(where(df, df$Origin == "London"))
```

5. Count total revenue with calls originating from revenue and terminating in Manchester:

```
sum(head(where(df, df$Origin == "London" &
  df$Dest=="Manchester"))$CallCharge)
```

Basically, there are two operations here:

- Filter all calls from London to Manchester :

```
head(where(df, df$Origin == "London" & df$Dest=="Manchester"))
```

- Then use the result of that to aggregate the value of the CallCharge column:

```
Sum(<FilterResultDataFrame>$CallCharge)
```

6. Register the dataset as a table to be operated on using SQL:

```
createOrReplaceTempView(df,"calldetails")
topCallDestinations = sql("select Dest, count(*) as callCnt from
   calldetails group by Dest Order by callCnt Desc")
show(topCallDestinations)
```

Java DataFrame manipulation – examples

Let us look at the same example with Java Programming Language.

1. Load the dataset as a DataFrame:

```
Dataset<Row> df = mySparkSession.read().json(fileName);
```

2. Print the top 20 records from the data frame:

```
df.show(20);
```

3. Display Schema:

```
df.printSchema();
```

4. Count the total number of calls originating from London:

```
df.filter("Origin == 'London'").show();
```

5. Count total revenue with calls originating from revenue and terminating in Manchester:

```
df.filter("Origin == 'London'").filter("Dest =='Manchester'").show();
```

6. Register the dataset as a table to be operated on using SQL:

```
df.createOrReplaceTempView("calldetails");
mySparkSession.sql(" SELECT Dest, count(*) as callCnt from
"+"calldetails "+"group by Dest "+"Order by callCnt Desc").show();
```

Reverting to an RDD from a DataFrame

We've seen how we can work with DataFrames; however, there might be cases where you might want to switch back to working with RDD. Fortunately, Spark provides the ability to switch back to RDD interface in Scala, Python, and Java. There is no way to revert back to an RDD from the R API.

`callDetailsDF` is the variable name for the DataFrame created in each of the following languages:

Example: Reverting to RDD using Scala API

```
val callDetailRecordsRDD = callDetailsDF.rdd;
```

Example: Reverting to RDD using Python API

```
callDetailRecordsRDD = callDetailsDF.rdd;
```

Example: Reverting to RDD using Java API

```
JavaRDD callDetailRecordsRDD = callDetailsDF.toJavaRDD();
```

Converting an RDD to a DataFrame

So we have seen how to create a DataFrame from a data source and get an RDD, but you'll be pleased to know that if you are working with RDDs and feel that for a certain set of operations a DataFrame would be more suitable, you can switch to a DataFrame. As you will have noticed, a DataFrame needs a bit more information than an RDD can provide so you will need to provide the schema to the Spark Framework. We'll use our CDR data, previously in a JSON format, and this time formatted as a CSV file to be loaded and operated upon. The data sample looks like this:

```
0797308107,0797131221,London,Birmingham,02/11/2016 01:51:41,549
0777121117,0777440392,Manchester,London,05/02/2016 01:26:54,2645
0797009202,0784243404,Victoria,Manchester,01/12/2016 21:12:54,1233
0777557705,0798420467,Twickenham,Victoria,07/11/2016 01:07:34,2651
0785434022,0779086250,Leeds,Scotland,02/11/2016 22:22:26,3162
0779716202,0795137353,Bradford,Virginia Water,05/01/2016 20:12:35,2246
0775490102,0775019605,Yorkshire,Ascot,04/12/2016 23:53:52,571
0787581376,0797043387,Birmingham,Bracknell,06/11/2016 20:31:49,3291
0789231956,0787649491,Coventary,Bradford,03/12/2016 12:15:17,2270
0785969980,0789993090,Wales,Yorkshire,06/02/2016 20:57:44,3420
```

Figure 4.15: Sample dataset

Example: Converting RDD to DataFrame using Scala API

We are going to use the `case` class syntax to create a call detail class, and then use that to create rows of `CallDetails` from the data file. You've looked at most of the syntax examples already:

Create a class:

```
case class CallDetail
   (OriginNumber: String,
     TermNumber: String,
     Origin: String,
     Term: String,
     callts: String,
     callCharge: Long)
```

Create a DataFrame from the RDD by splitting the data using the separator *comma* and then applying the `CallDetail` class. We then use the individual attributes and map them to the CallDetail object. Finally, we use the `toDF` method to create a DataFrame:

```
val callDetailsDataFrame = sc.textFile("/home/spark/sampledata/cdrs.csv")
   .map(callDetail => callDetail.split(","))
   .map(attributes => CallDetail
     (attributes(0),
     attributes(1),
     attributes(2),
     attributes(3),
     attributes(4),
     attributes(5).toInt))
   .toDF()
     callDetailsDataFrame.show()
```

Example: Converting RDD to DataFrame using Python API

```
from pyspark.sql import Row
  #Loading text File
  dataFile = sc.textFile("/home/spark/sampledata/cdrs.csv")
  #Splitting textFile rows into individual columns
  dataFileSplitIntoColumns = dataFile.map(lambda l: l.split(","))
  #Applying Schema
  callDetailRecords = dataFileSplitIntoColumns.map(lambda cd:
Row(OriginNum=cd[0],TermNum=cd[1],Origin=cd[2],Term=cd[3],datetime=cd[4],ca
llCharge=int(cd[5]))))
  #Creating a DataFrame
  callDetailsDF=spark.createDataFrame(callDetailRecords)
  #Perform usual DataFrame operations
  callDetailsDF.show(5)
```

Example: Converting RDD to DataFrame using Java API

The following screenshots gives an example for converting RDD to DataFrame using Java:

```java
import java.io.Serializable;

public class CallDetailRecord implements Serializable {

        private String originNumber;
        private String termNumber;
        private String origin;
        private String termDest;
        private String dateTime;
        private long callCharges;

        public String getOriginNumber() {return originNumber;}
        public String getTermNumber() {return termNumber;}
        public String getOrigin() { return origin;}
        public String getTermDest() {return termDest;}
        public String getDateTime() {return dateTime;}

        public void setDateTime(String dateTime) {this.dateTime = dateTime; }
        public void setTermDest(String termDest) {this.termDest = termDest;}
        public long getCallCharges() {return callCharges;}
        public void setOrigin(String originDest) {this.origin = originDest;}
        public void setCallCharges(long callCharges) {this.callCharges = callCharges;}
        public void setOriginNumber(String originNumber) {this.originNumber = originNumber;}
        public void setTermNumber(String termNumber) {this.termNumber = termNumber;}
    }
```

Figure 4.16: Creating the CallDetailRecord class to encapsulate the data

The following screenshot shows how to create a RDD and converting DataFrames using Java:

```
JavaRDD<String> dataFile = sc.textFile(fileName);

JavaRDD<CallDetailRecord> cdr = dataFile.map(new Function<String,CallDetailRecord>(){
    public CallDetailRecord call(String line) throws Exception{
        String[] parts = line.split(",");
        CallDetailRecord cdr = new CallDetailRecord();
        cdr.setOriginNumber(parts[0]);
        cdr.setTermNumber(parts[1]);
        cdr.setOrigin(parts[2]);
        cdr.setTermDest(parts[3]);
        cdr.setDateTime(parts[4]);
        cdr.setCallCharges(Long.parseLong(parts[5]));
        return cdr;
    }
});


Dataset<Row> cdrDataFrame = mySparkSession.createDataFrame(cdr, CallDetailRecord.class);
cdrDataFrame.show();
```

Figure 4.16: Creating an RDD and converting it to a DataFrame

Other data sources

Spark supports reading data from a variety of data sources via the DataFrame interface. As we have seen earlier, a DataFrame can be used to create a temporary view, which allows you to run SQL queries over its data.

Parquet files

Apache Parquet is a common columnar format available to any project in the Hadoop ecosystem, regardless of the choice of data processing framework, data model, and programming language. Parquet's design was based on Google's Dremel paper and is considered to be one of the best performing data formats in a number of scenarios. We'll not go into too much detail around Parquet, but if you are interested you might want to have a read at `https://parquet.apache.org/`. In order to show how Spark can work with Parquet files, we will write the CDR JSON file as a Parquet file, and then load it before doing some basic data manipulation.

Example: Scala – Reading/Writing Parquet Files

```
#Reading a JSON file as a DataFrame
val callDetailsDF =
spark.read.json("/home/spark/sampledata/json/cdrs.json")
# Write the DataFrame out as a Parquet File
callDetailsDF.write.parquet("../../home/spark/sampledata/cdrs.parquet")
# Loading the Parquet File as a DataFrame
val callDetailsParquetDF = spark.read.parquet
"/home/spark/sampledata/cdrs.parquet")
# Standard DataFrame data manipulation
callDetailsParquetDF.createOrReplaceTempView("callDetails")
val topCallingPairs = spark.sql("select Origin,Dest, count(*) as cnt from
callDetails group by Origin,Dest order by cnt desc")
```

```
scala> topCallingPairs.show(5)
+----------+----------+---+
|    Origin|      Dest|cnt|
+----------+----------+---+
|Birmingham|Birmingham|  4|
|Birmingham|  Scotland|  2|
|   Bradford|  Bradford|  2|
|  Yorkshire|     Wales|  2|
|  Coventary| Bracknell|  2|
+----------+----------+---+
only showing top 5 rows
```

Figure 4.18: Parquet file data manipulation using Scala API

Example: Python – Reading/Writing Parquet Files

```
#Reading a JSON file as a DataFrame
callDetailsDF = spark.read.json("/home/spark/sampledata/json/cdrs.json")
# Write the DataFrame out as a Parquet File
callDetailsDF.write.parquet("cdrs.parquet")
# Loading the Parquet File as a DataFrame
callDetailsParquetDF = spark.read.parquet("cdrs.parquet")
# Standard DataFrame data manipulation
callDetailsParquetDF.createOrReplaceTempView("calldetails")
topCallLocsDF = spark.sql("select Origin,Dest, count(*) as cnt from
calldetails group by Origin,Dest order by cnt desc")
```

Example: R – Reading/Writing Parquet Files

```
#Loading a JSON file as a DataFrame
callDetailsDF <- read.df("/home/spark/sampledata/json/cdrs.json","json")
```

```
#Writing the DataFrame out as a Parquet
write.parquet(callDetailsDF,"cdrs.parquet")
#Reading Parquet as a DataFrame
callDetailsParquetDF <- read.parquet("cdrs.parquet")
#Data Manipulation of Parquet Data
createOrReplaceTempView(callDetailsParquetDF,"parquetFile")
topCallLocsDF <- sql("select Origin,Dest, count(*) as cnt from calldetails
group by Origin,Dest order by cnt desc")
head(topCallLocsDF)
```

Example: Java – Reading/Writing Parquet Files

```
#Loading a JSON file as a DataSet of Row objects
Dataset<Row> callDetailsDF = mySparkSession.read().json(fileName);
#Writing a Parquet File
callDetailsDF.write().parquet(parquetFileName);
#Reading a Parquet file of Dataset of Row objects
Dataset<Row> callDetailsParquetDF = mySparkSession.read().parquet
parquetFileName);
#Parquet file data manipulation
callDetailsParquetDF.createOrReplaceTempView("callDetails");
Dataset<Row> topLocDF = mySparkSession.sql("select Origin,Dest, count(*) as
cnt from calldetails group by Origin,Dest order by cnt desc");
topLocDF.show(5);
```

Working with Hive

Hive is a data warehousing infrastructure based on Hadoop. Hive provides SQL-like capabilities to work with data on Hadoop. Hadoop, during its infancy was limited to MapReduce as a computer platform, which was a very engineer-centric programming paradigm. Engineers at Facebook in 2008 were writing fairly complex Map-Reduce jobs, but realised that it would not be scalable and it would be difficult to get the best value from the available talent. Having a team that could write Map-Reduce Jobs, and be called upon was considered a poor strategy and hence the team decided to bring SQL to Hadoop (Hive) due for two major reasons:

- An SQL-based declarative language while allowing engineers to plug their own scripts and programs when SQL did not suffice.
- Centralized metadata about all data (Hadoop based datasets) in the organization, to create a data-driven organization.

Spark supports reading and writing data stored in Apache Hive. You would need to configure Hive with Apache Spark.

Hive configuration

Hive has a large number of dependencies that are not provided with Spark. Hive dependencies need to be provided on the classpath for Spark, on all the worker nodes for Spark to load them automatically. Three major configuration files are required for the configuration, and need to be placed in the conf/ directory of your Spark installation:

- `hive-site.xml`: Hive site is generally used for setting the values for the entire Hive configuration. You'll need this file if you are connecting to an external hive installation.
- `core-site.xml`: This file is needed for all the relevant security configuration.
- `hdfs-site.xml`: This file is required for the relevant HDFS configuration.

You can create a SparkSession with Hive support using the `enableHiveSupport()` option, which will provide connectivity to the Hive metastore, support for Hive **SERDE**, and the **UDF**. You can enable hive support without an existing hive installation, which will mean that a local `metastore_db` powered by Derby will automatically be created for you. Once you have configured your `spark.sql.warehouse.dir` during the session instantiation, your tables will be created in the specified directory. As always make sure you have allowed the user starting the Spark session sufficient privileges on the warehouse-directory to be able to write into the directory. We'll demonstrate working with a local hive metastore in the following examples, where we will create a session that has hive support enabled, create a new table, and load the CDRs data into the hive table before querying and manipulating it. We'll be using Hive-QL, which is a variant of SQL.

Figure 4.19: Working with the local Hive metastore

Python, R, and Java API provide similar support. Let's have a quick look at the code examples for Python, Java, and R.

Example: Python – Spark SQL – Hive Integration

```
# Creating a Spark session with hive Support
customSparkSession = SparkSession.builder \c
appName("Ptyhon Sparl SQL and Hive Integration ") \
config("spark.sql.warehouse.dir","spark-warehouse") \
enableHiveSupport() \
getOrCreate()
# Creating a Table
customSparkSession.sql("CREATE TABLE IF NOT EXISTS cdrs
(callingNumber STRING, calledNumber String, origin String, Dest
String,CallDtTm String, callCharge Int)
ROW FORMAT DELIMITED FIELDS TERMINATED BY ',' ")
# Loading Data into Hive CDRs table
customSparkSession. sql("LOAD DATA LOCAL INPATH
'/home/spark/sampledata/cdrs.csv' INTO table cdrs")
# Viewing the Loaded data
customSparkSession.sql("SELECT * from cdrs LIMIT 5").show()
# Viewing top 5 Origin destination Pairs
customSparkSession. sql(" SELECT origin, dest, count(*) as cnt from cdrs
group by origin, dest order by cnt desc LIMIT 5").show()
```

```
>>> customSparkSession.sql("SELECT origin, dest, count(*) as cnt from cdrs group by \
... origin, dest order by cnt desc LIMIT 5").show()
+----------+----------+---+
|   origin|      dest|cnt|
+----------+----------+---+
|Birmingham|Birmingham|  4|
| Yorkshire|     Wales|  2|
|Birmingham|     Ascot|  2|
|  Bradford|  Bradford|  2|
| Coventary| Bracknell|  2|
+----------+----------+---+
```

Figure 4.20: Viewing the top five origin/destination pairs

Example: R – SparkSQL – Hive Integration

```
# Creating Spark Session with hive Support
sparkR.session(enableHiveSupport=TRUE)
# Creating a table to hold CDRs
sql("CREATE TABLE IF NOT EXISTS cdrs(callingNumber STRING, calledNumber
String,
origin String, Dest String,CallDtTm String, callCharge Int) ROW FORMAT
DELIMITED FIELDS TERMINATED BY ','")
```

```
# Loading data
sql("LOAD DATA LOCAL INPATH '/home/spark/sampledata/cdrs.csv' INTO table
cdrs")
# Finding top paired origin/destinations
sql(" SELECT origin, dest, count(*) as cnt from cdrs group by origin, dest
order by cnt desc LIMIT 5")
```

```
> head(sql(" SELECT origin, dest, count(*) as cnt from cdrs group by origin, dest order by cnt desc LIMIT 5"))
       origin        dest cnt
1 Birmingham Birmingham   4
2  Yorkshire      Wales   2
3 Birmingham      Ascot   2
4   Bradford   Bradford   2
5  Coventary  Bracknell   2
```

Figure 4.21: Viewing the top five origin/destination pairs

Example: Java – Spark SQL – Hive Integration

```
# Create Spark Session with Hive Support
SparkSession mySparkSession = SparkSession.builder()
    .master("local")
    .appName("Java Spark-SQL Hive Integration ")
    .enableHiveSupport()
    .config("spark.sql.warehouse.dir", sparkWarehouseDir)
    .getOrCreate();
# Create Table
mySparkSession.sql("CREATE TABLE IF NOT EXISTS "
    +" CDRs (callingNumber STRING, calledNumber String, "+" origin String,
Dest String,CallDtTm String, callCharge Int) "
    +" ROW FORMAT DELIMITED FIELDS TERMINATED BY ','");
# Load CDRs data
mySparkSession.sql("LOAD DATA LOCAL INPATH '"+fileName+"' "
    +"INTO TABLE CDRs");
#Manipulating the data using Hive-QL
mySparkSession.sql(" SELECT origin, dest, count(*) as cnt "
    +" FROM CDRs "
    +" GROUP by origin, dest "
    +" ORDERR by cnt desc "
    +" LIMIT 5").show();
```

SparkSQL CLI

Spark provides **SparkSQL CLI** to work with the Hive metastore service in local mode and execute queries input from the command line.

You can start the Spark-SQL CLI as follows:

```
./bin/spark-sql
```

Configuration of Hive is done by placing your `hive-site.xml`, `core-site.xml`, and `hdfs-site.xml` files in conf/. You may run `./bin/spark-sql --help` for a complete list of all available options.

Working with other databases

We have seen how you can work with Hive, which is fast becoming a defacto data warehouse option in the open source community. However, most of the data in the enterprises beginning with Hadoop or Spark journey is to stored in traditional databases including Oracle, Teradata, Greenplum, and Netezza. Spark provides you with the option to access those data sources using JDBC, which returns results as DataFrames. For the sake of brevity, we'll only share the Scala example of connecting to a Teradata database. Please remember to copy your database's JDBC driver class to all nodes in the cluster, and make it available for the drivers and executors to load into the JVM:

```
val teradataDBCDF = spark.read
    .format("jdbc")
    .option("url", "jdbc:teradata://localTD, TMODE=TERA")
    .option("dbtable", "dbc.tables")
    .option("user", "admin")
    .option("password", "suP3rUser")
    .load()
```

Once you have the dataframe, you can operate on your dataframes as normal, by either operating on them directly or registering them as a temp table and using them for SQL data manipulation.

References

The following list of references have been used for the various topics of this chapter. You might want to go through these specific sections to get more detailed understanding of individual sections.

1. https://databricks.com/blog/2016/07/14/a-tale-of-three-apache-spark-apis-rdds-dataframes-and-datasets.html
2. https://databricks.com/blog/2016/08/15/how-to-use-sparksession-in-apache-spark-2-0.html

3. `https://parquet.apache.org/`

4. **Setting up SparkR**: `https://www.youtube.com/watch?v=A5cBAPoidsg`

5. `http://spark.apache.org/docs/latest/sql-programming-guide.html`

6. **Structured Streaming**: `https://www.youtube.com/watch?v=1a4pgYzeFwE&feature=youtu.be`

7. **Catalyst Optimizer**: `https://www.youtube.com/watch?v=UBeewFjFVnQ&t=39s`

Summary

In this chapter, we have covered details around Spark SQL, the DataFrame API, the Dataset API, Catalyst optimiser, the nuances of SparkSession, creating a DataFrame, manipulating a DataFrame, converting a DataFrame to RDD, and vice-versa before providing examples of working with DataFrames. This is by no means a complete reference for SparkSQL and is perhaps just a good starting point for people planning to embark on the journey of Spark via the SQL route. We have looked at how you can use your favorite API without consideration of performance, as Spark will choose an optimum execution plan.

The next chapter is one of my favorite topics – Spark MLLib. Spark provides a rich API for predictive modeling and the use of Spark MLLib is increasing every day. We'll look at the basics of machine learning before providing users with an insight into how the Spark framework provides support for performing predictive analytics. We'll cover topics from building a machine-learning pipeline, feature-engineering, classification and regression, clustering, and a few advanced topics including identifying the champion models and tuning a model for performance.

5
Spark Streaming

All of us have been there. We go on to a new e-commerce website where we haven't bought anything before, like a new gadget, and decide to purchase it. As soon as we hit the checkout button, within a couple of seconds we get a message on our mobile phone from the credit card company asking if it was really us who was making the purchase. Let this sink in for a moment... The company has captured the transaction, realized it is not a usual transaction (some outlier detection mechanism), and made a call within a span of a few seconds.

It's a connected world out there, and streaming has become part and parcel of our digital life whether it is fraud detection, optimum ad placement, website monitoring, or self-driving cars. Sensors rule the roost, and pick up every bit of information you can possibly imagine ranging from the temperature fluctuations of your car's engine to your personal heart beat every second. The abundance of sensors has led to data that is being generated in huge volumes and high velocity, two of the famous "*Vs*" of big data.

We have worked with data at rest on local or distributed filesystems, in SQL or NOSQL databases, but what we have not touched upon is the challenges of data in-motion. The challenges include managing the stream, handling late-arriving data, fault-tolerance semantics, and perhaps getting the value out before the data becomes stale. Spark Streaming is an API that provides you the ability to work with streams of data.

This chapter will focus on the following key topics, such as:

- What is Spark Streaming?
- Discretized streams
- Sliding window operations
- Caching, persistence, and checkpointing
- Fault tolerance

- Structured streaming
- Key differences between discretized streams and structured streams

Let's get started!

What is Spark Streaming?

Spark Streaming was introduced in Spark 0.7 in early 2013, with the objective of providing a fault-tolerant scalable architecture that could provide second-scale latency, with a simple programming model and integrated with batch and interactive processing. The industry had given into the idea of having separate platforms for batch and streaming operations, with Storm and Trident being the popular streaming engines of choice in the open source community. Storm would provide at least once semantics while Trident would provide exactly-once semantics. Spark Streaming revolutionized the concept of streaming by allowing users to perform streaming and batching within the same framework and by emphasizing the idea that users should not be worried about the state maintenance of objects. It is now one of the most popular Spark APIs and according to a recent Spark survey carried out by DataBricks, more than 50% of the users consider Spark Streaming as the most important component of Spark.

Spark Streaming is an extension of the core Spark API, and major effort has been done to keep the API for batch and streaming applications relatively similar. Spark Streaming allows you to ingest data from a variety of sources such as Flume and Kafka, and filesystems such as HDFS, S3, Amazon Kinesis, and even live Twitter feeds, which is the favorite for most people demoing Spark-Streaming on stage. The data can be stored in storage engines such as HDFS, S3, or a variety of databases. You may choose to publish dashboards based on the information coming from Spark Streaming. You can also apply machine learning algorithms (learning and scoring) and graph algorithms to data streaming in the Spark framework.

Figure 5.1: Spark Streaming overview

As of today, Spark provides two different programming models for streaming:

- Spark Streaming as **Discretized Streams (Dstream)**
- Structured Streaming (still in Alpha as of November 2016)

We'll go through the DStream API as that is currently in production, but by the latter half of this chapter we will introduce you to the Structured Streaming API, which will take away some of the pain points of writing streaming applications. Having said that DStream API is still miles ahead of many other APIs in the market today.

DStream

It's good news for folks who have been paying attention to RDDs, because DStream is essentially dividing a live stream of data into smaller batches of n seconds, and processing each individual batch as an RDD in Spark. In the following figure, the StreamingContext uses a *10* second interval to join the data arriving and creating an RDD, which is passed onto Spark for further processing as per the user's program declarations. As seen earlier, the input can be from a variety of sources. Spark provides the usual powerful programming interfaces in Java, Scala, and Python to work with the Streaming API.

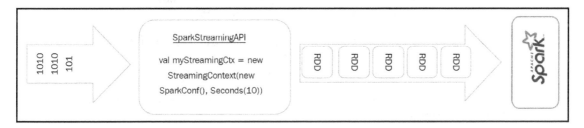

Figure 5.2: Spark Streaming overview – a mini-batch of 10 seconds

StreamingContext

The StreamingContext is the main entrance point to Spark Streaming applications and is equivalent to SparkContext that we have been using until now to work with Spark RDDs. The StreamingContext is configured the same way as SparkContext, but includes the additional parameter – the batch duration, which can be in milliseconds, seconds, or minutes.

Let's look at a simple streaming example, where we will use the netcat utility to write the data onto a network socket. Our streaming application will listen to the network socket to read the data from the socket, and perform a word count on the incoming data. This is a relatively simple example often used to demonstrate Spark Streaming as it removes complexities of other third-party systems generating or consuming streams.

Let's look at the examples in all three APIs (Scala, Java, and Python). We need to open two Terminal windows, whereby on one window we will run our Spark example, and on the other window we will run the netcat utility.

Let's look at the Scala version of the streaming program.

We are essentially creating listening to port 9988, and performing a word count on the incoming traffic:

```scala
import org.apache.spark._
import org.apache.spark.streaming._

object StreamingWordCount {
  def main(args: Array[String]){
    // Create a streaming context - Donot use local[1] when running locally
  val conf = new
SparkConf().setMaster("local[2]").setAppName("NetworkWordCount")
    val ssc = new StreamingContext(conf, Seconds(5))

    // Create a DStream that connects to hostname: port and fetches
       information at the start of streaming.
    val lines = ssc.socketTextStream("localhost", 9988)

    // Operate on the DStream, as you would operate on a regular stream
    val words = lines.flatMap(_.split(" "))

    // Count each word in each batch
    val pairs = words.map(word => (word, 1))
    val wordCounts = pairs.reduceByKey((x, y) => x + y)
    // Print on the console
    wordCounts.print()
    ssc.start() // Start the computation
    ssc.awaitTermination() // Wait for the computation to terminate
    }
}
```

Using netcat utility:

We are using the netcat utility to stream data to port 9988 using the `nc` utility available on most versions of Linux operating systems:

```
nc -lk 9988
```

 Spark Streaming has been designed to be used in batch mode and not interactive mode. For a quick reference, if you want to build your Spark application you may want to follow this link: `http://bit.ly/2fj3aPB`.

The code would generate the output based on the contents that you paste in the window where you have started your netcat utility:

```
spark@ubuntu:/spark/spark-2.0.1$ nc -lk 9988
Spark uses the Hadoop core library to talk to HDFS and other Hadoop-supported
storage systems. Because the protocols have changed in different versions of
Hadoop, you must build Spark against the same version that your cluster runs.
```

Figure 5.3: Netcat utility – port 9988

We are running the net cat utility, and simply pasting the contents of README.md on the window. On the other side, you can see that the streaming application is listening at port 9988, and applies the business logic that we wrote in our streaming application:

```
16/10/27 10:08:50 INFO DAGScheduler: Job 1 finished: print at StreamingWordCount.scala:22, took 0.346818 s
-------------------------------------------
Time: 1477588130000 ms
-------------------------------------------
(systems.,1)
(Because,1)
(runs.,1)
(same,1)
(have,1)
(build,1)
(uses,1)
(changed,1)
(talk,1)
(cluster,1)
...
```

Figure 5.4: Spark Streaming WordCount application

As you saw in the code, our interval was 5 seconds, so after 5 seconds, the streaming application again tries to apply the business logic of the WordCount application, but because the data stream is empty, it does not print anything:

```
16/10/27 10:08:55 INFO DAGScheduler: Job 3 finished: print at StreamingWordCount.scala:22, took 0.040047 s
-------------------------------------------
Time: 1477588135000 ms
-------------------------------------------
```

Figure 5.5: Streaming application – after 5 seconds

Let's decipher this Streaming WordCount program before we go into code examples in Java and Python.

Steps involved in a streaming app

Let's look at the steps involved in building a streaming application.

1. The first thing is to create a Streaming context. This can be done as shown in the preceding code example. If you have a SparkContext already available, you can reuse the SparkContext to create a Streaming context as follows:

   ```
   val ssc = new StreamingContext(sc, Seconds(5))
   sc = Spark Context reference
   ```

   Seconds(5) is the batch duration. This can be specified in milliseconds, seconds, or minutes.

   It is important to note that in local testing, while specifying the master in the configuration object, do not use local or local[1]. This will mean that only a single thread will be used for running the tasks locally.

   If you are using an input stream based on a receiver, such as, Kafka, Sockets, or Flume, then the single thread will be utilized to run the receiver, leaving you with no threads to process the incoming data. You should always allocate enough cores for your streaming application.

   While running on a cluster, you need to make sure that the number of threads specified is more than the number of receivers, otherwise you'll be in a situation where you will not have enough free resources to perform the computation and process the data.

2. The next step is to get a **Discretized Stream** (**DStream**) from a source generating the data stream. In our example, we were listening to a text on a particular socket:

```
val lines = ssc.socketTextStream("localhost", 9988)
```

The stream context provides options to read from a number of different sources, also referred to as the core/basic sources.

3. Once the DStream is available, DStream operations are applied in parallel to each batch RDD in the stream. Operations such as `flatMap()`, `map()`, `filter()`, and so on can be applied to the batches in addition to output operations.

4. You can then start the stream by calling the `start()` method on the Streaming context. Once a start is called, your streaming application will start receiving data until the processing is stopped due to an error or a manual intervention. The processing can manually be stopped using the `streamingContext.stop()` method. You need to remember that once the streaming context has been started, you cannot add any further operations. A stopped context cannot be restarted, and you have to create a new streaming context.

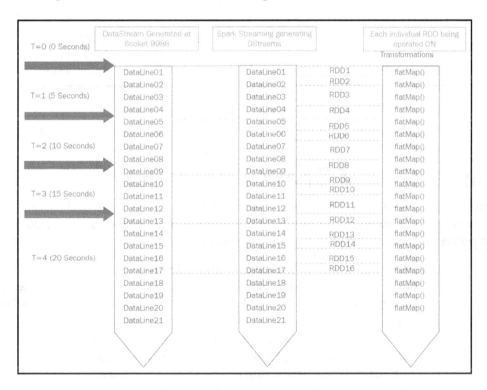

Figure 5.6: DStream representation

The operations that we apply on a DStream will be applied once per batch duration (in our case, 5 seconds), so irrespective of how much data you receive during the batch interval, the operation is applied only once. The Spark UI perhaps presents the most succinct view of Spark's micro-batch architecture, running a new batch after your specified batch interval.

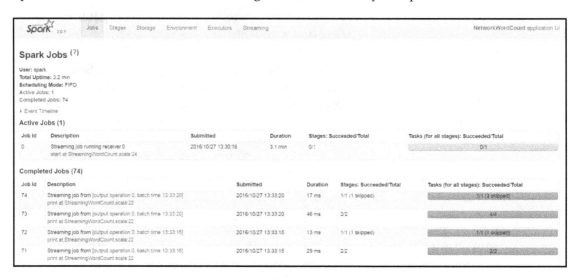

Figure 5.7: Spark UI showing micro-batch architecture

Architecture of Spark Streaming

Now that we have seen Spark Streaming in action, let's take a step back and try to understand what a stream processing engine should do. On a high level, a distributed stream processing engine uses the following execution model:

1. Receive data from other data sources: This could be web server logs, credit card transactions, Twitter sources, other sensor devices, and so on. Some of the most popular ingestion systems include Apache Kafka, Amazon Kinesis, and so on.

2. Apply business logic: Once the data is received, any distributed stream processing engine will apply the business rules (in a distributed manner). This can include filtering logs, aggregating information, checking for potential fraud, and identifying potential marketing offers. The list is endless, but this is perhaps the reason why you build a streaming application and reduce your reaction time to events of interest.

3. Once you have applied your business rules: You would potentially want to store the results in an external storage system (such as HBase, HDFS, or Cassandra), or perhaps send messages to a message broker queue such as Kafka.

Spark has adopted a distributed processing framework by discretizing the streaming data into micro-batches (based on your specified time-interval). The data is received in parallel by receivers before being buffered into the work node memory.

Spark then performs the computation based on the locality info of the data available in the worker memory, enabling the architecture to load-balance and provide optimum fault recovery.

In addition, each batch of data is a Resilient Distributed Dataset (RDD), which is the basic abstraction of a fault-tolerant dataset in Spark. Once data is available as an RDD, it can be processed as a traditional Spark RDD.

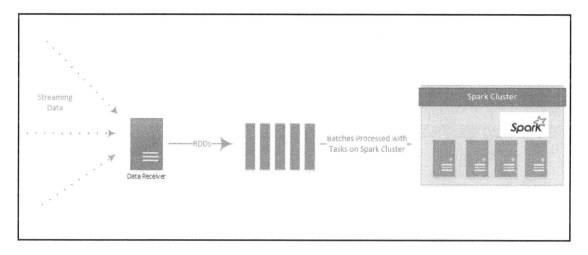

Figure 5.8: Spark's micro-batch architecture

Spark will split the incoming stream of data into micro-batches to allow for fine-grained allocations of computation to resources. For a simple job where a data stream is partitioned by key, the job's tasks will be naturally load balanced across the workers – some workers will process a few longer tasks, others will process more of the shorter tasks. This is unlike the traditional stream processing where a slow worker with more computation will become a bottle neck for the system. It is important to understand that in Spark, tasks are scheduled dynamically based on available resources. Spark also offers a fast failure and recovery from straggler tasks. Since the computation is divided into small tasks, failed nodes can be relaunched in parallel on all the other nodes in the cluster, thus evenly redistributing all the recomputations across many nodes and hence providing a swift recovery from any node failure.

Spark Streaming also provides similar fault-tolerance for DStreams as for RDDs, which means if input data is still available, Spark can recompute the state from its lineage. Since the data is replicated across at least two nodes by default, Spark can handle single worker node failures. Using lineage on a long-running process especially in the context of streaming application can be extremely tricky and hence Spark provides support for check-pointing, which means the current state can be saved to a reliable system such as HDFS, S3, and so on, and hence during recovery Spark Streaming will only go to the latest checkpoint rather than re-evaluating the entire stream.

The following streaming job flow clearly shows the execution of Spark Streaming within components of the Spark framework:

1. A streaming context launches receivers, which are tasks running within the **Executors** responsible for data collection from input source and saving it as RDDs. Remember that there are two types of receivers: reliable receivers, which send an acknowledgement to the reliable source when the data has been received and stored in Spark with replication, and unreliable receivers, which do not send any acknowledgement to the source.
2. The input data is cached in memory and also replicated to other executors for fault tolerance. By default, it is replicated across two nodes. Spark can therefore survive single node failures.
3. Streaming context would then run jobs based on the batch interval to process this data.
4. The output operations in the job then output the job in batches.

The following diagram explains the various steps in the streaming job:

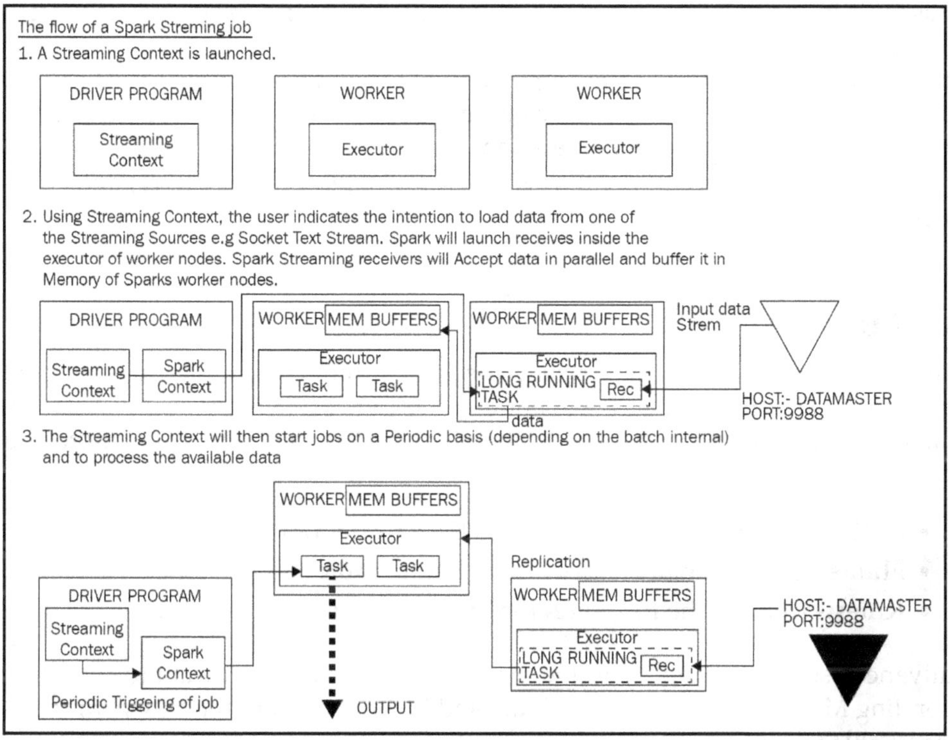

Figure 5.9: Spark Streaming job execution flow

Having looked at the execution model, let's look at the three major areas of Spark Streaming, which include:

- Input sources
- Transformations
- Output operations

Input sources

Spark supports working with a number of different sources, some of which are out of the box and other through additional maven linkages. Please do note that this is not an exhaustive list, and you should always refer to the Spark documentation to see what is new, as Spark is growing at a rapid pace with new sources being added with every release.

Core/basic sources

Spark has built-in support for a number of different sources and these are often referred to as core sources. The method to create DStream from existing sources is available with Streaming context. In the very first example, we looked at the socket text stream, which is one of the popular sources; however, streaming context offers options to read data from network or file-based sources using operations such as `binaryRecordStream()`, `fileStream()`, `queueStream()`, `receiverStream()`, `socketStream()`, and `textFileStream()`.

Advanced sources

In addition to the core sources, the strong eco-system around Spark provides support for an ever-growing list of data sources. These popular message brokers are systems that are seeing an increasing use in the real-time data integration market. These advanced sources include:

- **Kafka** (refer to the *References* the for **Kafka Integration Guide**).
- **Flume** (refer to the *References* the for **Flume Integration Guide**).
- **Kinesis** (refer to the *References* the for **Kinesis Integration Guide**).

These advanced sources cannot be tested in Spark Shell, unless you want to download the corresponding Maven dependencies and Jars and include them in the classpath for `Spark-Shell` to be able to resolve.

While traditionally there was limited support for some of these sources in Python, as of Spark 2.0.1 Kafka, Kinesis, and Flume are available with the Python API as well.

Custom sources

While there is generally support for most popular sources for Spark Streaming in the open source community, you can also implement your custom receivers. You should look at the following related information if you want to implement a custom receiver `http://spark.apache.org/docs/latest/streaming-custom-receivers.html`.

Transformations

DStreams transformations can be viewed as two distinct groups based on their state. The two groups can be stated as follows.

Stateless transformations are transformations that can be operated on individual batches without regard for the previous state of the batch. We've already seen a stateless transformation in our preceding examples code (`Map`, `FlatMap`, and `ReduceByKey`). While looking at the code you may feel that the stateless transformations are being applied to the entire DStream; however, internally each operation is applied to an individual RDD within the DStream. For example, in our previous example, a DStream is composed of multiple RDDs, with each RDD representing a line of text being received from the socket connection, and each transformation is applied on an individual RDD rather than all the RDDs within the DStream.

Stateless transformations can also combine data from multiple DStreams within each batch interval using various join operations. The available join operations include `join()`, `leftOuterJoin()`, `union()`, and `cogroup()`.

Stateful transformations are transformations where the results from previous batches are used to compute the results of the current batch. This is quite common in mini-batch approaches where you might want to look at a user's behavior over the past few batches to compute the current values. For example, in a telecom marketing campaign you might want to see if the user has sent 50 SMS's over the past hour before you can make them an offer of 5 free SMS's or an upgrade to an SMS bundle. Stateful transformations include transformations that act over a sliding window of time periods and `updateStateByKey()`, which is the user to track states across events for each key. We have discussed checkpointing earlier in this chapter, and it is important to note that checkpointing needs to be enabled for all Stateful transformations.

Sliding window operations

A sliding window is a popular technique when you want to operate on RDDs over a given duration compared to operating based on the duration given during the `ssc` configuration. As seen earlier, a batch interval basically means the interval after which the system generates RDDs based on the data received. For example, if you set the batch interval as *1* second, every 1 second, the system will generate RDDs from the received data.

A window operator however is defined by two parameters rather than one, both of which are rather self explanatory:

- **Window length**: Window length is the duration of the window
- **Slide interval**: Slide interval is the interval at which the window will slide or move forward.

These two intervals must be a multiple of the batches internal of the source DStream. Let's say you are collecting tweets about a particular topic, for example, your store's annual sale with the Hashtag `#PPSaleOffer` every 1 second, but you would like to know the sentiment of people reacting to your sale, and you would like to know the sentiment of people about the sale. You could use the sliding window functions to achieve that.

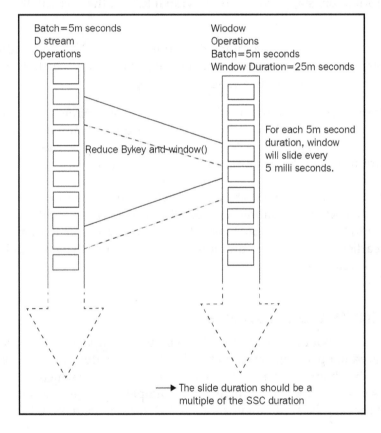

Figure 5.10: Spark Streaming sliding window operations

The default behavior of window operations is to slide at the same interval as the `ssc` duration. For example, as depicted in *Figure 5.10*, a sliding window defined on a 5 millisecond batch duration will slide 5 milliseconds. Spark allows you to define any slide duration, as long as it is a multiple of your batch duration.

The two main window operations include:

- `countByWindow()`: `CountByWindow()` returns a rather simple count of the elements in the stream.
- `reduceByKeyAndWindow()`: `reduceByKeyAndWindow()` has two variants:
    - `reduceByKeyAndWindow(func, windowLength, slideInterval, [numTasks])`: As the name indicates this is essentially a reduce function, and the reduce function is passed in as a parameter. When the function is called on a discretized stream of key/value pairs, it returns a new discretized stream which returns the values aggregated using the `func` operating over the batches in the window defined by the `windowLength` and `slideInterval`.
    - `reduceByKeyAndWindow(func, invFunc, windowLength, slideInterval, [numTasks])`: This is a rather more efficient version of `reduceByKeyAndWindow()` as the reduce is calculated incrementally using the output of reduce values from the previous window. Let us assume that you are performing a sentiment analysis based on a window of 10 minutes, and your slide interval is 2 minutes. For those of you who are unaware of what sentiment analysis is, you might want to look at `http://bit.ly/Sentiment_Analysis`. For an aggregate sentiment over the window using this approach, you can add the average sentiment for the tweets coming in, and subtract the average sentiment for the tweets leaving the window. Please do note that this is only applicable to functions which have a corresponding inverse reduce function.

Code examples for `ReduceByKeyAndWindow()` using Twitter streaming example can be found at `http://bit.ly/TwitterStreamingExample`.

Output operations

Output operations allow the data computed via transformations to be pushed out to external systems. Output operations start the actual execution of DStream transformations just like actions within RDDs. At the time of writing, the following output operations are supported:

Operation	Meaning	Scala	Java	Python
Print()	Print the first 10 elements of every DStream batch on the driver node. Primary usage is development and debugging.	x	x	Pprint()
saveAsTextFiles(prefix, [suffix])	Save the contents of DStream as TextFiles with filenames generated based on the prefix and suffix passed as arguments.	x	x	x
saveAsObjectFiles(prefix,[suffix])	Saving contents as sequence files of serialized Java objects.	x	x	N/A
saveAsHadoopFiles(prefix,[suffix])	Save the contents as Hadoop files.	x	x	N/A

| foreachRDD(func) | forEachRDD() is used to pass a generic function func to each RDD generated from the Stream. func will be executed in the driver program: however, the fact that you are operating over an RDD means that the functions that you are using on that RDD such as map(), filter() will still run on the worker nodes. It is important to realize that the data is not sent back onto the driver until a collect() is called. | X | X | X |

X = available in the API   N/A = not available in the API

Caching and persistence

Caching and persistence are two key areas that developers can use to improve performance of Spark applications. We've looked at caching in RDDs, and while DStreams also provide the persist() method, the persist() method on a DStream will persist all RDDs within the DStream in memory. This is especially useful if the computation happens multiple times on a DStream, which is especially true in window-based operations.

It is for this reason that developers do not explicitly need to call a persist() on window-based operations and they are automatically persisted. The data persistence mechanism depends on the source of the data, for example, for data coming from network sources such as sockets or Kafka, data is replicated across a minimum of two nodes by default.

The difference between `cache()` and `persist()` are:

- `cache()`: Persists the RDDs of the DStream with the default storage level (`MEMORY_ONLY_SER`). Cache() under the hood and calls the `persist()` method with the default storage level.
- `persist()` is overloaded with two variants:
  - You can either use `persist()` without parameters which will persist the RDDs of this DStream with the default storage level.
  - You can also use `perisist(level: StorageLevel)`, which can persist the RDDs of the DStream with the given storage level. You cannot change the storage level of the DStream after the streaming context has been started.

Checkpointing

A streaming application, as given in examples earlier such as fraud detection and next-best offer, typically operate 24/7 and hence it is of the utmost importance that the framework is resilient enough to recover from failures (which will happen). Spark Streaming provides the option to checkpoint information to a fault-tolerant storage system so that it can recover from failures. Checkpointing consist of two major types:

- **Metadata checkpointing**: Metadata checkpoint is essential if you would like to recover from driver program failures. As an application architect/engineer you would want to save the metadata about your job, that is, information defining the streaming computation to be performed to a fault-tolerant system such as HDFS or S3. If the node running the driver program fails, you will have to fall back on this checkpoint to get to the latest state of your application. A typical application metadata will include the following:

  1. **Configuration:** The initial configuration used to define the application.
  2. **DStream operations:** The operations that constitute the particular DStream.
  3. **Incomplete batches:** Currently running batches whose jobs are queued, but have not completed yet.

- **Data checkpointing**: Data checkpointing is necessary when you would want to recover from failures of stateful transformations. While Spark can recompute the RDD from the lineage information, it is often necessary, especially in case of stateful transformations (discussed previously), to save the generated RDDs to reliable storage.

  They are periodically checkpointed to reliable storage (for example, HDFS) to cut off the dependency chains.

Setting up checkpointing

To configure checkpointing, you will need to set up a checkpoint location on a reliable and fault-tolerant filesystem such as HDFS or S3. You need to understand the streaming behavior so that you can incorporate that in your programs:

1. First run the program.
2. A new streaming context is set up, and then a `start()` call is made.
3. Restart from failure.
4. Streaming context is recreated from the checkpoint data in the checkpoint directory.

Setting up checkpointing with Scala

Let us look into an example of setting up checkpointing using Scala:

```
def createStreamingContext (conf: SparkConf,checkpointPath: String):
StreamingContext = {
  val ssc = new StreamingContext( <ConfInfo> )
  .... other code ...
  ssc.checkPoint(checkpointDirectory)
  ssc
}

#Create a new context or get one from the last checkpoint
val context = StreamingContext.getOrCreate(checkpointDirectory,
createStreamingContext _)
..
context. .... # Perform your usual operation
#Start the context
context.start()
context.awaitTermination()
```

Setting up checkpointing with Java

Let us look into an example of setting up checkpointing using Java:

```
#Setup a factory that will return Streaming Contexts
avaStreamingContextFactory contextCreationFactory = new
JavaStreamingContextFactory() {
  @Override
  public JavaStreamingContext createStreamingContext() {
    JavaStreamingContext jsc = new JavaStreamingContext(...);
    JavaDStream<String> lines = jssc.socketTextStream(...);
    jsc.checkpoint(checkpointDirectory);
    return jsc;
  }
};
JavaStreamingContext context =
JavaStreamingContext.getOrCreate(checkpointDirectory,
contextCreationFactory);

.... other code ...
jsc.checkPoint(checkpointDirectory)

#Start
jsc.start()
#Await Terminationation
jsc.awaitTermination()
```

Setting up checkpointing with Python

Let us look into an example of setting up checkpointing using Python:

```
# Function to create and setup a new StreamingContext
def createStreamingContext():
ssc = new StreamingContext(...)
lines = ssc.socketTextStream(...) # Create DStreams from your preferred
data Stream, in this case a socket connection
...
ssc.checkpoint(checkpointDirectory) # set checkpoint directory
return ssc
# Will get a streaming context from checkpoint if restarted
# Will get a new Streaming context if first time.
streamingCtx = StreamingContext.getOrCreate(checkpointDirectory,
functionToCreateContext)
# Additional stream setup operations
streamingCtx. ...
# Start the context
streamingCtx.start()
```

```
streamingCtx.awaitTermination()
```

Automatic driver restart

After enabling `getOrCreate()`, you are still not done. You would need to enable automatic driver recovery after failure. Typically, monitoring apps within your infrastructure will continuously monitor the health of the Driver Manager, before deciding to restart it. All different cluster managers including the most famous ones such as Standalone, YARN, and Mesos support automatically restarting the driver. The details of this are out of the scope of this book. Please refer to relevant document of YARN, Mesos, and the Standalone scheduler to achieve this.

DStream best practices

- Setting the right batch interval is most crucial for Spark Streaming. Your batch processing time should be less than the batch interval. You should monitor end-to-end delay for each batch, and if they are consistent and comparable to the batch size, your system can be considered stable. If your batch processing time is bigger than your batch interval , you will run out of memory. You can use `spark.streaming.receiver.maxRate` to limit the rate of the receiver.
- Transformations will determine the amount of memory used by Spark Streaming. If you are maintaining a large key table using `updateStateByKey,` do account for the memory required.
- Each Spark receiver runs within an executor and needs a single core. If you are configuring parallel reads using multiple receivers, make sure that `spark.cores.max` is configured by taking the receiver slots in the account.
- Spark generates N number of blocks per n batch interval milliseconds. For example, during a 5 millisecond batch interval, 5 blocks are generated. The blocks are distributed by the block manager of the current executor to the Block manager of other executors and the driver is updated about the location of the blocks for further downstream processing. An RDD is created on the driver for the blocks generated during the batch interval and the blocks during the interval are partitions of the RDD. Each partition is a separate task in Spark. The map tasks on the blocks are processed in the executors irrespective of the block interval. A higher value of `spark.locaity.wait` increases the chances of processing blocks on the local nodes.

- You can either rely on the block interval or batch interval to determine the partitions or alternatively call `inputStream.repartition(numPartitions)`. This will increase the parallelism, but will of course incur the cost of network overhead during the reshuffle.
- With multiple DStreams, each DStream will convert into an RDD and eventually into a job. You can union the DStreams to form a bigger stream and hence a bigger RDD.

Fault tolerance

In a streaming application there are typically three types of guarantees available, as follows:

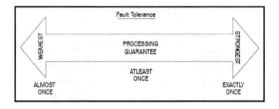

Figure 5.11: Typical guarantees offered by a streaming application

In a streaming application, which generally comprises of data receivers, transformers, and components, producing different output failures can happen.

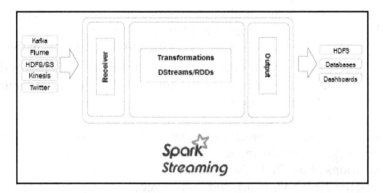

Figure 5.12: Components of a streaming application

Worker failure impact on receivers

When a Spark worker fails, it can impact the receiver that might be in the midst of reading data from a source.

Suppose you are working with a source that can be either a reliable filesystem or a messaging system such as Kafka/Flume, and the worker running the receiver responsible for getting the data from the system and replicating it within the cluster dies. Spark has the ability to recover from failed receivers, but its ability depends on the type of data source and can range from at least once to exactly once semantics.

If the data is being received from fault-tolerant systems such as HDFS or S3, Spark Streaming will provide exactly once semantics.

However, if data is based on reliable sources, the fault-tolerance mechanics depend on the type of receiver and the kind of failure. We have already mentioned the case of a reliable and unreliable receiver. In the event of a reliable receiver, generally an acknowledgement is sent after the replication to other nodes, and in case the failure happens before replication has occurred, no acknowledgement will be sent. This will result in the data being sent to the receiver again, and hence no data loss. This type of receiver provides at least once semantics.

In the event of an unreliable receiver, the data that has not yet been replicated will be lost.

The driver node failure is of particular concern, as all of the data that has been received and replicated in memory will be lost. This is particularly an issue for Stateful transformations, which keep the data in the driver's memory.

Worker failure impact on RDDs/DStreams

RDDs and DStreams provide semantics exactly once. We know that RDD can recompute from its lineage; as long as the input data is available there is no loss of data.

Worker failure impact on output operations

In the event of a worker failure, the output operations by default provide semantics at least once, as the operation that saves data to external systems might execute more than once. This might not be problematic in some cases; however, if you want to achieve semantics exactly once you will need to engineer the system to make use of transactions, so that each update gets pushed only once.

Spark's `saveAs****File()` operations automatically take care of multiple updates by ensuring that only one copy of the output file exists.

What is Structured Streaming?

We've covered discretized streams in quite a lot of detail. However, if you have been following the Spark news recently, you may have heard of the new DataFrame/DataSet-based streaming framework named Structured Streaming. Why is there a need for a new streaming framework? We've talked about how revolutionary the concept of Spark Streaming using DStreams was, and how you can actually combine multiple engines such as SQL, Streaming, Graph, and ML to build a data pipeline, so why the need for a new engine altogether?

Based on the experience with Spark Streaming, the team at Apache Spark released that there were a few issues with DStreams. The top three issues were as follows:

- As we have seen in the preceding examples, DStreams can work with the batch time, but not the event time inside the data.
- While every effort was made to keep the API similar, the Streaming API was still different to RDD API in the sense that you cannot take a Batch job and start running it as a streaming application.
- As we saw in the last section, you have to handle fault tolerance especially for drivers using the checkpointing or output operations and make sure that you either use transactions or idempotent updates to achieve semantics exactly once. While this was common for people working with other streaming frameworks, the team at Apache Spark decided that this is not what the developer of a streaming app should focus their energy on and be worried about.

The complexities of the DStream API resulted in the vision of creating an API that works for both batch and streaming and with the user simply mentioning the intention to ingest data in streaming or batch fashion, and letting the Spark framework worry about the integrity details.

Just think for a moment… what is a stream of data?… It is typically similar structure data arriving in multiple batches where sometimes the batch can be short (5 minutes) and sometimes the batch can be long (say 1 hour/4 hours, and so on). I remember while working with Teradata (my old employer), we were working with applications where data would arrive in mini-batches and get appended to the same table. The table was considered an infinite table (despite always being of a finite size). The same approach has now been bought to Spark streaming, essentially creating an infinite table. You might want to read the whole table, or just the freshly arriving data.

The Spark framework has adopted a similar approach by removing all differences from the Batch and Streaming APIs. The only difference is that in streaming the table is unbounded, while in batch applications the table is considered static.

Let's compare and contrast the Streaming and Batch APIs for a moment, and understand the intricacies of converting a batch application into a streaming application. We'll revert back to our old CDR dataset, and continuously report on calls originating from London with a revenue of over 200 cents. Let's look at the code example of a batch application before looking at the streaming application.

The following is a batch application:

```
val cdrSchema = new
StructType().add("OriginNum","String").add("TermNum","String").add("Origin"
,"String").add("Term","String").add("CallTs","String").add("CallCharge","in
teger")

val cdrs =
spark.read.schema(cdrSchema).json("/home/spark/sampledata/json/cdrs.json")

val callsFromLondon =
cdrs.select("Origin","Dest","CallCharge").where("CallCharge >
200").where("Origin = 'London'")

callsFromLondon.write.format("parquet").save("/home/spark/sampledata/stream
ing/output")
```

I am using the preceding code example in the batch application, and have recently been asked by the management to build a report using the preceding information, that refreshes every 1 minute. In the old days, I would have had to go through a lot of hassle and have a rethink on the architecture of the application before I could convert it into a streaming job. Let's attempt that with Spark using Structured Streaming and see the beauty and simplicity of it:

```
val cdrSchema = new
StructType().add("OriginNum","String").add("TermNum","String").add("Origin"
```

```
,"String").add("Term","String").add("CallTs","String").add("CallCharge","in
teger")

val cdrs =
spark.readStream.schema(cdrSchema).json("/home/spark/sampledata/json/cdrs.j
son")

val callsFromLondon =
cdrs.select("Origin","Dest","CallCharge").where("CallCharge >
200").where("Origin = 'London'")

callsFromLondon.writeStream.format("parquet").start("/home/spark/sampledata
/streaming/output")
```

At the time of writing, the preceding code works for Spark 2.0.0; however, this API is experimental and subject to change. So please do not use this in your production workloads until it has been released for general availability. As you can see, converting a batch application into streaming is relatively simple.

Let's look at this from an architectural perspective.

Spark Streaming now treats the input data as an infinite unbounded table, with every new item in the stream appended to the bottom of the table as a new row. From a developer's perspective, they are still working with a static table to obtain a final result set, which is written to an output sink. However, any query that the developer writes on what they think is still a batch like operation is transformed into a streaming execution plan by the Spark optimizer. Spark will take the responsibility of maintaining the state to update the result once a new set of rows arrive. From a developer's perspective, they are responsible for specifying triggers to control when to update the results.

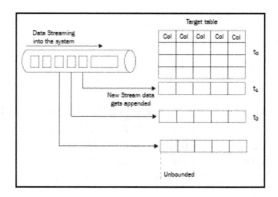

Figure 5.13: Structured Streaming – unbounded table

In summary, from a processing perspective, a user simply expresses queries using the Batch API, and Spark builds incremental plans to run them in a streaming fashion.

The following diagram from the Apache Spark documentation web page (`https://spark.a pache.org/docs/latest/structured-streaming-programming-guide.html#programmin g-model`) explains the programming model for Structured Streaming in a very succinct way, and perhaps cannot be explained more clearly:

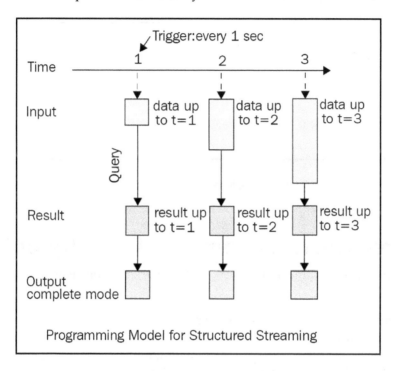

Figure 5.14: Structured Streaming – programming model

Under the hood

Under the hood, the optimization of a streaming application differs from a batch application in the sense that it creates incremental execution plans. The planner will use the knowledge to convert a streaming logical plan to a number of incremental execution plans used to process the next chunk of incoming streaming data. This is basically taking the Spark exaction plan for batch applications to the next level.

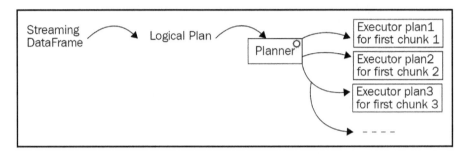

Figure 5.15: Incremental execution plan

Structured Spark Streaming API :Entry point

The entry point to a DataFrame and Dataset API is Spark Session, as we have seen previously.

- **Creation of Streaming Data Frames** – Spark Streaming DataFrames can be created through the `DataStreamReader` interface, which is returned by `SparkSession.readStream()`, as shown in the previous example. Since the API is similar to the static DataFrame API, you can specify options and schema. The built-in sources for the Streaming DataFrame in Spark 2.0 include:
- **FileSource**: Read the files written in a directory as a stream of data. Supports CSV, Text, JSON, and Parquet.
- **Socket Source (for Testing)**: Reads text data from a socket connection. The listening server socket is at the driver. This should only be used for testing as it does not provide any end-to-end fault-tolerance guarantees.

Output modes

An output is basically what gets written to the external storage and can be expressed in different modes, some of which were available in Spark Streaming. The following modes will be available with Spark Structured Streaming.

Append mode

The append mode means new rows that have arrived since the last trigger point will be appended to the result table and written to external storage. The append mode is the default mode and is only applicable to queries that do not have any aggregations, for example, queries with only select, map, flatMap, filter, join, and so on are supported.

Complete mode

The complete mode is relevant when the entire updated result table is written to the external storage. The complete mode is supported with aggregation queries; for example:

```
input.agg(count("*")).write.outputMode("complete").format("orc").startStrea
m("path")
```

Update mode

The update mode, as the name indicates, is relevant for rows that were updated in the result table since the last trigger, and these rows will be changed in the external storage. The update mode can only work with sinks that can be updated; for example, MySQL tables, and so on. At the time of writing, this mode was not available in Spark 2.0.

Output sinks

There are a few types of built-in output sinks.

- **File Sink**: Stores the output to a directory. The only format supported by Spark 2.0 is Parquet and the only output mode supported is the append mode.
- **Foreach Sink**: Available only to Java and Scala programming languages. For each processes each record and runs any specified computation. You have to implement ForEachWriter, which has methods that will get called whenever a sequence of row is generated as an output after a trigger.
- **Console Sink**: Very useful for debugging, as it prints everything to the console. You can enable append and complete modes. The output is stored in the driver's memory, so it should be used with caution.

- **Memory Sink**: Memory sink stores the output in memory on the driver side in an in-memory table providing both append and complete modes:

Sink	Supported Output Modes	Usage	Fault-tolerant	Notes

File Sink (Only Parquet as of Apache 2.0)	Append	`writeStream`
		`.format("parquet")`
		`.start()`
			Yes	Supports writes to partitioned tables. Partitioning by time may be useful.

Foreach Sink	All modes	`writeStream.` `.forEach(...) .start()`	Depends on ForeachWriter implementation	Allows arbitrary operations to be computed on output data.

Console Sink	Append, Complete	`writeStream`
		`.format("console")`
		`.start()`
			No	Testing and debugging purposes only.

Memory Sink	Append, Complete	`writeStream`
		`.format("memory")`
		`.queryName("table")`
		`.start()`
			No	Saves the output data as a table, for interactive querying. Table name is the query name.

Table 5.1: Sinks with Spark 2.0 Structured Streaming and corresponding settings (Apache Spark docs)

Failure recovery and checkpointing

Structured Streaming allows you the option to recover from failures. This is achieved using checkpointing and WAL. Checkpointing can be configured during the definition of the streaming data frame using the `checkpointlocation` option. The checkpoint location should be on a fault-tolerant system, and as of Spark 2.0 it has to be on HDFS compatible systems.

If we wanted to enable checkpointing on our earlier CDR examples, we could have done it as follows:

```
callsFromLondon.writeStream.format("parquet").option("checkpointlocation","
hdfs://nn:8020/mycheckloc").start("/home/spark/sampledata/streaming/output"
)
```

References

The following reference articles, YouTube videos, and blogs have been valuable in the information presented in this chapter, and in some cases provided more details around each section. Spark Streaming is a topic that perhaps requires an entire book on its own, and it would be difficult to do justice to this in 30 odd pages. I hope you can refer to the following references for further details and explanations:

1. http://bit.ly/2dDqmCS
2. http://spark.apache.org/docs/latest/streaming-programming-guide.html
3. https://parquet.apache.org/
4. **Setting up SparkR:** https://www.youtube.com/watch?v=A5cBAPoidsg
5. http://spark.apache.org/docs/latest/sql-programming-guide.html
6. https://databricks.com/blog/2015/07/30/diving-into-apache-spark-stre amings-execution-model.html
7. http://people.csail.mit.edu/matei/papers/2013/sosp_spark_streaming.p df
8. http://spark.apache.org/docs/latest/streaming-kafka-integration.html
9. http://spark.apache.org/docs/latest/streaming-flume-integration.html
10. http://spark.apache.org/docs/latest/streaming-kinesis-integration.ht ml
11. http://spark.apache.org/docs/latest/streaming-custom-receivers.html
12. https://databricks.com/blog/2016/07/28/structured-streaming-in-apach e-spark.html

Summary

In this chapter, we have covered details of Spark Streaming, and have spent most of the time explaining the constructs of discretized streams, and have also explained the new and upcoming Structured Streaming API. As mentioned, the Structured Streaming API is still in alpha mode, and hence should not be used for production applications.

The next chapter deals with one of my favorite topics – Spark MLLib. Spark provides a rich API for predictive modeling and the use of Spark MLLib is increasing every day. We'll look at the basics of machine learning before providing users with an insight into how the Spark framework provide support for performing predictive analytics. We'll cover topics from building a machine-learning pipeline, feature-engineering, classification and regression, clustering, and a few advanced topics including identifying the champion models and tuning a model for performance.

6
Machine Learning with Spark

We have spent a considerable amount of time understanding the architecture of Spark, RDDs, DataFrames and Dataset-based APIs, Spark SQL, and Streaming, all of which was primarily related to building the foundations of what we are going to discuss in this chapter, which is machine learning. Our focus has been on getting the data onto the Spark platform either in batch or in streaming fashion, and transforming it into the desired state.

Once you have the data in the platform, what do you do with it? You can either use it for reporting purposes, building dashboards, or letting your data scientists analyze the data to detect patterns, identify reasons for specific events, understand the behavior of customers, group them into segments to aid better decision making, or predict the future.

The power of Spark's MLLib stems from the fact that it lets you operate your algorithms over a distributed dataset, which can sometimes be its weakness too as not all algorithms can be parallelized and hence it primarily provides algorithms that are good for distributed processing. In this chapter, we'll cover the following topics:

- What is machine learning?
- Why machine learning?
- Types of machine learning
- Spark MLLib:
  - Spark Pipeline API
  - Feature engineering
  - Classification and regression
  - Clustering
  - Collaborative filtering

Let's get started!

What is machine learning?

Machine learning is a branch of AI that gives computers the ability to learn new patterns with little to no human intervention. The machine learning models learn from previous computations to produce more accurate results as more data is crunched. A very simple example is Facebook's face detection algorithm, which uses machine learning techniques to identify the people in the pictures, and gets refined over time. Machine learning has its roots in computation statistics and has been referred to as data mining, although data mining focuses more on the unsupervised learning part of machine learning. To some people machine learning is still science fiction; however, it is now being used in everyday life from predicting fraud, to recommending new products and services to customers, and predicting when your car needs a service.

Is machine learning a new phenomenon? Almost 75 years ago in the Bulletin of Mathematical Biophysics, *Warren S. Mculloch* (http://bit.ly/2eSkb1q) and *Walter Pitts* (http://bit.ly/2g0k1rC) provided the foundation of certain brain theories in a number of classical papers, including "*A Logical Calculus of the Ideas Immanent in Nervous activity*", which is credited as being strongly influential on the neural network theory and the theory of computation. This paper proposed the first mathematical model of a neural network. In 1957, the first **Perceptron algorithm** (http://bit.ly/2OOEBrS) was invented by *Frank Rosenblatt* (http://bit.ly/2g0o8DO) and while it was intended to be a hardware-based implementation, the first software implementation was done on IBM 704.

Neural networks couldn't meet the expectations due to limited computing power until it was revitalized in 1980s with the introduction of back-propagation of errors resulting in Multilayer Perceptrons. Classification and Regression tree methods were also embraced widely during 1980s, which along with relatively larger digital data sources and inexpensive hardware (comparatively) led to the foundation of contemporary machine learning. Machine learning today is a mathematically rigorous discipline that encompasses sophisticated modeling, optimization, and learning research; it has concrete applications in medicine, software, robotics, and traditional business problems. Particularly in the business problem domain, there is significant overlap among the fields of data science, data mining, and machine learning.The following figure is taken from a data mining primer course offered by the SAS Institute, a leader in business analytic in 1998:

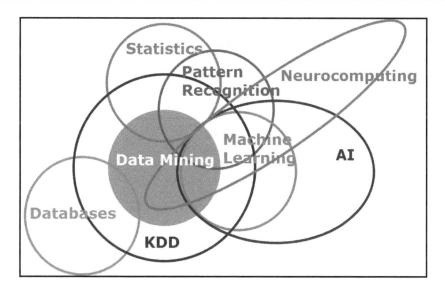

Figure 6.1: SAS data mining primer: 1998

SAS language was originally developed in 1966 with offering around statistics, after which multiple regression and **ANOVA** were added in 1968. SAS as a company moved into data mining with the **FASTCLUS** procedure, which implemented **KMeans** clustering (`http://b it.ly/2etJsk8`) in 1982 (34 years before this book was written).

If you have heard the buzz about machine learning in recent years, you might be asking yourself why do we need to care about a field of science that is almost 80 years old now, and why so much noise around it at the moment? If you look at **Gartner's Hype Cycle** for Emerging technologies, 2016, you will see machine learning at the peak of inflated expectations:

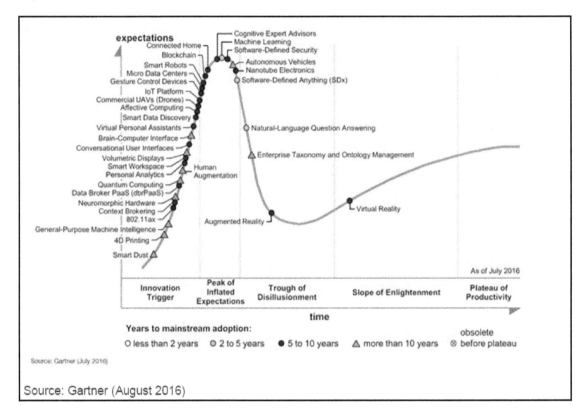

Source: Gartner (August 2016)

Figure 6.2: Gartner's Hype Cycle for emerging technologies, 2016

You might be asking yourself two questions:

- Why is machine learning an emerging technology?
- Why has it become so popular that it has made its way to Gartner's Hype Cycle?

Well machine learning is probably re-emerging as a technology, and there is a reason it has become so popular again. Modern data challenges are high-dimensional, which means new techniques are required to solve problems, which was not possible with traditional techniques. However, the techniques have always been around, so what has revolutionized machine learning? My sincere belief is that this has been made more popular by the new computing paradigms, the abundance of low-cost high-quality hardware, and richer data sources. These along with the need to outsmart the competition. Has necessitated the need to move on from reporting on the past to predicting the future as accurately as possible.

Traditional BI environments limit decision support by providing information on historical trends and leaving the decision making entirely with the end user. In a high-dimensional space, it becomes increasingly hard to point out a solution by looking at raw data. Consider an example of a telecom company, which wants to send out offers to its customers, and having limited number of call center agents it has to target the customers efficiently with the right offers, otherwise the entire exercise can be futile. Can a CMO look at a raw dataset and suggest which customers the offer should be sent to? How about using modern machine learning techniques to identify which customers are likely to accept a particular offer, and the possible upside to an acceptance, thus quantifying the success and failure of a particular marketing campaign.

It is important to understand that machine learning is neither a hype nor a fad, but is now fulfilling quite realistic expectations of solving problems, and helping humans/end users make better decisions. It is therefore a natural demand to create technology that surpasses our limited abilities to surmount the toughest challenges faced by businesses today.

Why machine learning?

While we have given some examples on why you need machine learning, it might be helpful to look at some of the sample use cases of machine learning. Machine learning is used by us on a daily basis from fraud detection, banking, credit risk assessment, to predicting customer churn and sales volumes. People who are from a statistics background might say, "*Hey – I have done all of that using simple statistics*". The answer is that you have probably used a lot of the techniques that we will discuss in this book using a different name, as there is a huge overlap between statistics, data mining, and machine learning.

Some example use cases include:

- **Credit risk**: To predict how likely is it for the borrower to meet its debt obligations under the agreed terms, financial institutions need to manage the credit risk inherent in the portfolio, in addition to the risks on individual credits or transactions.

- **Self-driving cars**: They are the talk of the town, with everyone planning to buy one. They make use of deep learning and machine learning by capturing the image of the scene from the camera, and then performing scene labeling using machine learning. Scene labeling essentially assigns a label to each pixel corresponding to the object to which the pixel belongs. Classifiers are built on top of this to predict an action. So for instance, if the region that you have identified as a car in the center of a frame gets larger in a subsequent frame, you're probably going faster than the car in front of you, and the action should be to apply brakes.
- **Sentiment analysis**: Sentiment analysis is the process of computationally identifying and categorizing opinions expressed in a piece of text, especially in order to determine whether the writer's attitude towards a particular topic, product, and so on, is positive, negative, or neutral. Businesses want to understand customer reaction to product launches on Twitter, Facebook, across the blogs, and look at a broader picture of customer likeliness of a particular product.
- **Fraud detection**: Identifying fraudulent transactions and anomaly detection is a common occurrence in daily life, and is one of the prime use cases of machine learning.
- **Cyber security**: Government agencies, leading banks, and other institutions are spending a lot of time and effort on utilizing machine learning for cyber security of sensitive installations and online banks. Machine learning algorithms are used to detect DOS attacks, and scale up the instances upon imminent threats.

Types of machine learning

There are four major categories of machine learning algorithms:

- **Supervised learning**: In supervised learning, we have a bunch of data that has already been labeled, and can be used to train a model, which can later be used to predict the labels of new and un-labeled data. A simple example could be data on a list of customers who have previously churned, or people who have defaulted on their loans. We can use this data to train a model, and understand the behaviors demonstrated by churners or loan-defaulters. Once we have trained a model, we can use this model to detect churners or loan-defaulters by looking at similar attributes, and identifying the likelihood of a person being a churner or a loan defaulter. This is also sometimes known as predictive modeling or predictive analytic. Example algorithms include:
  - **Decision trees**
  - **Regression**

- **Neural networks**
- **SVM**

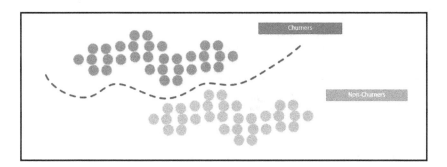

Figure 6.3: Supervised learning

- **Unsupervised learning:** In unsupervised learning, there is no pre-existing data with known labels. Using machine learning algorithms, you find areas in a multi-dimensional space that are similar to each other, and identify the structure and attributes of data that makes it similar to other data within the same area. A well known example of this is customer segmentation, where you want to identify customer segments based on the behavior. You may want to use unsupervised learning for fraud detection and cyber security. Example algorithms include:
    - **Clustering**
    - **Principal component analysis**

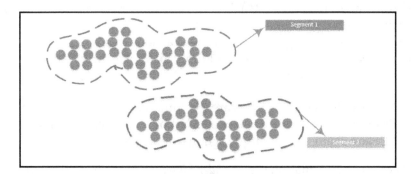

Figure 6.4: Unsupervised learning: clustering

- **Semi-supervised learning:** In semi-supervised learning you will use data that is partially labeled, and use estimation techniques to identify unlabeled data, thus providing superior performance over unsupervised learning, which is often CPU intensive. Example algorithms include:
  - **Clustering**
  - **Factorization machines**

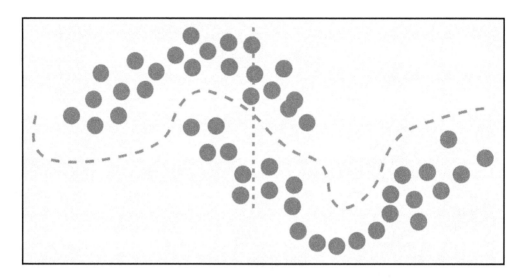

Figure 6.5: Semi-supervised learning: using partially labeled data

- **Reinforcement Learning** (**RL**): Reinforcement learning is a field within machine learning involving sequential decision making and learning from interaction. In reinforcement learning, an agent chooses actions that will maximize the expected cumulative reward over a period of time. Examples include gaming, such as casino games, Chess, or Go.

  Markov Decision Processes are a common technique. A Markov Decision Process (also called a Controlled Markov Chain) can be thought of as a Markov chain with multiple actions and rewards:

 For more information see *Satinder Singh's Reinforcement Learning Tutorial* at `http://hunch.net/~jl/projects/RL/RLTheoryTutorial.pdf`.

Introduction to Spark MLLib

MLLib stands for Machine Learning Library in Spark and is designed to make machine learning scalable, approachable, and easy for data scientists and engineers. It was created in the Berkley **AMPLab** and shipped with Spark 0.8.

Spark MLLib is a very active project with huge contributions from the community and an ever growing coverage of machine learning algorithms in the areas of classification, regression, clustering, recommendation, and other utilities such as feature extraction, feature selection, summary statistics, linear algebra, and frequent pattern matching.

Version 0.8 started small with the introduction of limited algorithms, such as:

- KMeans
- **Alternating Least Squares** (**ALS**)
- Gradient Descent (Optimization Technique)

From an API perspective, support for these algorithms was made available in the following programs:

- Java
- Scala

The amazing pace of MLLib can be gauged from the fact that within 3 months, version 0.9 was launched, which added the following:

- Naïve Bayes

The Python API was introduced in the same release. Version 1.0 bought new algorithms, such as:

- Decision trees
- **Principal Component Analysis** (**PCA**)
- **Singular Value Decomposition** (**SVD**)

This version received major performance boost with the introduction of sparse data for storage and computation.

Soon after, version 1.1 came up with an additional list of algorithms and utility functions, such as:

- Summary statistics
- Non active matrix factorization

- Streaming linear regression
- Word2Vec (feature xtraction)

Tree Reduce and Torrent Broadcast helped achieve 5.x performance gains.

The API and application part of the MLLib API lagged behind the innovation on the algorithms and performance side, and hence with version 1.2 a major improvement was introduced in the form of the pipeline API, which was necessary as the abundance of algorithms didn't mean anything unless the users were able to build production applications using the platform with ease and the whole process was simple for data scientists who could focus on the business problem rather than engineering the technical efficiency of a solution. In addition to the Pipeline API, version 1.2 also bought in additional algorithms, such as:

- Random forests
- Gradient boosting
- Streaming KMeans

Spark 1.3 was another mega release, which bought additional algorithms, such as:

- **Latent Dirichlet Allocation (LDA)**
- Multinomial Logistic Regression
- Gaussian mixture models
- Distributed block matrix
- Isotonic regression (calibration)

Support was added to import/export models. The list of algorithms was building up, and the developers were aware of Mahout's fate where a number of algorithms available in core Mahout had to be deprecated due to non-use in the field. A website called Spark Packages (`https://spark-packages.org`) was launched, to build a community of algorithms that are not mainstream, but still useful. At the time of writing, the website contains 291 Spark packages with a constant influx of new packages.

Version 2.0 is the major release for Spark, as DataFrame is now the primary API for Spark and RDD-based APIs have been put into maintenance mode, which means that new features/functions will not be added and only bugs will be fixed. RDD-based APIs are expected to be removed from Spark 3.0 and hence we won't spend any time on RDD-based MLLib APIs in this book.

Spark's MLLib, with the objective of making machine learning scalable and easy provides the following tools, and you would have seen each Spark release discussed previously added to at least one of these areas:

1. **ML algorithms**: Examples include classification, Regression, Clustering, and Collaborative filtering.
2. **Featurization**: Feature extraction, transformation, dimensionality reduction, and selection.
3. **Pipelines**: Tools for constructing, evaluating, and tuning ML pipelines.
4. **Persistence**: saving and loading algorithms, models, and pipelines.
5. **Utilities**: Linear algebra, statistics, and data handling.

Why do we need the Pipeline API?

Before digging into the details of the Pipeline API, it is important to understand what a machine learning pipeline means, and why we need a `Pipeline` API.

It is important to understand that you cannot have an efficient machine learning platform if the only thing you provide is a bunch of algorithms for people to use. Machine learning is quite an involved process, which involves multiple steps, and a machine learning algorithm itself is just one (though very important) part of the step. As an example, let's consider a text classification example, where you have a corpus of text, and you want to classify if that is a sports article or not a sports article. We would like to simplify it to a 1 and a 0, where a 1 indicates it is about sports and 0 indicates it is not about sports. This is a supervised machine learning flow, where we will use data with existing labels, to predict the labels for data with no labels.

You would need to collect this data. Preprocess it, sample it, divide it into a training/hold-out dataset, build a machine learning model, and then evaluate the test data based on the model that you have developed to understand the model prediction accuracy.

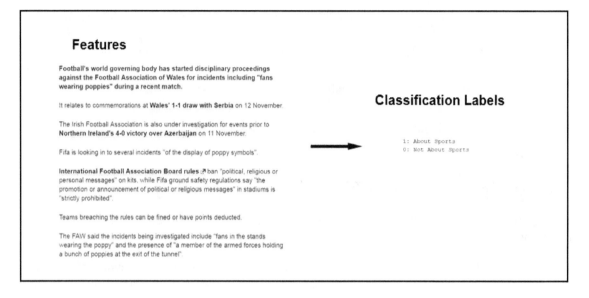

Figure 6.6: Classification example

A typical supervised learning flow would look like the following:

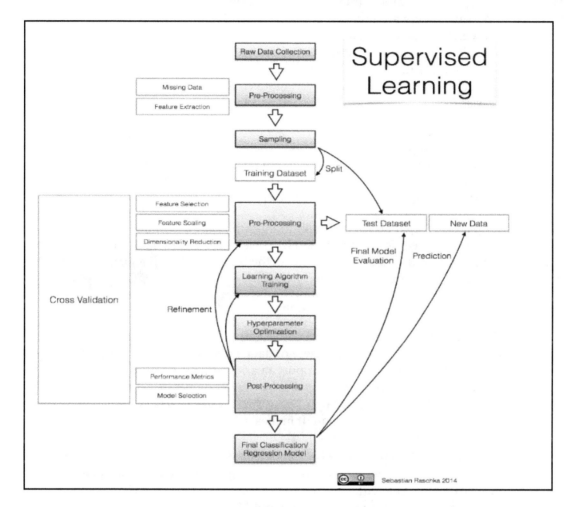

Figure 6.7: Typical machine learning flow in a supervised learning approach

As you can see from this process, there are various handovers between data preparation tasks, feature engineering, model tuning, and validation and this handover needs to be as seamless as possible. There are multiple algorithms involved in the process and output of one algorithm will be translated to input into another algorithm with the sole objective of being able to make predictions about the future or unknown data. Each of the algorithms, be it for feature engineering, model tuning, or validation has its own set of tuning parameters, which makes the entire task even more cumbersome, especially if you are using different libraries to perform different functions and translating between the various algorithms.

Big data means bigger pipelines, which results in bigger problems. A single tuning mistake in one algorithm will result in the garbage flowing out as a result, and then amplifying the problem at the end of the pipeline. What you need is a high-level API where you can define a workflow, and only care about features rather than worrying about metadata.

This is what Spark ML Pipeline API is used for. It is built on the familiar DataFrame API that we have seen in the earlier chapters, and has taken inspiration from Pandas backed by Spark SQL engine and thus enabling users to get the best execution plan irrespective of the developer-facing API being used.

The key abstractions of an ML pipeline include:

1. **DataFrames**: DataFrames are the core concept (and is not limited to the **ML Pipeline** API) that can hold variety of data including text, feature vectors, labels, and predictions. DataFrames support a variety of basic and structured data types in addition to ML vector types and can be created implicitly or explicitly from an RDD. Columns within a DataFrame have a schema attached to them, which is generally a name of the column. It makes it easier to manipulate the DataFrame with the name associated with it.

2. **Transformer**: A Transformer is an algorithm that can transform one DataFrame to another DataFrame. A machine learning algorithm is a Transformer because it inputs a data frame with features and outputs a DataFrame with predictions. Technically speaking, a transformer would implement a `Transform()` method, which would convert one DataFrame into another, usually by adding one or more columns. For example, you might have an input data set that will be used to train a model. A feature transformer uses the data frame to take the input data set (for example, a text column), and converts it into a set of feature vectors, and hence produces an output that includes the feature vectors in addition to the input data. This is the default behavior and it is done under the hood.

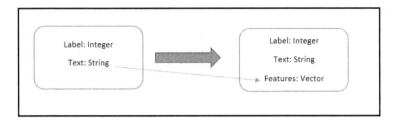

Figure 6.8: ML Pipeline API – transformation abstraction

3. **Estimator** – An Estimator is an algorithm that takes a DataFrame as an input and returns a model. Basically, you train your labels and features to train a model so that it can predict labels and features. As an example, a learning algorithm is an estimator that trains a DataFrame and produces a model. An Estimator generally implements a method `fit()`, which takes a DataFrame as an input (typically produced by a Transformer), and produces a Model (which itself is a Transformer). An example could be `LinearRegression`, which is an Estimator, and calling `fit()` on the `LinearRegression` trains a `LinearRegressionModel`, which is a model. The model can be considered a special type of Estimator, because if you look at it, essentially it takes a text and a set of features and produces a prediction.

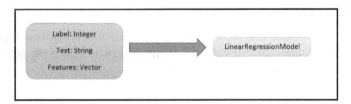

Figure 6.9: ML Pipeline API – Estimator Abstraction

The following figure shows you that a model essentially is a special type of estimator:

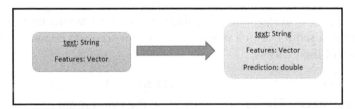

Figure 6.10: ML Pipeline API – Model as a special Estimator

4. **Evaluator:** The Evaluator is the final part of the flow that takes the final data frame and returns some value. This can be a metric, for example, comparing labels and prediction columns to come up with **Area Under Curve (AVC)** or **Mean Squared Error (MSE)**. We'll be using the Evaluator in our case studies in Chapter 9, *Building a Recommendation System* and Chapter 10, *Customer Churn Prediction*.

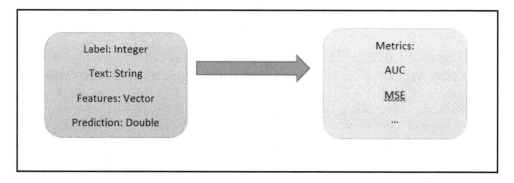

Figure 6.10: ML Pipeline API – Evaluator abstraction

5. **PipelineModel**: PipelineModel is the overarching abstraction of a pipeline. A PipelineModel is a type of a transformer as it takes a DataFrame and outputs a DataFrame with predictions.
6. **Pipeline**: A pipeline is a type of estimator. Our full workflow starts with a DataFrame of labels and texts, and at the end produces a pipeline model that can produce predictions about our data set.
7. **Parameter**: All transformers and Estimators now share a common API for specifying parameters.

How does it work?

A pipeline is a sequence of stages and each stage is either a Transformer or an Estimator. The stages are run in a sequence in a way that the input frame is transformed as it passes through each stage of the process:

- **Transformer stages**: The transform() method on the DataFrame
- **Estimator stages**: The fit() method on the DataFrame

A pipeline is created by declaring its stages, configuring appropriate parameters, and then chaining them in a pipeline object. For example, if we were to create a simple classification pipeline we would tokenize the data into columns, use the hashing term feature extractor to extract features, and then build a logistic regression model.

Please ensure that you add Apache Spark ML Jar either in the class path or build that when you are doing the initial build.

Scala syntax – building a pipeline

This pipeline can be built as follows using the Scala API:

```
import org.apache.spark.ml.classification.LogisticRegression
import org.apache.spark.ml.linalg.{Vector,Vectors}
import org.apache.spark.ml.param.ParamMap
import org.apache.spark.ml.feature.{HashingTF, IDF, Tokenizer}

val textTokenizer = new
Tokenizer().setInputCol("corpus").setOutputCol("tokenizedWords")

/* HashingTF and CountVectorized can be used to generate term frequencies.
HashingTF utilizes that hashing trick and is a very fast and space-
efficient way of turning arbitrary features into a vector or a matrix.*/
val hashingTermFrequency = new
HashingTF().setNumFeatures(1000).setInputCol(tokenizer.getOutputCol).setOut
putCol("features")
val logisticRegression = new
LogisticRegression().setMaxIter(10).setRegParam(0.01)
val pipeline = new Pipeline().setStages(Array(tokenizer,
hashingTermFrequency, logisticRegression))
```

Now that you have a pipeline, you can fit the pipeline on a training data set to get a Logistic Regression model as follows:

```
val model = pipeline.fit(trainingDataset)
```

The preceding pipeline model is depicted in the following figure, where the dashed lines will only happen during the pipeline fitting:

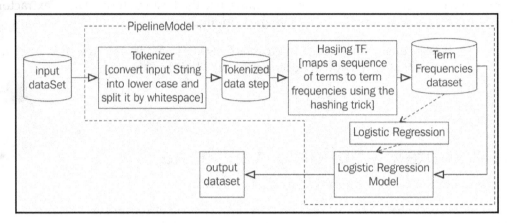

Figure 6.11: Pipeline model

Let's quickly see this in action. In the following code example, we are building a pipeline model. The business case is that we have a set of documents, and we are predicting whether they relate to football or not. If the corpus of text relates to football, we have a label of *1* and if the text does not relate to football, we have a label of *0*. Our ML pipeline will consist of three different stages:

1. Tokenization of the data.
2. HashingTF.
3. Logistic Regression Model.

Building a pipeline

Let's look at the code examples in Scala:

```
import org.apache.spark.ml._
import org.apache.spark.ml.classification.LogisticRegression
import org.apache.spark.ml.feature._
import org.apache.spark.ml.linalg.Vector
import org.apache.spark.sql.Row

// Prepare training documents from a list of (id, text, label) tuples.
//Label 1= Sports, and 0= Not Sports

val trainingDS = spark.createDataFrame(Seq((0L, "ronaldo zidane goals score
```

```
ball studs", 1.0),
(1L, "obama trump clintons whitehouse policy inflation", 0.0),
(2L, "corner penalty worldcup eurocup barcelona messie", 1.0),
(3L, "hadoop mapreduce spark goal pig hive", 0.0))).toDF("id", "text",
"label")


// Configure an ML pipeline, which consists of three stages: tokenizer,
hashingTF, and lr.
val textTokenizer = new
Tokenizer().setInputCol("text").setOutputCol("words")
val hashingTF = new
HashingTF().setNumFeatures(1000).setInputCol(textTokenizer.getOutputCol).se
tOutputCol("features")
```

We create a Logistic Regression Model instance which will be used in the pipeline building phase. Since we are building a model, and estimating coefficients, we need to provide a max number of iterations to prevent it from performing lengthy iterative loops. The regularization parameter is a control on your fitting parameters.

```
val logisticRegressionModel = new LogisticRegression()
logisticRegressionModel.setMaxIter(30)
logisticRegressionModel.setRegParam(0.01)

//Creating a pipeline with three stages in sequence.
val pipeline = new Pipeline().setStages(Array(textTokenizer, hashingTF,
logisticRegressionModel))

// Fit the pipeline to training documents.
val model = pipeline.fit(trainingDS)
```

Now that we have a pipeline, which we had fitted on a particular training set to create a model, we can use the model to test it based on our test data set. In the preceding code, while building the training data set, we provided the labels for our documents. However, while doing a prediction, we will provide a dataset with no labels, and see how the pipeline assigns labels to the dataset. The code for making predictions on test documents is as follows.

Predictions on test documents

Let's look at how the prediction works on test documents in Scala:

```
// Prepare test documents, which are unlabeled (id, text) tuples.
val testDataSet = spark.createDataFrame(Seq(
    (4L, "corner ball goal score" ),
```

```
    (5L, "sort hive optimzer columnar"),
    (6L, "ronaldo messie eurocup"),
    (7L, "database parquet orc avro"))).toDF("id", "text")
```

```
// Make predictions on test documents. We are using the model to predict
the test data, and then selecting a subset of columns which are then
viewed.
  model.transform(testDataSet).select("id", "text", "probability",
"prediction").collect().foreach {
      case Row(id: Long, text: String, prob: Vector, prediction: Double) =>
println(s"($id, $text)
        --> prob=$prob, prediction=$prediction")
}
```

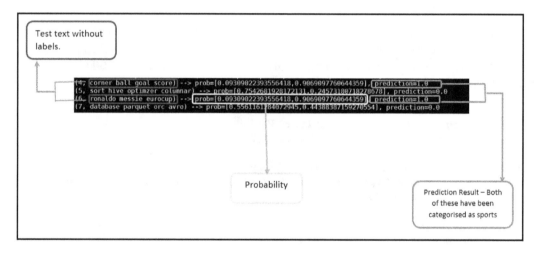

Figure 6.12: Prediction results using the pipelineModel from the pipeline

Python program – predictions on test documents

Let's look at the Python version of the program and see how this prediction works on test documents:

```
from pyspark.ml import Pipeline
from pyspark.ml.classification import LogisticRegression
from pyspark.ml.feature import HashingTF, Tokenizer


# Create a dataframe using labelled data set
trainingDataSet = spark.createDataFrame([
    (0, "ronaldo zidane goals score ball studs", 1.0),
```

```
    (1, "obama trump clintons whitehouse policy inflation", 0.0),
    (2, "corner penalty worldcup eurocup barcelona messie", 1.0),
    (3, "hadoop mapreduce spark goal pig hive", 0.0)], ["documentId",
"corpus", "label"])

# Configure an ML pipeline, which consists of three stages:
# texttokenization, hashingTF, and logisticRegressionmodel.

textTokenizer = Tokenizer(inputCol="corpus", outputCol="words")
hashingTF = HashingTF(inputCol=textTokenizer.getOutputCol(),
outputCol="features")
logisticRegressionModel = LogisticRegression(maxIter=30, regParam=0.01)
pipeline = Pipeline(stages=[textTokenizer, hashingTF,
logisticRegressionModel])

# Fit the pipeline to training documents.\
#Returns a model which can then be used with other data sets for
prediction.

model = pipeline.fit(trainingDataSet)

# Create a dataset which contains unlabelled documents of data
testDataSet = spark.createDataFrame([
    (4, "corner ball goal score" ),
    (5, "sort hive optimzer columnar"),
    (6, "ronaldo messie eurocup"),
    (7, "database parquet orc avro")], ["documentId", "corpus"])


# Make predictions on test documents and print columns of interest from the
predictions.

prediction = model.transform(testDataSet)
selectedColumns = prediction.select("documentId", "corpus", "prediction",
"probability")
for eachRow in selectedColumns.collect():
print(eachRow)
```

The results are very similar to our Scala program, where we get correct predictions for corpus related to sports barring `documentId`=7. However please do look at the probability which gives a clue to the confidence of the prediction.

```
Row(documentId=4, corpus=u'corner ball goal score', prediction=1.0, probability=DenseVector([0.1672, 0.8328]))
Row(documentId=5, corpus=u'sort hive optimzer columnar', prediction=0.0, probability=DenseVector([0.6906, 0.3094]))
Row(documentId=6, corpus=u'ronaldo messie eurocup', prediction=1.0, probability=DenseVector([0.0825, 0.9175]))
Row(documentId=7, corpus=u'database parquet orc avro', prediction=1.0, probability=DenseVector([0.5, 0.5]))
```

Figure 6.13: Prediction results using the PipelineModel from the pipeline

Hopefully, this quick introduction to pipeline will have given you some confidence when attempting to build your machine learning pipelines. This is an introductory level chapter, so we'll move on to giving you an overview of what else you can expect in the Spark MLLib. For detailed code examples, we would refer you to the Spark documentation on the Apache website (`http://spark.apache.org/docs/latest/ml-guide.html`). The folks at Apache are doing a tremendous job of maintaining top-quality and up-to-date documentation of what is available within the library.

Feature engineering

Feature engineering is perhaps the most important topic in machine learning. The success and failure of a model to predict the future depends primarily on how you engineer features to get a better lift. The difference between an experienced data scientist and a novice would be their ability to engineer features from the data sets given, and this is perhaps the most difficult and time consuming aspect of machine learning. This is where the understanding of business problems is the key. Feature engineering is basically an art more than it is a science, and basically it is needed to frame the problem. So what is feature engineering?

Feature engineering is the process of transforming raw data into features that better represent the underlying business problem to the predictive models, resulting in improved model accuracy on unseen data

Due to the importance of feature engineering, Spark provides algorithms for working with features divided into three major groups:

- **Feature Extraction:** Extracting features from raw data
- **Transformations:** Modification of features
- **Selection:** Selection of a smaller set of features from a larger set

We'll now look at each of these in more detail.

Feature extraction algorithms

Let's look at some of the feature extraction algorithms which are quite key in any machine learning process.

Algorithm Name	High Level Overview
TF-IDF	Term Frequency-Inverse Document Frequency is used in text mining to understand what the importance of a word is to a document in a collection or corpus. The `tf-idf` weight is a weight often used in information retrieval and text mining (more details can be found at `http://bit.ly/2g qN8PV`).
Word2Vec	Word2vec is a computationally-efficient predictive model for learning word embeddings from raw text. The model maps each word to a unique fixed-size vector (more details can be found at `http://bit.ly/2g2i7oB`).
CountVecmtorizer	CountVectorizer converts a collection of text documents to a matrix of token counts (more details can be found at `http://bit.ly/2gfv2Be`).

Feature transformation algorithms

Let's look at some of the feature transformation algorithms which are quite key in any machine learning process.

Algorithm Name	High Level Overview
`Tokenizer`	`Tokenization` is a process (as already seen in previous examples), where we take a piece of text (line of text) and split it into individual terms (usually words). By default, a white space is used for `tokenization`; however, you can use the `RegexTokenizer` class to perform more advanced `tokenization` (more details can be found at `http://bit.ly/2gfy1Ke`).
`StopWordsRemover`	Stop words are words that are insignificant to the body of text, and are generally filtered before processing of natural language of text. `StopWordsRemover` can take a sequence of strings, and drop all stop words from the input. Stop words can either be passed as a parameter, or loaded by calling `StopWordsRemover.loadDefaultStopWords(language)` for certain languages supported by Spark (more details can be found at `http://bit.ly/2fBjmL0`).

n-gram	`n-gram` is an advanced Tokenizer, which is often used to transform features into `n-grams`. N-Gram emits a sequence of n items from a given sequence of text or speech. Google has an N-Gram Viewer, which can be accessed here `https://books.google.com/ngrams/`. For more details on `n-gram` functionality, visit `http://bit.ly/2gJgLjU`.
Binarizer	`Binarizer` is the process of converting numerical features to binary 0 or 1 features. The process is quite simple where the algorithm takes an input and output column in addition to a threshold value. Features with values greater than the threshold are `Binarized` to 1.0, and features with values less than threshold are `Binarized` to 0.0. More details can be found at `http://bit.ly/2gryzPZ`.
PCA	PCA, an acronym for **Principal Component Analysis (PCA)**, is a technique focused on emphasizing the variation and strong patterns in the data set by successive attempts made of finding a linear combination of a set of variables that have maximum variance. In essence it is a dimensionality reduction technique. More details can be found at `http://bit.ly/2g2oaJT`.
StringIndexer	`StringIndexer` is a very useful utility method that can help encode a string column of labels to a column of label indices. The indices are in `[0, numLabels)`, ordered by label frequencies, so the most frequent label gets index 0. More details can be found at `http://bit.ly/2g2mMa0`.
IndexToString	An `IndexToString` is an inverse of `StringIndexer` as it uses a column of label indices to get the original labels. A common use case is to produce indices from labels with `StringIndexer`, train a model with those indices, and retrieve the original labels from the column of predicted indices with `IndexToString`. More details can be found at `http://bit.ly/2fjp8Cw`.
PolynomialExpansion	Polynomial feature expansion is the process of expanding your features into polynomial space, which is created by an n degree combination of your dimensions. Polynomial expansion increases the number of predictors. More details can be found at `http://bit.ly/2fyhuPS`.

`DiscreteCosineTransform`	**Discrete Cosine Transform (DCT)** linearly transforms n length data (that is, a set of numbers, for example, a0, a1, ..., an) in the time domain another N length valued sequence into the frequency domain. More details can be found at `http://bit.ly /2fjueOU`.
`OneHotEncoder`	Categorical variables are often used and encoded as numerical variables in order to be used as a feature in a given model. If you have a column with values `[house, banglow, flat, house]`, you may encode them as `[0,1,2,0]`, which means you have given them an ordinal characteristic that is not desirable as you have implied house `< banglow < flat`. One-hot encoding is necessary for the proper representation of these elements. One-hot encoding (`http://en.wikipedia.org /wiki/One-hot`) maps a column of label indices to a column of binary vectors, with at most a single one-value. This encoding allows algorithms that expect continuous features, such as Logistic Regression, to use categorical features. One-hot encoding offers increases in prediction accuracy of the models. More details can be found at `http://bit.ly/2fybkiF`. 	ID	CATEGORY		ID	CATEGORYVECTOR	|---|---|---|---|---|	0	A		0	2,[0],[1.0]		1	B		1	2,[],[]		2	C		2	2,[1],[1.0]		3	A		3	2,[0],[1.0]		4	A		4	2,[0],[1.0]		5	C		5	2,[1],[1.0]	 Figure 6.14: Usage of one-hot encoder to encode categorical variables

This is not a comprehensive list as Apache Spark is continuously improving its list of feature transformations. For more details, please visit `http://bit.ly/2grwIqx`.

Feature selection algorithms

Apache Spark also provides feature selection algorithms. At the time of writing, only three were included in the release, and more are expected to be added soon:

Algorithm Name	Details
VectorSlicer	Vector Slicer is quite useful in feature extraction from vector columns. **Input** = Feature vector **Output** = Feature vector with sub-array of original features. More details can be found at `http://bit.ly/2gqZ1p7`.
RFormula	RFormula selects columns specified by an R model formula. At the moment a limited set of R operators are supported such as: ~ => Separate target and the terms. + => Concat terms. – => Remove Term : => Interaction . => all columns except Target More details can be found at `http://bit.ly/2fjsJAp`.
ChiSqSelector	`ChiSqSelector` stands for Chi-Squared feature selector. `ChiSqSelector` uses the Chi-Squared test of independence to decide which features to choose. More details can be found at `http://bit.ly/2fyccnr`.

Classification and regression

Apache Spark provides a number of classification and regression algorithms. The main algorithms are listed as follows.

Classification

In machine learning and statistics, classification is the problem of identifying to which of a set of categories (sub-populations) a new observation belongs, on the basis of a training set of data containing observations (or instances) whose category membership is known. Typically in classification cases, the dependent variables are categorical. A very common example is classification of e-mail as spam versus not spam. The major algorithms that come with Spark include the following:

- Logistic regression
- Decision tree classifier
- Random forest classifier
- Gradient- boosted tree classifier
- Multilayer perceptron classifier

- One-vs-Rest classifier
- Naïve Bayes

Regression

In machine learning and statistics, Regression is a process by which we estimate or predict a response based on the model trained based on previous data sets. Regression predicts a value from a continuous set, whereas classification predicts belonging to a class. Regression assumes that there is a relationship between the input and targets. Regression techniques often use maximum likelihood estimations. The following major regression algorithms are included with Apache Spark:

- Linear Regression.
- Generalized Linear Regression.
- Decision Tree Regression.
- Random Forest Regression.
- Gradient-boosted tree regression.
- Survival Regression.
- Isotonic Regression.

Clustering

For the most part of this chapter, we have primarily focused on supervised machine learning techniques where we train a model based before using it for predictions. Clustering is an unsupervised machine learning technique, used in customer segmentation, pattern recognition, image analysis, information retrieval, bioinformatics, data compression, and computer graphics.

Apache Spark provides various clustering algorithms, including:

- K-Means
- Latent Dirichlet Allocation (LDA)
- Bisecting K-Means
- Gaussian Mixture Models

Collaborative filtering

Most of us will have used eBay, Amazon, or any other popular web retailer. And most of us will have seen recommendations based on our past choices. For example, if you buy an electric toothbrush, Amazon would recommend you some extra brush heads as these items normally go together. All of these suggestions are based on recommended systems, which are typically based on collaborative filtering techniques.

Collaborative filtering algorithms recommend items (this is the *filtering* part) based on preference information from many users (this is the *collaborative* part). The collaborative filtering approach is based on similarity; the basic idea is people who liked similar items in the past will like similar items in the future.

In the following example, Adrian likes the movies Mission Impossible, Skyfall, Casino Royale, and Spectre. Bob likes the movies Skyfall, Casino Royale, and Spectre. Andrew likes the movies Skyfall and Spectre.

To recommend a movie to Andrew, we calculate that users who liked Skyfall and also liked Casino Royale, so Spectre is a possible recommendation for Andrew:

	MI	Skyfall	Spectre	Casino Royale
Adrian	5	4	5	5
Bob		5	4	5
Andrew		5	?	4

Figure 6.15: Movie recommendations example

Collaborative filtering techniques aim to fill the missing entries of a user-item association matrix. Apache Spark supports collaborative filtering in which users and products are described by a small set of latent factors that can be used to predict missing entries. Spark ML uses the **Alternating Least Squares (ALS)** technique to learn these factors using the following parameters:

- numBlocks

- Rank
- maxIter
- regParam
- alpha
- nonnegative

For the purpose of this chapter, that is all we are going to discuss. However, we will discuss recommendation systems in much more detail in Chapter 9, *Building a Recommendation System* where we'll build a recommendation engine. For further details on APIs, please visit http://bit.ly/2fk8vXh.

ML-tuning – model selection and hyperparameter tuning

Model development is one of the major tasks. However an important ML task is the selection of the best model from among a list of models, and tuning the model for optimal performance. Tuning can obviously be done for the individual steps or the entire pipeline model, which would include multiple algorithms, feature engineering, transformations and selections.

MLLib supports model selection using the following tools:

- Cross Validator
- Train Validation Split

We will look at Model Tuning in Chapter 9, *Building a Recommendation System,* on Recommendations to see how we can minimize mean squared error, one of the characteristics of a good model.

References

The following articles, blog posts, and videos were used as a resource during the preparation of this chapter. However, these are also important from the perspective of further reading.

1. https://support.sas.com/resources/papers/proceedings14/SAS313-2014.pdf

2. http://www.minicomplexity.org/pubs/1943-mcculloch-pitts-bmb.pdf

3. http://psycnet.apa.org/psycinfo/1959-09865-001

4. http://www.sascommunity.org/sugi/SUGI82/Sugi-82-121%20Sarle.pdf

5. https://www.hakkalabs.co/articles/spark-mllib-making-practical-machine-learning-easy-and-scalable

6. http://spark.apache.org/docs/latest/ml-pipeline.html

7. http://www.slideshare.net/databricks/practical-machine-learning-pipelines-with-mllib

8. https://databricks.com/blog/2015/01/07/ml-pipelines-a-new-high-level-api-for-mllib.html

9. http://machinelearningmastery.com/discover-feature-engineering-how-to-engineer-features-and-how-to-get-good-at-it/

10. http://www.haberdar.org/discrete-cosine-transform-tutorial.htm

11. >http://stackoverflow.com/questions/17469835/one-hot-encoding-for-machine-learning

12. https://www.quora.com/What-is-one-hot-encoding-and-when-is-it-used-in-data-science

Summary

In this chapter we have covered details around machine learning basics, types of machine learning, introduction to Spark MLLib, introduction to Pipeline API, examples of building a Pipeline API and then highlighting the algorithms provided by Spark around feature engineering, classification, regression, clustering and collaborative filtering.

Machine learning is an advanced topic, and it is impossible to cover the depth and breadth of the topic in such a small chapter. However, I hope this chapter gives you a flavor of what is available within Spark and where you can go to for further information. The references section contains the details of the topics. For machine learning, I would recommend *Practical Machine Learning* or *Master Machine Learning with Spark* both of which have been published by Packt Publishing and are really good books to give your more in-depth understanding of machine learning.

The next chapter covers GraphX, which is quite a hot topic. We'll cover the basics of graph processing, before going into the details of the offerings from Apache regarding GraphX.

7
GraphX

Machine learning is an interesting topic, and if you are reading this book cover to cover, you might be wondering what topic can perhaps overshadow the impressive capability in the day-to-day use machine learning. Well if you haven't heard of graphs before (not graphics!), this is the chapter where we will cover the interesting topic of graphs. We'll look at the following major topics, such as:

- Graphs in everyday life
- What is a graph?
- Why are Graphs elegant?
- What is GraphX?
- Graph operators in Spark
- Graph algorithms in Spark
- Examples of graph algorithms

Let's get started with this interesting chapter!

Graphs in everyday life

You are on Facebook and being a privacy freak you lie about almost everything on your profile including your personal information, but Facebook is still able to recommend a huge number of people that you have met in daily life, and acquaintances that you might have met a decade ago. If you weren't smart enough, you would think that it is magic. If you are still wondering about this mystery (without thinking it is magic), you aren't the only one. This mystery led to a full scale investigation by the Irish Data Protection Commissioner; however, what we all believe today is that Facebook hasn't been malicious about their suggestions, but rather has used Graph algorithms to the most optimum effect. When you sign-up for Facebook, you may allow Facebook access to your contacts (desktop, e-mail, and phone numbers), and using these details Facebook would try to find other users who have similar information on their contacts and build an initial social circle of friends and family. The questions that you might find invasive, such as which school you went to, and which city/area you lived are actually in very useful in building that initial social graph.

Once the social graph is built, Facebook can look at your Graph and predict people that you should most likely connect to now and in the future. This is actually based on some clever graph algorithms, where Facebook can run pretty sophisticated analysis on the structure of the networks and identify how closely related are two people, and if a certain person in a group is actually the heart and soul of the group, and is important for the group to stay connected.

Facebook isn't the only company trying to understand the structure of communities, as all major social media companies including Twitter, LinkedIn, Google, and major telecommunication companies, are looking into ways to understand their community of users. For example, let's take another example of telecommunication companies. Your mobile service provider has access to all of your data including calling patterns such as who you call, when you call them (business hours, out-of-office hours), how frequently you call them (twice a day, every weekend), and based on this information it will build some pretty sophisticated social networks identifying the influencers of the network and the outliers and detect communities of users based on this rich set of information.

So graphs are common place in our daily lives, and in almost everything we touch, but what exactly is a graph?

What is a graph?

A graph is a mathematical representation of linked data. It is a study of relationships or relationships objects, and it is formed by vertices (also known as nodes or points), which are connected by edges (also known as arcs or lines). A graph may be directed or undirected, where a directed graph implies that edges have direction associated with them, while an undirected graph implies that the edges do not have a direction associated with them.

A graph is therefore represented as an ordered pair of $G=(V,E)$ where V is a set of vertices, nodes, or points connected by E, which is a set of edges, arcs, or lines. For example, in *Figure 7.1*, we have a set of vertices numbered 1 to 7, and certain vertices are connected by more than one edges, for example, 4 connected to vertices 1,2,3,6 while 7 is only connected to 6.

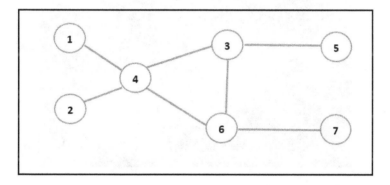

Figure 7.1: An example of a Graph

In computer science, graphs are used to represent networks of communication such as data organization, a set of computational devices, and the flow of communication. We have seen some examples of graph theory in social networks and telecommunication earlier; however, graph theory has many uses including, but not limited to:

- Linguistics
- Study of molecules in chemistry and physics
- Sociology
- Biology and conservation efforts
- Mathematics

If you think about it even the World Wide Web is a graph, with multiple pages (vertices) connected to each other via hyperlinks.

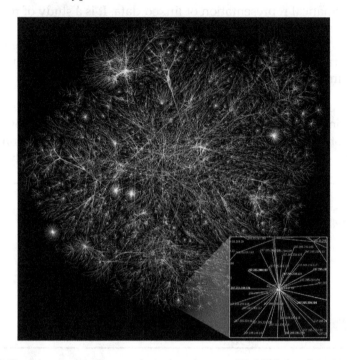

Figure 7.2: Partial map of the Internet based on January 15, 2005 data found on opte.org

From a historic perspective, the paper published by *Leonhard Euler* on the *Seven Bridges of Konigsberg* in 1736 is widely regarded as the first paper in the history of Graph Theory. The Seven Bridges of Konigsberg is a notable problem in mathematics, and Euler's non-resolution of the problem formed the basis of what we know as graph theory. In the city of Konigsberg, Prussia (now known as Kaliningrad, Russia) two large islands were connected to each other and the mainland by seven bridges. Euler proves that there was no way to devise a walk through the city such that:

- You cross the bridge and only once
- The islands could only be reached by the bridges
- Every bridge once accessed must be crossed to the other end
- The starting and ending point can be different

You can read more about the problem on Wikipedia, but the objective of mentioning this history is that graph theory has been around for some time, but has now become more popular due to the advent of new and popular graph processing frameworks and the power of computing available to us at a much cheaper cost.

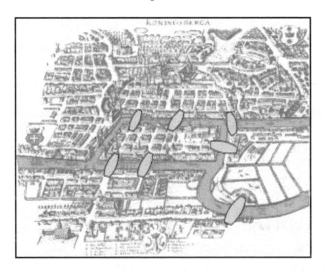

Figure 7.3: Map of Königsberg in Euler's time showing the actual layout of the seven bridges, highlighting the river Pregel and the bridges

Why are Graphs elegant?

Graphs are elegant and provide a simpler way to frame complex problems within the computer sciences domain. Graph problems are typically **NP-Complete** and are therefore useful for study in computational complexity. Graphs are used to model different scenarios from routing algorithms to finite state machines, and if you go into a bit more detail, you will see that graph algorithms can be parallelized in a much better way.

Google realized the importance of graphs, visualized the web as a series of connected web pages via hyperlinks, and created a competitive advantage by building the fastest search engine around.

The simplicity of Graph computation can be gauged from the fact that all the algorithms operate in the same pattern, that is, access the directly connected neighbors of a particular vertex. The beauty of this approach is that you can easily parallelize this over an MPP environment.

Consider the following graph:

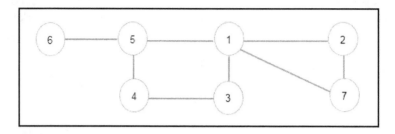

You can have any particular algorithm that can operate on the graph, but from an execution perspective, the algorithm itself while calculating the value at a particular vertex only needs to access the neighboring edges. You may need to iterate over the interim result to produce a final result, but the algorithm itself can be easily parallelized.

What is GraphX?

Spark **GraphX** is not the first system to bring graph parallel computation to the mainstream, as even before this project, people used to perform graph computation on Hadoop, although they had to spend considerable time to build a graph on Hadoop. This resulted in creation of specialized systems such as **Apache Giraph** (an open source version of **Google's Pregel**), which ensured that the graph processing times come down to a fraction of what they were on Hadoop. However, graph processing is not isolated, and is very similar to MLLib where you have to spend time to load the data and pre-process it before running a machine learning pipeline. Similarly, the full data processing pipeline isn't just about running a graph algorithm, and graph creation is an important aspect of the problem, including performing post-processing, that is, what to do with the result. This was beautifully presented in a *UC Berkley AmpLab* talk in 2013 by *Joseph Gonzalez* and *Reynold Xin*.

The following figure is taken from the slides that they presented, and clearly explains where most of the time was spent with traditional graph parallel systems:

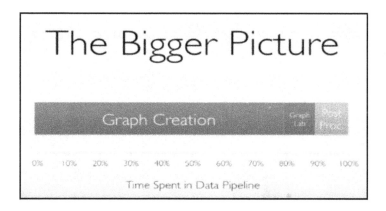

Figure 7.4: Traditional graph parallel systems – amount of time spent in data pipeline

GraphX projects combine the powerful aspects of Spark (for exmple, RDDs, fault-tolerance, and task-scheduling) with GraphLab, which provides the GraphAPI (graph representation and efficient execution) to build a single system that can build the entire pipeline.

By bringing the flexibility of the Spark architecture, GraphX overcomes the limitations from traditional graph parallel systems by providing support for the construction of graphs and the post-processing of graphs, in addition to providing an interactive interface. Since Apache Spark provides DataFrames, SQL, streaming, machine learning, and graph processing as a part of the same framework, you do not need to maintain multiple platforms.

GraphX is exciting because you can seamlessly transition from data tables to graphs and vice-versa, and combine the best of both worlds.

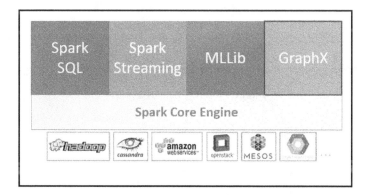

Figure 7.5: Apache Spark GraphX

Creating your first Graph (RDD API)

For the RDD API, the basic class in GraphX is called a `Graph`
(`org.apache.spark.graphx.Graph`), which contains two types of RDDs as you might
have guessed:

- Edges
- Vertices

In the following graph, you can see we have a number of different vertices, namely *Fawad,
Aznan, Ben, Tom,* and *Marathon.*

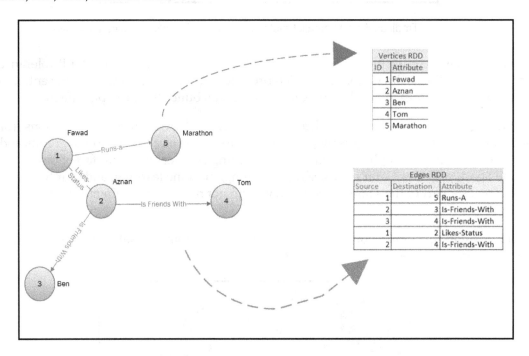

Figure 7.6: Depiction of a graph

This is a labeled graph where the edges and vertices have labels associated with them.

Following the Graph, we will look at a code example, where we:

- Create the vertices
- Create the edges
- Instantiate a graph object
- View the vertices configured with the graph

The following code example can be used to create a Graph similar to the one shown in the preceding figure.

Code samples

Let's look at the code example:

```
import org.apache.spark.graphx._

val myVertices = sc.parallelize(Array(
  (1L, "Fawad"),
  (2L, "Aznan"),
  (3L, "Ben"),
  (4L, "Tom"),
  (5L, "Marathon"))
)

val myEdges = sc.parallelize(Array(
  Edge(1L, 5L, "Runs-A"),
  Edge(2L, 3L, "is-friends-with"), Edge(3L, 4L, "is-friends-with"),
  Edge(1L, 2L, "Likes-status"),
  Edge(2L, 4L,"Is-Friends-With")))

val myGraph = Graph(myVertices, myEdges)
myGraph.vertices.collect
//Find all Vertices where the name property in Vertice="Fawad"
myGraph.vertices.filter{ case (id,name)=> name=="Fawad" }.count
//Collect All vertices where the name property is "Marathon"
myGraph.vertices.filter{ case (id,name)=> name=="Marathon" }.collect()
```

GraphX also provides options to build a graph from a collection of vertices and edges in an RDD or available on disk.

Graphs can be loaded from a disk using the `GraphLoader()` class available in `org.apache.spark.graphx.GraphLoader`. The `GraphLoader()` class has an `edgeListFile()` method, which can be used to build a graph. The `edgeListFile()` method accepts the following parameters:

- `SparkContext`: SC
- Path to the file: String
- Canonical Orientation: Boolean parameter to define whether to orient the edges in a positive direction.
- `numEdgePartitions`: Number of partitions for the `edgeRDD` – This defines the parallelism
- `edgeStorageLevel`: The desired storage level for the edge partitions (MEMORY, DISK, HYBRID)
- `vertexStorageLevel` – The desired storage level for vertex partitions. (MEMORY, DISK, HYBRID)

This method will skip all the lines that begin with `#`.

Let us consider an example of a file with a million call records, with very simple information of the calling and the called number. This data is not a real dataset, as in a proper call record you will see much more information rather than simply the calling number and called number. The `edgeListFile()` method is automatically creating vertices as mentioned by the edges:

```
spark@ubuntu:~/sampledata/graphx$ head callrecords.txt
#January Call Records
#CallingNumber CalledNumber
0777652429     0777738147
0785760097     0785595912
0778083047     0796000705
0797535374     0774714482
0789871662     0795122518
0774707226     0788034752
0794247598     0795300158
0789482464     0796298977
```

Figure 7-7: Sample call records

We will now use the `GraphLoader.edgeListFile()` to load these `CallRecords` as a graph. Please note that all the vertex and edge attributes are set to 1, as you can see in the following screenshot:

```
scala> val myGraph = GraphLoader.edgeListFile(sc,"/home/spark/sampledata/graphx/callrecords.txt")
myGraph: org.apache.spark.graphx.Graph[Int,Int] = org.apache.spark.graphx.impl.GraphImpl@41232f59

scala> myGraph.vertices.count()
res16: Long = 198948

scala> myGraph.edges.count()
res17: Long = 100000

scala> myGraph.edges.take(1)
16/12/10 01:36:52 WARN Executor: 1 block locks were not released by TID = 8914:
[rdd_441_0]
res18: Array[org.apache.spark.graphx.Edge[Int]] = Array(Edge(774000131,787935778,1))

scala> myGraph.vertices.take(1)
res19: Array[(org.apache.spark.graphx.VertexId, Int)] = Array((778684014,1))
```

Figure 7.8: Loading via GraphLoader

We can also create a Graph from other RDDs of vertices and edges. The following methods in the Graph (`org.apache.spark.graphx.Graph`) can be used to achieve this:

- `Graph.apply`: Allows for creating a graph from RDDs of vertices and edges. Duplicate vertices are picked arbitrarily and vertices found in the edge RDD but not the vertex RDD are assigned the default attribute.
- `Graph.fromEdges`: Allows for creating a graph from only an RDD of edges, automatically creating any vertices mentioned by edges and assigning them the default value.
- `Graph.fromEdgeTuples`: Allows for creating a graph from only an RDD of edge tuples, assigning the edges the value 1, and automatically creating any vertices mentioned by edges and assigning them the default value. It also supports de-duplicating the edges.

Basic graph operators (RDD API)

We have already looked at some basic RDD operators while discussing the RDD API earlier in this book. Graphs also support basic operators to help create new graphs and manipulate them. The two major classes for graphs are:

- org.apache.spark.graphx.Graph: This is an abstract class that represents a graph with arbitrary objects associated with vertices and edges. This class provides basic operations to access and manipulate the data associated with the vertices and edges, as well as the underlying structure. Like the RDD API, graph API provides a functional structure in which mutating operations would return a new Graph object.
- org.apache.spark.graphx.GraphOps: The GraphOps class contains additional functionality for graphs. All operations are expressed in terms of efficient GraphXAPI. This class is implicitly constructed for each graph object and can be obtained from the ops value member as follows. You do not need to explicitly get a GraphOps object as Scala implicitly will let the GraphOps operators automatically appear as members of the Graph.

```
scala> val myGraphOps = myGraph.ops
myGraphOps: org.apache.spark.graphx.GraphOps[String,String] = org.apache.spark.graphx.GraphOps@d9fe131

scala> myGraphOps.inDegrees.count
res7: Long = 4

scala> myGraph.inDegrees.count
res8: Long = 4
```

Figure 7.9: Getting a GraphOps object

List of graph operators (RDD API)

Let's look at the commonly used graph operators. Please note in the Class column C, that abbreviation GO stands for org.apache.spark.graphx.GraphOps and G for org.apache.spark.graphx.Graph:

The following table of functions provide detailed information about the graph:

C	Method	Description
GO	numEdges()	The number of edges in the graph.
GO	numVertices()	The number of vertices in the graph.
GO	inDegrees()	The in-degree of each vertex in the graph.
GO	outDegrees()	The out-degree of each vertex in the graph.
GO	degrees()	The degree of each vertex in the graph.

The following table of functions provide the views of graphs as collections:

C	Method	Description
G	vertices	An RDD containing the vertices of the graph and their associated attributes.
G	edges	An RDD containing the edges of the graph and their associated attributes.
G	triplets	An RDD containing the edge triplets, which are edges along with the vertex data associated with the adjacent vertices.

The following table of functions are used to transform the attributes of a vertex and edge:

C	Method	Description
G	mapVertices	Transforms each vertex attribute in the graph using a map function.
G	mapEdges	Transforms each edge attribute using the map function, passing it a whole partition at a time.
G	mapTriplets	Transforms each edge attribute a partition at a time using the map function, passing it adjacent vertex attributes as well.

The following table of functions are used to modify the graph structure.

C	Method	Description
G	reverse	Reverse all the edges in the graph. This can be useful when trying to compute the inverse PageRank.
G	subgraph	Restricts the graph to only the vertices and edges that satisfy the predicates passed in as arguments.
G	mask	The mask operator constructs a subgraph by returning a graph that contains the vertices and edges that are also found in the input graph. This can be used in conjunction with the subgraph operator to restrict a graph based on the properties in another related graph.
G	groupEdges	Merges multiple edges between two vertices into a single Edge.

The following functions help you join other RDDs with the graph

C	Method	Description
GO	joinVertices	Joins the vertices with an RDD and then applies a function from the vertex and RDD entry to a new vertex value.
G	outerJoinVertices	Joins vertices with entries in the table RDD and merges the results using mapFunc(), which is passed as an argument.

The following are some of the most important functions. They let the developer aggregate information about the adjacent triplets:

C	Method	Description
GO	collectNeighborIds	Collects the neighbor vertex IDs for each vertex.
GO	collectNeighbors	Collects the neighbor vertex attributes for each vertex.
G	aggregateMessages	Aggregates values from neighboring edges and vertices of each vertex.

Following table shows Iterative graph-parallel computation:

C	Method	Description
GO	pregel	Executes a Pregel-like iterative vertex-parallel abstraction. The user-defined vertex-program `vprog` is executed in parallel on each vertex receiving any inbound messages and computing a new value for the vertex. The `sendMsg` function passed as an argument is then invoked on all out-edges and is used to compute an optional message to the destination vertex. The `mergeMsg` function, which is a commutative association function, is used to combine messages destined to the same vertex. On the first iteration, all vertices receive the initial message and on subsequent iterations if a vertex does not receive a message then the vertex program is not invoked. This function iterates until there are no remaining messages, or for `maxIterations` iterations.

Following table shows Basic Graph Algorithms:

C	Method	Description
GO	pageRank	Runs a dynamic version of PageRank, returning a graph with vertex attributes containing the PageRank and edge attributes containing the normalized edge weight.
GO	connectedComponents	Computes the connected component membership of each vertex and returns a graph with the vertex value containing the lowest vertex ID in the connected component containing that vertex.
GO	triangleCount	Computes the number of triangles passing through each vertex.
GO	stronglyConnectedComponents	Computes the strongly connected component (SCC) of each vertex and returns a graph with the vertex value containing the lowest vertex ID in the SCC containing that vertex.

Caching and uncaching of graphs

If you remember in the earlier chapters, we discussed the caching of RDDs, which basically referred to the fact that if you intend to use a particular RDD multiple times, you will need to cache the RDD, otherwise the Spark framework will recompute the RDD from scratch every time it is called.

Graphs (like RDDs) are not persisted in memory by default, and caching is the ideal option when using the graph multiple times. The implementation is quite similar where you simply call the cache on the Graph object:

```
myGraph.cache()
```

Uncaching unused objects from memory may improve performance. Cached RDDs and graphs remain memory resident until they are evicted due to memory pressures in an LRU order. For iterative computations, intermediate results from previous iterations will fill up the cache, resulting in slow garbage collection due to memory being filled up with unnecessary information.

Suggested approach: Uncache intermediate results as soon as possible, which might mean materializing a graph and using materialized datasets in future iterations. Pregel API is recommended for Iterative computations due to its ability to unpersist intermediate results.

Graph algorithms in GraphX

GraphX supports sophisticated Graph processing and while you can build your own graph algorithms, GraphX provides a number of algorithms as a part of GraphX directly available as methods of graph or `GraphOps` objects. The three major components that GraphX supports include:

- PageRank
- Connected components
- Triangle counting

PageRank

PageRank measure the importance of a vertex in the graph. For example, a Twitter user with lots of Twitter followers, or a LinkedIn user with lots of LinkedIn connections and followers is often considered influential and ranked highly.

GraphX supports both static and dynamic versions of PageRank, where static PageRank runs for a fixed number of iterations, while a dynamic PageRank runs until convergence (changes less than the tolerance level after each iteration).

Let's look at a very simple example. We have a set of call detail records (dummy data), and we are trying to identify the most important person in the community. There are other metrics, but one of the ways to identify an important person or position is by looking at the number of inward connections. In our example, we have the following structure of the file:

1. Calling Number
2. Called Number

We also have another reference data file, which contains the list of users to whom these numbers belong. In real life, you will have a data set from a CRM system, but the objective of joining a graph with an RDD remains essentially the same.

```
spark@ubuntu:~/sampledata/graphx$ cat cdrs.txt
#callingnumber callednumber
7917559559 7788410276
7841027521 7788410276
3321345671 7788410276
7841027521 3321345671
7788410276 7917559559
3321345671 4678923134
4678923134 7788410276
0990099009 34044013413
0990099009 7788410276
```

Figure 7.10: Call detail records to be used for the example

The usernames list contains eight users, and the structure is a simple CSV file with the first column referring to the phone number, and the second column referring to the name of the person.

```
spark@ubuntu:~/sampledata/graphx$ cat usernames.csv
7917559559,James
7788410276,Timmy
7841027521,Bondoo
3321345671,Sultan
3321345671,Raees
4678923134,Roger
990099009,Andrew
4044013413,Adrian
```

Figure 7.11: Usernames list

We'll now look at the code example that utilizes the PageRank algorithm to identify the most important vertices in the data set.

Code example — PageRank algorithm

The following code shows an code example for PageRank algorithm:

```
import org.apache.spark.graphx.{Graph, VertexRDD, GraphLoader}

val cdrGraph =
GraphLoader.edgeListFile(sc,"/home/spark/sampledata/graphx/cdrs.txt")
val influencers = cdrGraph.pageRank(0.0001).vertices
val usersList =
sc.textFile("/home/spark/sampledata/graphx/usernames.csv").map{line =>
  val fields = line.split(",")
  (fields(0).trim().toLong, fields(1))
}

val ranksByUsername = usersList.join(influencers).map {
  case (id, (username, userRank)) => (username, userRank)}
  println(ranksByUsername.collect().mkString("\n"))
```

If you look at the result of the PageRank example, you will see that user **Timmy** is the highest ranked individual. If we have a quick look at the original data set, we will see that the number **7788410276** belongs to **Timmy**, and he is on the receiving end of five of the nine calls, outnumbering every other individual.

James received just one call, but he is ranked as the second highest influential individual. Can you figure out why? This is because James is the only one who has been called by **Timmy**, the highest ranked individual and hence James is a person of high influence.

```
scala> println(ranksByUsername.collect().mkString("\n"))
(James,2.295398410507568)
(Bondoo,0.15)
(Andrew,0.15)
(Timmy,2.5239981300089043)
(Roger,0.24084375)
(Sultan,0.21375)
(Raees,0.21375)
```

Figure 7.12: Result of PageRank on our fictional data set

Connected components

Let us consider the example of a social network where you will have various clusters of people connected to each other, but the clusters themselves might not be connected. The goal of finding the connected components is to find these clusters. The connected components algorithm labels each connected component of the graph with the ID of its lowest-numbered vertex. Let's look at our CDR data set, and see how we can find connected components using GraphX.

Code example — connected components

The following code shows an code example for Connected components algorithm:

```
import org.apache.spark.graphx._

val cdrGraph =
GraphLoader.edgeListFile(sc,"/home/spark/sampledata/graphx/cdrs.txt")
val connectedVertices = cdrGraph.connectedComponents().vertices
val usersList =
sc.textFile("/home/spark/sampledata/graphx/usernames.csv").map{line =>
  val fields = line.split(",")
  (fields(0).trim().toLong, fields(1))
}

val connectedComponentsByUsers = usersList.join(connectedVertices).map {
  case (id, (username, cc)) => (username, cc)
}
println(connectedComponentsByUsers.collect().mkString("\n"))
```

Triangle counting

Triangle counting is very useful in social network analysis. Due to the limitations on the size of this book, we cannot go any further than explaining the basic structure of a triangle in a graph. Suppose you are friends with Rob and Steven on Facebook, and Rob and Facebook are also friends with each other. You three will make up a triangle. GraphX makes it very easy to find such graph structures in a large graph. Spark's `triangleCount()` method on the graph object will return triangle counts.

Spark GraphX documentation has more detail on the topic and I would strongly recommend looking at the latest documentation available at `http://bit.ly/2hjcdOK`.

GraphFrames

Having seen GraphX over the course of this chapter, have you not wondered what happened to DataFrame? If you are reading/following this book cover to cover, you might be asking yourself why is there a switch between RDD and the DataFrame API? We saw that DataFrame has become the primary API for Spark, and all new optimizations can only be benefitted from if you are using a DataFrame API, so why is there no DataFrame API for GraphX?

Well the reality is that there is a lot of focus on **GraphFrames,** which is the DataFrame based API for graphs in Spark. There are certain motivations to have a DataFrame based API for Spark and some of these stem from some shortcomings of GraphX.

Why GraphFrames?

GraphX poses certain challenges, for example:

- **Supports Scala only**: The promise of Spark lies in the fact that you can have the same set of algorithms available to a wide variety of users, who can program in Java, Scala, Python, or R. GraphX only supports Scala API. This is a serious limitation and is hindering GraphX's adoption at the same rate as Streaming, SQL, or machine learning.
- **Only RDD interface**: As you have seen, GraphX only supports an RDD interface, which is quite a serious limitation. See the following point.
- **No access to new Spark optimizations**: The majority of the Spark optimizations are through Catalyst query optimization and via Tungsten Memory management. Not using DataFrames limits your ability to make use of those optimizations.

Due to these limitations it was necessary to write a GraphFrames library that supports the following major goals:

- Simplify interactive queries on Graphs
- Support Motif-finding for structural pattern search
- Benefit from DataFrame optimizations

Motif finding is the method by which you can search structural patterns within a Graph object. This is typically available with Graph databases such as **Neo4J** and **Titan,** but it is not supported by GraphX or **Apache Giraph.**

Basic constructs of a GraphFrame

GraphFrames is constructed from two basic constructs:

1. **Vertices DataFrame**: A vertices DataFrame is any DataFrame where each row is treated as a Vertex. The frame will have an `id` column for the ID of the vertex, which can be any data type from the catalyst provided data types. At the time of writing, an `id` column is mandatory for a dataframe that has to be used as a vertice.

2. **Edges DataFrame**: An edges DataFrame has one edge per row. It should have at least two columns `src` and `dst`, which refer to the vertices DataFrame, and defines the connection between two vertices. Any extra columns are additional attributes for the edge datframe.

Let's consider the following example of a social graph, where the investigation agencies are trying to apprehend users who are involved in content around *Terrorism* and *Hate Speech*, both of which are killers for the wellbeing of a society. We are looking at users who create, share, or like such content. Of course, this is a simplistic example and a social graph is much more complex, but the essence still remains the same.

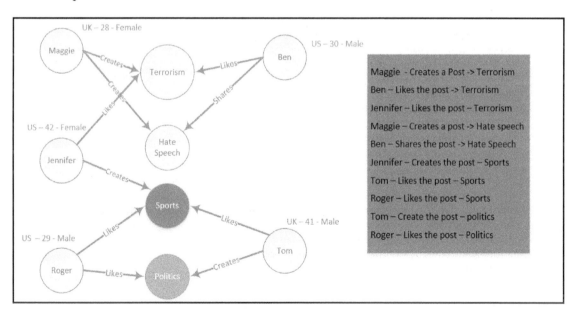

Figure 7.13: Social media content – terrorism analysis

Remember that the DataFrames graph at the time of writing is not part of the Spark project directly, but is available through the Spark Packages website. We can load it simply by specifying the package before starting the Spark-Shell. This can be done as follows:

```
./bin/spark-shell --packages graphframes:graphframes:0.3.0-spark2.0-s_2.11
```

The following code example can be used to set up a graph DataFrame:

```
import org.graphframes.GraphFrame
//Creating a Vertices Data Frame - Remember to specify the "id" column
val vertices = spark.createDataFrame(List(
   ("Maggie","UK",28,"Female"),
   ("Jennifer","US",42,"Female"),
   ("Roger","US",42,"Male"),
   ("Ben","US",30,"Male"),
   ("Tom","UK",41,"Male"),
   ("Terrorism","N/A",0,"N/A"),
   ("Hate-Speech","N/A",0,"N/A"),
   ("Sports","N/A",0,"N/A"),
   ("Politics","N/A",0,"N/A"))).toDF("id","Country","Age","Gender")

//Creating an Edges Data Frame - Remember to specify the "src" and "dst"
//columns
val edges = spark.createDataFrame(List(
   ("Maggie","Terrorism","Creates"),
   ("Ben","Terrorism","Likes"),
   ("Maggie","Hate-Speech","Creates"),
   ("Jennifer","Terrorism","Likes"),
   ("Maggie","Terrorism","Creates"),
   ("Ben","Hate-Speech","Shares"),
   ("Jennifer","Sports","Creates"),
   ("Roger","Sports","Likes"),
   ("Roger","Politics","Likes"),
   ("Tom","Sports","Likes"),
   ("Tom","Politics","Creates"))).toDF("src","dst","relationship")

// Creating the Graph Frame by passing the vertices and edges data frames
to the GraphFrame class constructor.
  val terrorAnalytics = GraphFrame(vertices,edges)
//You can run degrees on this GraphFrame as follows
  terrorAnalytics.degrees.show()
```

```
scala> terrorAnalytics.degrees.show()
+-----------+------+
|         id|degree|
+-----------+------+
|   Jennifer|     2|
|Hate-Speech|     2|
|      Roger|     2|
|        Tom|     2|
|     Sports|     3|
|     Maggie|     3|
|        Ben|     2|
|   Terrorism|    4|
|   Politics|     2|
+-----------+------+
```

Figure 7.14: GraphFrame degrees

Motif finding

Motif finding refers to finding structural patterns within the graph. This has been typically a feature of graph databases, and it helps to find recurrent or statistically significant patterns of a graph.

GraphFrame supports a simple domain-specific language to express queries for finding the relevant patterns.

For example:

(v1) -[e1] -> (v2) refers to a an edge *e1* from vertex *v1* to vertex *v2*.

The important points to note for the DSL are:

1. A vertex is enclosed in parenthesis, for example, *(v1)*.
2. An edge is enclosed by square brackets, for example, *[e1]*.
3. 3. An edge can be negated with the ! sign to indicate that the particular edge should not be present in the subgraph.
4. A pattern can be expressed as a union of edges and edge patterns can be joined with semicolons. For example, the following Motif *(person1)-[action1]->(person2); (person2)-[action2]->(person3)* specifies two edges from *person1* to *person2* to *person3*. As specified previously, in a social network the edge can be a like, share, or content creation.

5. Within a pattern, names can be assigned to vertices and edges. For example, *(person1)-[action1]->(person2)* has three named elements; vertices *person1*, *person2*, and edge *action1*. These names can then be used to build complicated patterns, and the resultant dataframe will contain these as column names.

6. Within the pattern you can specify an empty `vertice()` or an empty edge `[]`.

7. You can additionally apply filters to the results of the `find()` operation.

Looking at this example, if we want to understand people who are involved with creating and sharing posts on social media involving terrorism, we can find the relevant subgraph as follows:

```scala
scala> terrorAnalytics.find("(a)-[e]->(b)").filter("e.dst='Terrorism'").select("a.id").distinct().show()
+--------+
|      id|
+--------+
|Jennifer|
|  Maggie|
|     Ben|
+--------+
```

Figure 7.15: Social media content – terrorism analysis: finding culprits

This is quite a powerful analysis tool and it can certainly help in more advanced analytic. To keep this chapter within sanity's limit, we'll now move on. However, I will certainly recommend looking at the GraphFrames documentation available at `http://graphframes.github.io/user-guide.html#motif-finding`.

GraphFrames algorithms

GraphFrames provides the complete list of GraphX algorithms, some of which are wrappers on the GraphX API, while others have been written from scratch.

The following algorithms are available in GraphFrames at the time of writing:

Algorithm	Use Cases	GraphX Wrapper/DF Implementation
PageRank	Finds important vertices	GraphX Wrapper
Connected Components	Finds groups of components, communities	GraphX Wrapper
Strongly Connected Components	Finds groups of components, communities	GraphX Wrapper
Label Propagation	Finds groups of components, communities	GraphX Wrapper
Shortest Path	Finds path between a set of vertices	GraphX Wrapper
SVD Plus Plus	X	GraphX Wrapper
Breadth-First Search	Finds path between a set of vertices	DataFrame Implementation
Triangle Counting	Find subgraphs – use cases in SNA	DataFrame Implementation

Loading and saving of GraphFrames

Using the DataFrames API gives GraphFrames the ability to load and save GraphFrames using the same DataFrame API:

```
//Loading vertices/edges from a Parquet Source
val vertices = spark.read.parquet(....)
val edges=spark.read.parquet(...)
val graph = GraphFrame(vertices,edges)

//Saving a data frame to a Parquet Source
graph.vertices.write.parquet(....)
graph.edges.write.parquet(....)
```

Comparison between GraphFrames and GraphX

It is important to look at a quick comparison between GraphX and GraphFrames as it gives you an idea as to where GraphFrames are going. Joseph Bradley, who is a software Engineer at Databricks, gave a brilliant talk on GraphFrames and the difference between the two APIs. The talk is available at `http://bit.ly/2hBrDwH`. Here is a summary of the comparison:

	GraphFrames	**GraphX**
Core APIs	Scala, Java, Python	Scala only
Programming Abstraction	DataFrames	RDDs
Use Cases	Algorithms, Queries, Motif Finding	Algorithms
VertexIds	Any type (in Catalyst)	Long
Vertex/edge attributes	Any number of DataFrame columns	Any type (VD,ED)
Return Types	GraphFrames/DataFrames	Graph [VD,ED] or RDD [Long,VD]

GraphX <=> GraphFrames

If you have invested heavily into GraphX already and are wondering how you will migrate your existing code to GraphFrames, you are about to receive some good news. Apache Spark provides seamless conversions between GraphX and GraphFrames:

```
GraphFrame = myGraphFrame
```

```
GraphX = myGraph
```

Converting from GraphFrame to GraphX

You can convert a GraphFrame to GraphX. However, vertex and edge attributes are Rows in order to handle IDs of non-Long Type. As you might remember, GraphX only supports IDs of Long Type, whereas GraphFrames is more flexible:

```
val myGraph:Graph[Row,Row]= myGraphFrame.toGraphX
```

Converting from GraphX to GraphFrames

You can also covert from GraphX to GraphFrames as well:

```
val myGraphFrame:GraphFrame = GraphFrame.fromGraphX(myGraph)
```

References

The following books, articles, blog, posts and videos have been referred to when writing this book to and can aid as additional reference for the reader.

1. http://www.wiley.com/WileyCDA/WileyTitle/productCd-047064754X.html
2. http://www.minicomplexity.org/pubs/1943-mcculloch-pitts-bmb.pdf
3. https://en.wikipedia.org/wiki/Leonhard_Euler
4. https://en.wikipedia.org/wiki/Seven_Bridges_of_K%C3%B6nigsberg
5. https://www.usenix.org/system/files/conference/osdi12/osdi12-final-167.pdf
6. http://snap.stanford.edu/data/cit-HepTh.html
7. https://www.youtube.com/watch?v=mKEn9C5bRck&t=1370s
8. http://spark.apache.org/docs/latest/graphx-programming-guide.html
9. http://spark.apache.org/docs/latest/api/scala/index.html#org.apache.spark.graphx.Graph
10. http://spark.apache.org/docs/latest/api/scala/index.html#org.apache.spark.graphx.GraphOps
11. http://graphframes.github.io/quick-start.html
12. http://graphframes.github.io/user-guide.html
13. http://spark.apache.org/docs/latest/api/scala/index.html#org.apache.spark.graphx.Graph

Summary

In this chapter, we have covered details around GraphX, looked at various operations and algorithms of GraphX, before moving on to GraphFrames, which is a very similar programming API to what we had recently worked with in recent chapters. I hope that this chapter has given you a starting point and helped you understand the importance of graph analytics in addition to working with practical examples of GraphX and GraphFrames. If you would like to learn more, I would recommend looking at the *Apache Spark Graph Processing* by *Rindra Ramamonjison, Packt Publishing*.

The next chapter is focussed around setting up Spark in a clustered environment including Standalone scheduler, YARN, and Mesos. We will then cover two case studies before wrapping up with an `Appendix`, *There's More with Spark* of helpful topics.

8
Operating in Clustered Mode

We have covered the functional and exciting aspects of Spark and how it provides a whole range of APIs in the areas of streaming, machine learning and graph. However, we have not gone into the details of how does Spark work across multiple machines, which is necessary for working with bigger data sets. Spark framework is a cluster agnostic framework and can run on multiple clusters. In this chapter we are going to cover the following key topics:

- What is a Cluster?
- What is Standalone cluster mode?
- Deploying Spark on a Standalone cluster
- What is YARN?
- Deploying Spark on YARN
- What is Mesos?
- Deploying Spark on Mesos
- Optimization

I believe that while it is important to focus on the cool aspects of a data application like which algorithm to choose, how to build a data pipeline and so on, it is equal important to deploy the application so that the value from effort spent on building the application can be realized.

Let's get started.

Clusters, nodes and daemons

Cluster, node, and daemon is the terminology that we will use throughout this chapter. It is important to build a common understanding of the context around which these terms are used during this chapter.

- **Cluster:** A cluster is a group of computers (nodes) that work together in many aspects, and are often viewed as a single system.
- **Node:** A node is an individual component in the cluster.
- **Daemon:** In multitasking computer operating systems, a daemon is a computer program that runs as a background process, rather than being under control of an interactive user.

So now that we have terminology out of the way, what exactly does Spark need to run on a cluster? How is it managed? Is it a master/slave architecture? All these are key questions and need to be answered to fully understand the way how Spark works on a set of machines that comprise a cluster. Let's refer to the classical Spark architecture diagram (reference `spark.apache.org/docs/latest`) to understand this in a bit more detail.

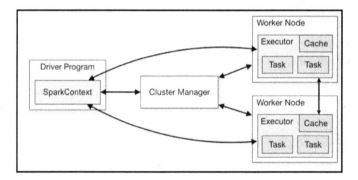

Figure 8.1: Spark Architecture Diagram

The key piece of this Architecture is the SparkContext running inside your driver program with the ability to connect to a wide number of cluster managers for example, Spark's standalone cluster manager, YARN, or Mesos. A spark application needs resources like CPU and RAM on the machines (nodes) that comprise a cluster, and the responsibility of a cluster manager is to allocate the resources to your driver program for the execution of your application. Once the necessary resources are acquired and allocated, the application comprised of JAR files or Python files are sent to the executors.

Once every executor has the specific application code, they are then sent instructions from the driver program which are executed as tasks on these executors.

Key bits about Spark Architecture

Let us go in more details regarding Spark Architecture:

1. **Application Isolation:** Each application gets its own executor processes, which span the lifetime of the application and run multiple tasks using threads. Application Isolation has great benefits like memory isolation, as each application's tasks run in separate JVMs. This benefits the driver as each driver will schedule its own tasks. However, there is also a drawback to this approach, which is data sharing. Data will need to be written to external systems if you would like to share it between various applications. This means that if two developers are working on large datasets, they will load the data in their own memory space, resulting in memory overhead. While there are other open-source projects out there that can help in data sharing this capability is not available by default on the Spark Framework.

2. **Cluster Manager Agnosticism**: We did discuss this earlier, but it is important to understand that one of the cool features about Spark is its cluster agnosticism. This means all Spark needs is the ability to work with a number of different cluster managers as long as they can allocate resources to Spark.

3. **Driver Program**: The driver program is the brains of the Spark, and basically runs the `main()` function of your Spark Program. It is therefore a single point of failure as well. It must stay alive and connected to its executors through its lifetime, accept incoming connections, and if possible configured as close to the cluster as possible (on the same LAN if possible) due to its need of frequent communication with the executors. A driver program can be monitored by its WebUI which typically starts at port 4040. If you have other applications running at port 4040, Spark will try to start the UI on port 4041, 4042, and so on.

Running Spark in standalone mode

A standalone mode is basically when Spark uses its default mode provided with the application and does not use one of the externally provided cluster managers like YARN or Mesos. In this section, we'll look at the following key topics:

- Installing Spark Standalone on a cluster
- Starting the cluster
  - Manually
  - Launch-Scripts
- Launching an application in the cluster

- Monitoring
- Configuring High-Availability
  - Configuring Stand-by masters with ZooKeeper
  - Recovery with the FileSystem

Installing Spark standalone on a cluster

In our example we are going to build a 6 node Spark cluster, and have a windows machine submit Spark jobs to the cluster. We'll not develop a new Spark program, but rather submit the examples provided with the Spark Framework for the purpose of this exercise. Our architecture looks something like the following image:

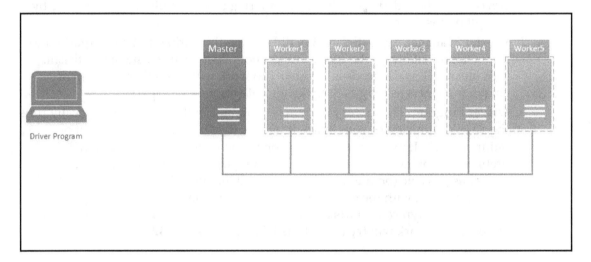

Figure 8.2: Spark Standalone Cluster Deployment

The installation of a standalone cluster is very simple, you need to place a compiled version of Spark on each node on the cluster. The pre-compiled version or source can be downloaded from `http://spark.apache.org/downloads.html`. I prefer to download the latest source and compile it. If you are looking for information around building Spark, you should refer to the following help page from the Apache Spark website at `http://spark.apache.org/docs/latest/building-spark.html`. You might want to simply download the binaries to simplify the process as a first time user.

Starting a Spark cluster manually

As discussed earlier, a Spark cluster needs to have a Spark master. Spark comes with shell scripts which can be used to setup a Spark master or a Spark worker. The script that we use to start a Spark master is available in the `sbin` directory.

```
./sbin/spark-master.sh
```

When you startup a master daemon on one of the node, you'll get the following output. You'll see certain ports and URL's written to the log file, which are important as these will be used later on to start the workers and also monitor the Spark cluster.

The three important pieces of information are:

1. Spark master service port and URL
2. Spark master UI port and URL
3. Leader notification

If you look at the log produced while starting the master, you'll see the key piece of information listed here. For example, the Spark master service is started on port 7077, while the URL is important as it will be required to start the workers and connect to the Spark master server. The URL for the master is: `spark://sparkmaster.demo.com:7077`

```
Using Spark's default log4j profile: org/apache/spark/log4j-defaults.properties
16/12/18 06:37:15 INFO Master: Started daemon with process name: 22588@sparkmaster
16/12/18 06:37:15 INFO SignalUtils: Registered signal handler for TERM
16/12/18 06:37:15 INFO SignalUtils: Registered signal handler for HUP
16/12/18 06:37:15 INFO SignalUtils: Registered signal handler for INT
16/12/18 06:37:15 WARN NativeCodeLoader: Unable to load native-hadoop library for your platform... using bu
16/12/18 06:37:15 INFO SecurityManager: Changing view acls to: root
16/12/18 06:37:15 INFO SecurityManager: Changing modify acls to: root
16/12/18 06:37:15 INFO SecurityManager: Changing view acls groups to:
16/12/18 06:37:15 INFO SecurityManager: Changing modify acls groups to:
16/12/18 06:37:15 INFO SecurityManager: SecurityManager: authentication disabled; ui acls disabled; users
  view permissions: Set(); users  with modify permissions: Set(root); groups with modify permissions: Set()
16/12/18 06:37:16 INFO Utils: Successfully started service 'sparkMaster' on port 7077.
16/12/18 06:37:16 INFO Master: Starting Spark master at spark://sparkmaster.demo.com:7077
16/12/18 06:37:16 INFO Master: Running Spark version 2.0.2
16/12/18 06:37:16 INFO Utils: Successfully started service 'MasterUI' on port 8080.
16/12/18 06:37:16 INFO MasterWebUI: Bound MasterWebUI to 0.0.0.0, and started at http://10.37.101.3:8080
16/12/18 06:37:16 INFO Utils: Successfully started service on port 6066.
16/12/18 06:37:16 INFO StandaloneRestServer: Started REST server for submitting applications on port 6066
16/12/18 06:37:16 INFO Master: I have been elected leader! New state: ALIVE
16/12/18 06:37:19 INFO Master: Registering worker 10.37.101.8:44277 with 16 cores, 125.0 GB RAM
16/12/18 06:37:25 INFO Master: Registering worker 10.37.101.10:59136 with 16 cores, 125.0 GB RAM
```

Figure 8.3: Starting up Spark master

In addition Spark master has a UI referred to as the Master UI in the logs that can be viewed on Port *8080*. The full master UI URL in our logs file is `http://10.37.101.3:8080`. We'll look at what the master UI contains in a later screenshot.

We'll now need to start the remaining workers. We have 5 workers here, so each one will be started by a command like the following:

```
./sbin/spark-slave.sh spark://sparkmaster.demo.com:7077
```

Where `spark://sparkmaster.demo.com:7077` is the URL for the Master service.

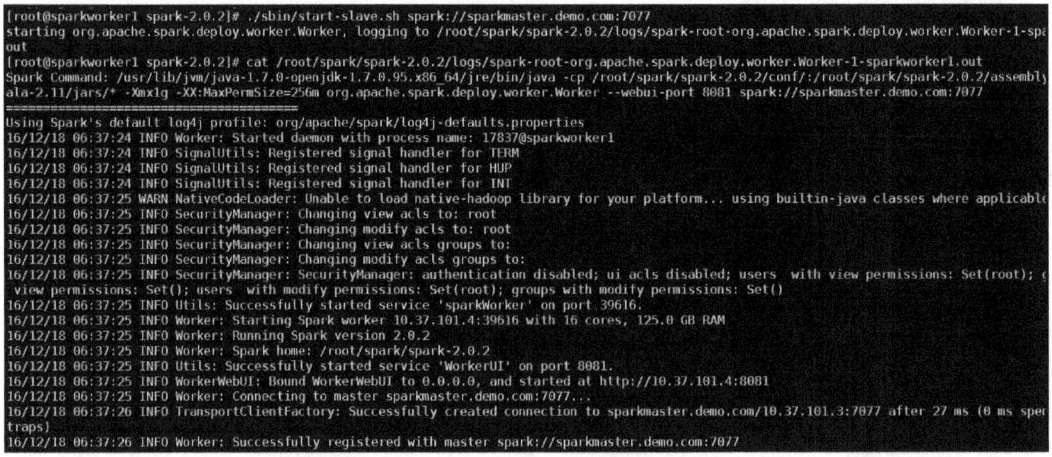

Figure 8.4: Starting up Spark Worker

For brevity's sake we'll skip the remaining snapshots of the workers starting, but essentially you have to start the worker daemon on each of the nodes you want to be a part of the cluster. Each worker will have a WorkerUI which starts on port 8081 of the worker node by default.

Once you have started all 5 workers, you can connect to the Spark MasterUI to look at the details of the cluster. This will give you a high level overview of the current status of the cluster. The Master UI can be split into following major portions:

- Cluster overview
- Workers overview
- Running applications overview
- Running drivers overview
- Completed applications overview
- Completed drivers overview

Cluster overview

The top portion of the MasterUI provides you an overview of the overall cluster. In our case, we are running on a cluster which has 5 workers each configured with 16-cores, and 128 GB of RAM. This will give us a total of 80 cores, and approximately 640 GB of memory to work with. Of course, this will vary based on your specific cluster configuration. The top portion of the MasterUI also shows the memory in use, number of running applications, and current status of the master.

Spark Master at spark://sparkmaster.demo.com:7077

2.0.2

URL: spark://sparkmaster.demo.com:7077
REST URL: spark://sparkmaster.demo.com:6066 *(cluster mode)*
Alive Workers: 5
Cores in use: 80 Total, 0 Used
Memory in use: 625.2 GB Total, 0.0 B Used
Applications: 0 Running, 0 Completed
Drivers: 0 Running, 0 Completed
Status: ALIVE

Figure 8.5: Master UI – Cluster Overview

Workers overview

The second important piece of information provided by Spark is in the second section of the UI, which indicates the total number of configured workers, their current status and also provides direct link to the Worker UI. You can also see the amount of memory used on each worker and if there is a memory skew happening.

Workers

Worker Id	Address	State	Cores	Memory
worker-20161217125808-10.37.101.8-59424	10.37.101.8:59424	ALIVE	16 (0 Used)	125.0 GB (0.0 B Used)
worker-20161217125858-10.37.101.4-33677	10.37.101.4:33677	ALIVE	16 (0 Used)	125.0 GB (0.0 B Used)
worker-20161217130000-10.37.101.11-60702	10.37.101.11:60702	ALIVE	16 (0 Used)	125.0 GB (0.0 B Used)
worker-20161217130128-10.37.101.6-48740	10.37.101.6:48740	ALIVE	16 (0 Used)	125.0 GB (0.0 B Used)
worker-20161217130136-10.37.101.10-42666	10.37.101.10:42666	ALIVE	16 (0 Used)	125.0 GB (0.0 B Used)

Figure 8.6: MasterUI – Worker Overview

Running applications and drivers overview

The third portion of the screen shows the running applications, their name, number of cores allocated, memory per node, and current status. Let us run `SparkPi`, a program provided with Spark examples, and submit it to the cluster. We'll use Spark-submit to submit it to the cluster.

```
./bin/spark-submit
--class org.apache.spark.examples.SparkPi  /* Entry point to App */
--master spark://sparkmaster.demo.com:7077  /* Master URL*/
--deploy-mode cluster /* Deploy the Driver in the cluster (default client) */
./examples/target/scala-2.11/jars/spark-examples_2.11-2.0.2.jar /* App Jar */
10 /* Applicataion arguments */
```

Figure 8.7: Submission to the cluster

Once you submit the application to the cluster, the MasterUI will show the running applications, and optionally the running drivers. In this case we had decided to deploy our driver on the cluster, which is not a default option. If your client machine is far away from the worker machines, you can use the cluster mode to minimize network latency between the driver and the executors:

Running Applications

Application ID		Name	Cores	Memory per Node	Submitted Time	User	State	Duration
app-20161218074123-0001	(kill)	Spark Pi	79	1024.0 MB	2016/12/18 07:41:23	root	RUNNING	0.4 s

Running Drivers

Submission ID		Submitted Time	Worker	State	Cores	Memory	Main Class
driver-20161218074120-0001	(kill)	Sun Dec 18 07:41:20 EST 2016	worker-20161218063924-10.37.101.10-52292	RUNNING	1	1024.0 MB	org.apache.spark.examples.SparkPi

Figure 8.8: Running applications and drivers

Under the running applications you will have a link to the specific application that you had run, which gives more insights into how many executors your application had consumed. As you can see from the application UI, unlimited cores and executors were available to this application. It has used all 79 cores, but only 5 Executors (one on each worker). The amount of memory per executor was also 1 GB as opposed to 128 GB per machine.

In addition, you can also see the workers where the executors had been allocated.

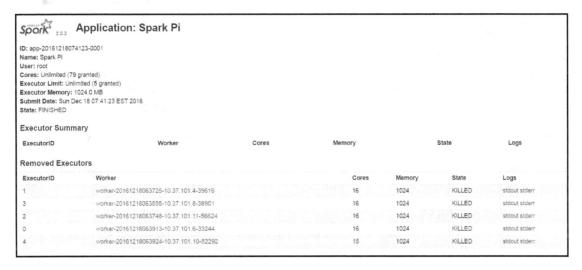

Figure 8.9: Spark application UI

Completed applications and drivers overview

The final area of the screen will show you all the previously completed applications, the time when they were submitted, the amount of memory they had consumed, and the total time that they took to complete.

In case you had requested driver programs to be deployed on the cluster, you will also see the completed drivers, and the specific worker where they were deployed.

Completed Applications

Application ID	Name	Cores	Memory per Node	Submitted Time	User	State	Duration
app-20161218074123-0001	Spark Pi	79	1024.0 MB	2016/12/18 07:41:23	root	FINISHED	4 s
app-20161218073933-0000	Spark Pi	79	1024.0 MB	2016/12/18 07:39:33	root	FINISHED	3 s

Completed Drivers

Submission ID	Submitted Time	Worker	State	Cores	Memory	Main Class
driver-20161218074120-0001	Sun Dec 18 07:41:20 EST 2016	worker-20161218063924-10.37.101.10-52292	FINISHED	1	1024.0 MB	org.apache.spark.examples.SparkPi
driver-20161218073931-0000	Sun Dec 18 07:39:31 EST 2016	worker-20161218063913-10.37.101.6-33244	FINISHED	1	1024.0 MB	org.apache.spark.examples.SparkPi

Figure 8.10: Completed applications and drivers overview

Using the Cluster Launch Scripts to Start a Standalone Cluster

We have seen how easy it was to launch a cluster with minimal effort. But, the cluster that we had set up was a relatively smallish cluster with only 5 worker nodes. Imagine, setting up a 5000 nodes cluster following the above steps. This will neither be easy nor maintainable especially in terms of adding/removing nodes from this cluster. Spark therefore provides options by which you can make sure you don't have to manually perform such configuration.

Before running any scripts you have to make sure that the workers are accessible from the master via SSH. You will need to provide either of the following:

1. Password-less ssh between the master and the workers.
2. Set `SPARK_SSH_FOREGROUND` option – Serially provide password for each worker.

In addition to the SSH configuration, you will need to create a configuration file in the `conf` directory called slaves, where you will enter the names of nodes which should be used as workers. You can use the `conf/slaves.template` file as a template, and use that to create your own slaves file. The slaves file for our cluster looks as follows:

```
# A Spark Worker will be started on each of the machines listed below.
sparkworker1
sparkworker2
sparkworker3
sparkworker4
sparkworker5
```

Figure 8.11: Slaves file in the conf directory

Spark provides a number of scripts that are available in the ./sbin directory and can be used to launch or stop your cluster. If you are familiar with Hadoop, you'll find these scripts familiar as they are based on Hadoop's deploy scripts.

start-master.sh	**Starts a master instance on the machine where script is executed**
start-slaves.sh	Starts a slave instance on each machine specified in conf/slaves file
start-slave.sh	Starts a slave instance on the machine where the script is executed
start-all.sh	Uses the conf/slaves to start the master and slave instances
stop-master.sh	Stops the master instance on the machine
stop-slaves.sh	Stops all slave instances using the conf/slaves file
stop-all.sh	Stops all the master and slave instances using conf/slaves file

After editing the conf/slaves file, we can start the master and slave instances using ./sbin/start-all.sh. If you look at the output log file, you'll see the URL for the Master UI. The output is similar to what we saw earlier.

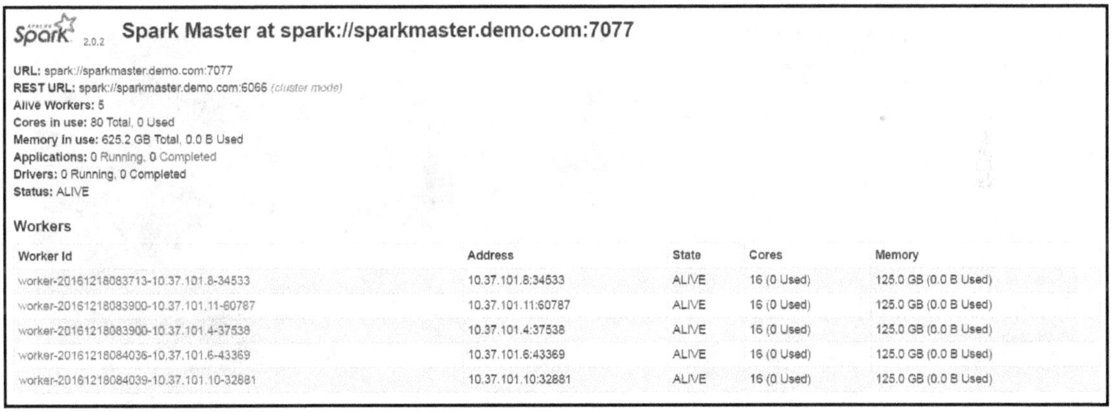

Figure 8.12: Starting cluster using the launch scripts.

Environment Properties

Spark environment properties can be configured using the conf/spark-env.sh file. A starter template file is available as spark-env.sh.template file. You can use that to build your own configuration and set appropriate properties including master Port, WebUI Port, Number of Worker Cores, Worker memory allocation and so on.

Connecting Spark-Shell, PySpark, and R-Shell to the cluster

We have already seen an example of submitting a pre-built application to the cluster. However discovery for data scientists is an important part of their daily activities. We have already used Scala shell, **PySpark,** and R-Shell through the various examples. If you would like to connect one of the existing Shells to the cluster, you need to pass the spark://IP:Port of the master. You can also pass the total executor cores that will be assigned to this application by the cluster.

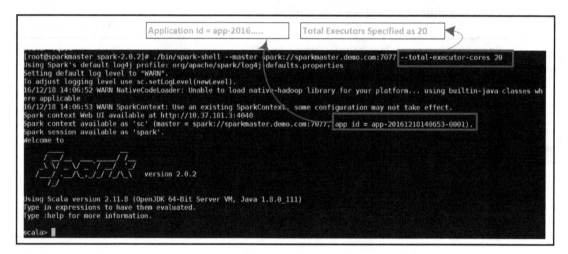

Figure 8.13: Running a scala-shell against the cluster

If we look at the Master UI, we'll see that as requested, only 20 cores are allocated to the application instead of the total 80 available.

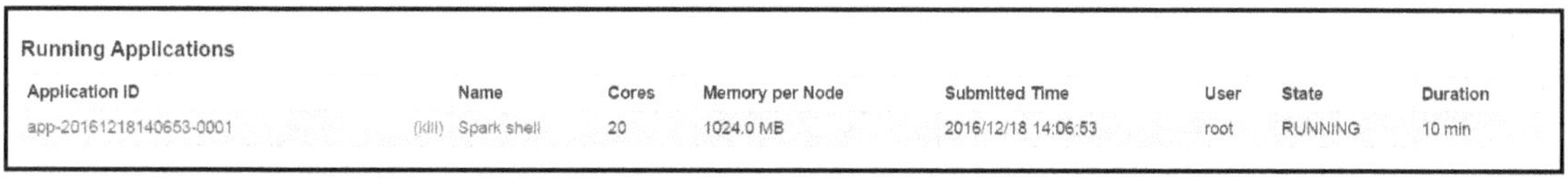

Running Applications

Application ID	Name	Cores	Memory per Node	Submitted Time	User	State	Duration
app-20161218140653-0001	(kill) Spark shell	20	1024.0 MB	2016/12/18 14:06:53	root	RUNNING	10 min

Figure 8.14: Master UI showing 20 cores allocated to the application

For brevity's sake we will not demonstrate the usage of other shells, but I hope you get the idea that passing the master-URL as a parameter will run the specific app on the cluster.

Resource scheduling

Standalone scheduler is quite limited in how it manages resources. By default it will use a simple FIFO scheduling, which is enough if you have a single user on the server and are OK with users having their applications queued. However, in most test & production scenarios you will want the cluster to share the resources with other users, but as we have seen above if you do not limit the resources, Spark allocates all the cores in the cluster to the application. For example, as you have seen earlier in the case of the Spark PI example, the entire 80 cores were allocated to our application. This is undesirable, and avoidable.

You can either ask the applications to behave and/or set a global maximum per application. For example, while setting up Spark configuration you can specify the maximum number of cores using the `spark.cores.max` property.

```
val conf = new SparkConf()
        .setMaster(...)
        .setAppName(...)
        .set("spark.cores.max", "10")
val sc = new SparkContext(conf)
```

You can then configure `spark.deploy.defaultCores` on the cluster manager process to change the default for applications. This is done in the `conf/spark-env.sh`. For example, Let's say we want all the applications to get a default of 2 cores unless they ask for more. This can be set using the following option:

```
export SPARK_MASTER_OPTS="-Dspark.deploy.defaultCores=2"
```

Running Spark in YARN

In the previous section, we covered Spark working in a Standalone cluster, and while on-premises deployment on Standalone clusters accounts for 42% of all Spark deployments, Spark deployment on YARN accounts for 36% of all on-premises deployments. These figures were taken from the Apache Spark survey report published by data bricks in June of 2016.

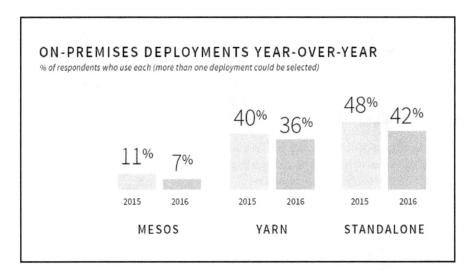

Figure 8.15: YARN deployments – Databricks survey report: Page 10 (Databricks.com)

YARN has been supported since 0.6 release of Apache Spark. In order to run your application on YARN you need to ensure you have the correct configuration files for your Hadoop cluster, and the following environment variables point towards the right location of these files:

- `HADOOP_CONF_DIR`
- `YARN_CONF_DIR`

These configuration files will be shipped to the YARN cluster and then distributed to all the containers running the application to make sure that they use same configuration.

When you run an application on YARN you have two deployment modes each with its own technicalities:

- **Deploy-Mode = client**: If you are running with a client deployment mode, the driver program will run inside the client process, and the application master for the YARN application is only used to request resources from YARN. This puts various burdens on the client including possibilities to make sure the client is not too far away from the cluster, and keeping it alive during the duration of the application.
- **Deploy-Mode = cluster**: It is generally recommended to use the cluster deployment mode as the driver program will run inside the application master which will be of course YARN managed. The client does not need to remain connected to the application, and you can get benefits of the driver program not being a single point of failure.

If you remember from our earlier discussion, when submitting a program with Standalone mode, we had to pass in the spark master location, however in the case of YARN since the location of the cluster is specified in the configuration files, you would just specify YARN as the master argument. We'll see this in the examples.

Spark with a Hadoop Distribution (Cloudera)

We are going to use **Cloudera** distribution for the demonstration exercises. Cloudera is quite a popular and mature Hadoop distribution, and you can easily deploy Hadoop across a single or multiple nodes using Cloudera Manager. The only downside of using a Hadoop distribution is that it might not support the latest Spark release, which are far too frequent for the distributors to keep track of. For example, at the time of writing the latest Spark release is 2.0 whereas Cloudera only supports Spark 1.6.

Figure 8.16: Cloudera Hadoop Distribution with Spark installed.

Let's look at submitting code to YARN via the interactive (shell) and batch interface. As you know the shell is a long running application and Spark will reserve the amount of memory in the cluster until the shell is operational. For batch applications, Spark will simply reserve the appropriate amount of containers requested, run the job, and return the results back.

Interactive Shell

Let's look at the interactive application first. In this case, we are running this from the Hadoop cluster itself, however you can run it from any location as long as Spark has access to your cluster configuration files.

```
-bash-4.1$ ./spark-shell
Setting default log level to "WARN".
To adjust logging level use sc.setLogLevel(newLevel).
Welcome to


      ____              __
     / __/__  ___ _____/ /__
    _\ \/ _ \/ _ `/ __/  '_/
   /___/ .__/\_,_/_/ /_/\_\   version 1.6.0
      /_/

Using Scala version 2.10.5 (Java HotSpot(TM) 64-Bit Server VM, Java 1.7.0_67)
Type in expressions to have them evaluated.
Type :help for more information.
Spark context available as sc (master = yarn-client, app id = application_1482330917317_0002).
SQL context available as sqlContext.
```

Figure 8.17: Running Spark-Shell on a Hadoop cluster

Let's look at how YARN has allocated resources for this application. We can view this from YARN Resource Manager UI, typically accessible at port 8088.

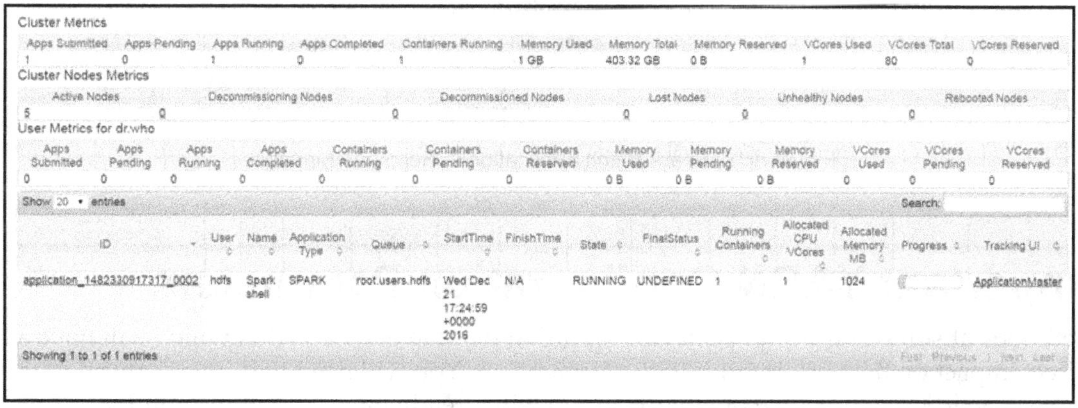

Cluster Metrics											
Apps Submitted	Apps Pending	Apps Running	Apps Completed	Containers Running	Memory Used	Memory Total	Memory Reserved	VCores Used	VCores Total	VCores Reserved	
1	0	1	0	1	1 GB	403.32 GB	0 B	1	80	0	

Cluster Nodes Metrics						
Active Nodes	Decommissioning Nodes	Decommissioned Nodes	Lost Nodes	Unhealthy Nodes	Rebooted Nodes	
5	0	0	0	0	0	

User Metrics for dr.who											
Apps Submitted	Apps Pending	Apps Running	Apps Completed	Containers Running	Containers Pending	Containers Reserved	Memory Used	Memory Pending	Memory Reserved	VCores Used	VCores Pending	VCores Reserved
0	0	0	0	0	0	0 B	0 B	0 B	0	0	0

Show 20 ▾ entries   Search:

ID	User	Name	Application Type	Queue	StartTime	FinishTime	State	FinalStatus	Running Containers	Allocated CPU VCores	Allocated Memory MB	Progress	Tracking UI
application_1482330917317_0002	hdfs	Spark shell	SPARK	root.users.hdfs	Wed Dec 21 17:24:59 +0000 2016	N/A	RUNNING	UNDEFINED	1	1	1024		ApplicationMaster

Showing 1 to 1 of 1 entries   First Previous 1 Next Last

Figure 8.18: Spark-Shell running on YARN

Batch Application

We are now going to submit a batch application from a different installation of Spark, a Windows machine and submit a batch application.

```
spark-submit
   --class org.apache.spark.examples.SparkPi
   --master yarn
   --deploy-mode cluster
   ../lib/spark-examples*.jar 10
```

The application doesn't take a long time to complete. At the same time we will also close our spark-shell to make sure we release the resources.

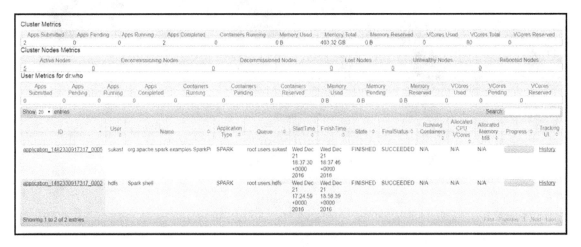

Figure 8.19: Spark Batch application in Resource Manager

Important YARN Configuration Parameters

Let's look at some of the important configuration parameters for YARN which will have a direct impact on the performance of the application. You will need to be very careful with these properties, and people familiar Hadoop will already have configured similar properties for their map reduce containers. While there are lots of other properties that you can set, we'll refer you to the documentation. We are just looking at the most common ones that developers tend to set for their applications.

Property Name	Default Setting	Meaning
`spark.yarn.am.memory`	512m	The amount of memory that will be allocated to the YARN application master when it is running in client mode. If you see the amount of memory allocated to our sample application it was 1gb default, but the reason was because it was using spark.driver.memory.
`spark.driver.memory`	1g	The amount of memory used for the driver process when the driver is run inside the Application Master.
`spark.driver.cores`	1	Number of cores used by the driver in YARN cluster mode. In the cluster mode, the driver program shares the core with the application master as both are running in the same JVM. For the client mode, spark.yarn.am.cores is used.

`spark.yarn.am.cores`	1 Number of cores used by the driver in YARN cluster mode. In the cluster mode, the driver program shares the core with the application master as both are running in the same JVM. For the client mode, spark.yarm.am.cores is used. spark.yarn.am.cores 1	Number of cores used by the YARN Application Master in the client mode.
`spark.yarn.max.executor.failures`	numExecutors *2	The application continues to run despite the failure of an executor. However, you can specify the number of failures that you can accept before eventually failing the application.
`spark.executor.cores`	1 = YARN mode	The number of cores to use on each executor. For YARN and standalone mode only.
`spark.executor.memory`	1g	
`spark.yarn.executor.memoryOverhead`	executorMemory*0.10	The amount of off-heap memory (in MBs) to be allocated per executor for things like VM overheads, interned strings, other native overloads.

`spark.yarn.driver.memoryOverhead`	driverMemory * 0.10	The amount of off-heap memory (in megabytes) to be allocated per driver in cluster mode.
`spark.yarn.am.nodeLabelExpression`	(none)	A YARN node label expression that restricts the set of nodes AM will be scheduled on. Only available on YARN >= 2.6
`Spark.yarn.executor.nodeLabelExpression`	(none)	A YARN node label expression that restricts the set of nodes executors will be scheduled on.
`Spark.yarn.principal`	(none)	Prinicpal to be used to login to the KDC, on a secure Hadoop cluster.

Hopefully this section should have given you a good starting point for configuring Spark applications with YARN. We'll now move on to our next section where we'll look at Spark working with Mesos.

Running Spark in Mesos

Mesos is an open source cluster manager started as a UC Berkley research project in 2008 and quite widely used by a number of organizations. Spark supports Mesos, and *Matei Zahria* has given a key note at Mesos Con in June of 2016. Here is a link to the YouTube video of the keynote: `http://bit.ly/2huK1aC`.

Before you start

If you haven't installed Mesos previously, the getting started page on the Apache website gives a good walk through of installing Mesos on Windows, MacOS, and Linux. Follow the URL `https://mesos.apache.org/gettingstarted/`.

1. Once installed you need to start-up Mesos on your cluster
2. Starting Mesos Master: `./bin/mesos-master.sh -ip=[MasterIP] -work-dir=/var/lib/mesos`
3. Start Mesos Agents on all your worker nodes: `./bin/mesos-agent.sh -master=[MasterIp]:5050 -work-dir=/var/lib/mesos`
4. Make sure Mesos is up and running with all your relevant worker nodes configured: `http://[MasterIP]@5050`

Make sure that Spark binary packages are available and accessible by Mesos. They can be placed on a Hadoop-accessible URI for example:

1. HTTP via `http://`
2. S3 via `s3n://`
3. HDFS via `hdfs://`

You can also install spark in the same location on all the Mesos slaves, and configure `spark.mesos.executor.home` to point to that location.

Running in Mesos

Mesos can have single or multiple masters, which means the Master URL differs when submitting application from Spark via mesos:

1. Single Master
2. Mesos://sparkmaster:5050
3. Multiple Masters (Using Zookeeper)
4. Mesos://zk://master1:2181, master2:2181/mesos

Modes of operation in Mesos

Mesos supports both the Client and Cluster modes of operation.

Client Mode

Before running the client mode, you need to perform couple of configurations:

1. `Spark-env.sh`
2. Export `MESOS_NATIVE_JAVA_LIBRARY=<Path to libmesos.so [Linux]>` or `<Path to libmesos.dylib[MacOS]>`
3. Export SPARK_EXECUTOR_URI=<URI of Spark zipped file uploaded to an accessible location e.g. HTTP, HDFS, S3>
4. Set `spark.executor.uri` to URI of Spark zipped file uploaded to an accessible location e.g. HTTP, HDFS, S3

Batch Applications

For batch applications, in your application program you need to pass on the Mesos URL as the master when creating your Spark context. As an example:

```
val sparkConf = new SparkConf()
              .setMaster("mesos://mesosmaster:5050")
              .setAppName("Batch Application")
              .set("spark.executor.uri", "Location to Spark binaries
                 (Http, S3, or HDFS)")

val sc = new SparkContext(sparkConf)
```

If you are using `Spark-submit`, you can configure the URI in the `conf/spark-defaults.conf` file using `spark.executor.uri`.

Interactive Applications

When you are running one of the provided spark shells for interactive querying, you can pass the master argument e.g.

```
./bin/spark-shell –master mesos://mesosmaster:5050
```

Cluster Mode

Just as in YARN, you run spark on mesos in a cluster mode, which means the driver is launched inside the cluster and the client can disconnect after submitting the application, and get results from the Mesos WebUI.

Steps to use the cluster mode

1. Start the `MesosClusterDispatcher` in your cluster:

   `./sbin/start-mesos-dispatcher.sh —master mesos://mesosmaster:5050`

   This will generally start the dispatcher at port 7077.

2. From the client, submit a job to the mesos cluster by `Spark-submit` specifying the dispatcher URL. Example:

   ```
   ./bin/spark-submit \
     --class org.apache.spark.examples.SparkPi \
     --master mesos://dispatcher:7077 \
     --deploy-mode cluster \
     --supervise \
     --executor-memory 2G \
     --total-executor-cores 10 \
     s3n://path/to/examples.jar \
   ```

Similar to Spark Mesos has lots of properties that can be set to optimize the processing. You should refer to the Spark Configuration page (`http://bit.ly/1BEwJky`) for more information.

Mesos run modes

Spark can run on Mesos in two modes:

1. **Coarse Grained** (default-mode): Spark will acquire a long running Mesos task on each machine. This offers a much cost of statup, but the resources will continue to be allocated to spark for the complete duration of the application.
2. **Fine Grained** (deprecated): The fine grained mode is deprecated as in this case each mesos task is created per Spark task. The benefit of this is each application receives cores as per its requirements, but the initial bootstrapping might act as a deterrent for interactive applications.

Key Spark on Mesos configuration properties

While Spark has a number of properties that can be configured to optimize Spark processing, some of these properties are specific to Mesos. We'll look at few of those key properties here.

Property Name	Meaning/Default Value
`spark.mesos.coarse`	Setting it to true (default value), will run Mesos in coarse grained mode. Setting it to false will run it in fine-grained mode.
`spark.mesos.extra.cores`	This is more of an advertisement rather than allocation in order to improve parallelism. An executor will pretend that it has extra cores resulting in the driver sending it more work. `Default=0`
`spark.mesos.mesosExecutor.cores`	Only works in fine grained mode. This specifies how many cores should be given to each Mesos executor.
`spark.mesos.executor.home`	Identifies the directory of Spark installation for the executors in Mesos. As discussed, you can specify this using `spark.executor.uri` as well, however if you have not specified it, you can specify it using this property.
`spark.mesos.executor.memoryOverhead`	The amount of memory (in MBs) to be allocated per executor.
`spark.mesos.uris`	A comma separated list of URIs to be downloaded when the driver or executor is launched by Mesos.
`spark.mesos.prinicipal`	The name of the principal used by Spark to authenticate itself with Mesos.

You can find lots of other properties at the Spark documentation page (`http://bit.ly/2hd tH0t`).

References:

The following blogs, videos and reference articles were used for the preparation of the content of this chapter. You might want to go through them for further reading.

1. `http://spark.apache.org/docs/latest/running-on-mesos.html`
2. `https://www.youtube.com/watch?list=PLGeM09tlguZQVL7ZsfNMffX9h1rGNVqnC&v=L029ZNBG7bk`
3. `http://go.linuxfoundation.org/mesoscon-north-america-2016-videos`

Summary

In this chapter we have covered the topics surrounding running Spark on different clusters including standalone, YARN, and Mesos. As with the rest of the book, the objective of this chapter is to get you started on Spark and is by no means a comprehensive guide to running Spark on these cluster managers. In fact, each cluster manager operation can span an entire book.

We've now covered most of the topics in this book, and will now look at practical examples and use cases over the course of the next two chapters. The objective of the next chapters is to make the reader go through a simple exercise of building a recommendation and churn model and understand how Spark can be utilized for this purpose.

9
Building a Recommendation System

In the last chapter, we covered the concepts around deploying Spark across various clusters. Over the course of this and the next chapter we will look at some practical use cases. In this chapter, we will look at building a Recommendation System, which is what most of us are building in one way or another. We'll cover the following topics:

- Overview of a recommendation system
- Why do you need a recommendation system?
- The long tail phenomenon
- Types of Recommendations
- Key problems in recommendations
- Content-based recommendations
- Collaborative filtering
- Latent factor models

This chapter will hopefully give you a good introduction to recommender systems, and then follow up with specific code examples to solve a real world use case of movie recommendations.

Let's get started.

What is a recommendation system?

We come across recommendation systems on almost a daily basis, whether you are buying stuff from Amazon, watching movies on Netflix, playing games on Xbox, finding news articles on Google, or listening to music with Spotify. These online applications recommend items based on your previous history, or users who have similar interests.

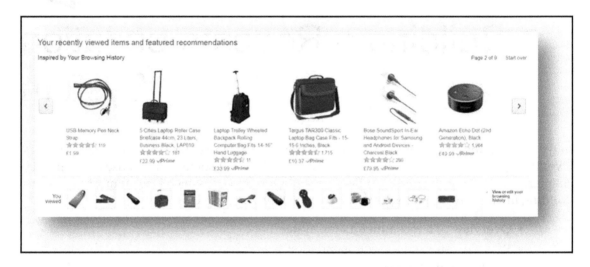

Figure 9.1: Recommendation system on Amazon

Why has recommendation become such a big thing in our lives when 15-20 years ago in a typical brick and mortar store this was unheard of? The answer lies in the fact that we are now in an era of abundance rather than scarcity. Let's drill down a bit more into this. 20 years ago, the number of products that a typical retailer stocked were limited. The reason is the limit of shelf space and expensive real estate cost.

Similarly, our favourite movie shop would only contain a limited number of movies and our book seller would contain a limited number of books. I still remember 20 years ago walking at least 10 miles to find a Pascal book going through various shops, since it was not a hot item, and was not stocked by a majority of the booksellers in Islamabad. The Web as you know has no such shelf space limitation, and hence the number of movies available on Netflix is much more than any typical movie store. Similarly, the number of products available on Amazon and eBay are multiple times more than any other retailer in the world right now. What has made this possible? This has been possible due to a **Long Tail** phenomenon (`https://www.wired.com/2004/10/tail/`). The idea is that if you rank items by popularity, which is based on the number of sales of a particular item, a retail store would only sell items that exceed a certain threshold, which typically is the cost of holding the item in stock. This is depicted in *Figure 9.2*:

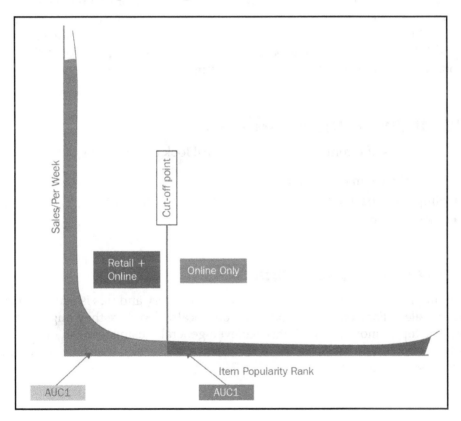

Figure 9.2: The Long Tail phenomenon

The Long Tail phenomenon is observed when you look at items that are popular in terms of the unit sales, and less popular items with lower sales. A retailer would typically only stock items that are popular and give it the best value for money, whereas the less popular items (to the right of the cut-off point) are only stocked by online shops. This phenomenon applies to all sorts of items including books, movies, songs, news articles, and the piece of the curve towards the right of the cut-off point is called the Long-tail.

The more interesting thing is that if you compute the area under the curve, for example *AUC1*, the green shaded area for the items available online and in the retail store compared to the red shaded area, which are the items that are only available online, you will find that the *AUC2* is normally as big, if not bigger than the *AUC1*. These online items cannot be found in a retail store, and the fact that there are so many of them it is hard to find them, and in most cases users would not know either the exact name or you will need to introduce users to these new products. The fact that you now have a lot more choice on the products, means you require better filters, and the answer to this is a recommendation engine. There are many well-known cases where products that were previously not good sellers, did tremendously well after being plugged into recommendation engines.

Types of recommendations

There are three types of recommendations, and we'll look into each one of these:

- Manual recommendations
- Simple aggregated recommendations based on popularity
- User specific recommendations

Manual recommendations

This is the simplest and the oldest way of recommendations, and this is even relevant for traditional retailers. For example, if you visit your local video store they might have an aisle displaying the top 10 movies, and that is achieved generally using some manual process. On popular websites, you can see a list of favorites or staff picks, which do not take into account any user interaction.

Simple aggregated recommendations based on Popularity

Many online stores have moved on from the manual recommendation system to another simpler way of recommending items to the users. On many websites, the default mechanism is to pick up the top 10 items currently selling and display them as popular items. Similarly, if you go to YouTube, you can see the most popular videos or trending videos. Similarly if you go to Twitter, you can see the latest trending topics that users are tweeting about. Such recommendations while based on general user activity are not specific to any particular user, and are typically based on the aggregate activity of the user.

User-specific recommendations

In order to get the best engagement from users you have to tailor your recommendations to the specific users rather than manually picking them or basing them on high-level aggregates. Users are more likely to watch a movie that is similar to the one that they had watched earlier, or read a book that is similar to the books that they like to read rather than watching a movie or reading a book from the Top-10 list. These sorts of recommendations are the hardest to get right, and they provide the best results and hence are the focus of this specific chapter.

User specific recommendations

During the remainder of this chapter, we will focus on user-specific ratings. Let's start by considering a model of the recommendation system.

Let's assume:

C = Set of customers.

I = Set of items (could be movies, books, news items, and so on).

R = Set of ratings. This is an ordered set, where higher numbers indicate the high likeness of a particular item, whereas the lower value indicates a low likeness of a particular item. Generally this is represented by a real value between 0 and 1.

Let's define a utility function u, which looks at every pair of customers and items and maps it to a specific rating:

u: $C * I \rightarrow R$

Let's give an example of a utility matrix, for a set of movies and users:

	Godfather I	Godfather II	Good Will Hunting	A Beautiful Mind
Roger			1	0.5
Aznan	1	0.7	0.2	
Fawad	0.9	0.8	0.1	
Adrian			1	0.8

A utility matrix is generally a **sparse matrix**, as users rate fewer movies than they watch. The areas where ratings are missing can be either due to users not bothering about rating the movies or simply the fact that they have not bothered to rate the movies at all. The objective of a recommendation system is to find out these missing values, and identify the movies that the users might have rated highly and then recommend them to the users.

Key issues with recommendation systems

There are three key issues with recommender systems in general:

1. Gathering known input data
2. Predicting unknown from known ratings
3. Evaluating Prediction methods

Gathering known input data

The first interim milestone in building a recommendation system is to gather the input data, that is, customers, products, and the relevant ratings. While you already have customers and products in your CRM and other systems, you would like to get the ratings of the products from the users. There are two methods to collect product ratings:

- **Explicit**: Explicit ratings means the users would explicitly rate a particular item, for example, a movie on Netflix, a book/product on Amazon, and so on. This is a very direct way to engage with users and it typically provides the highest quality data. In real life, despite the incentives given to rate an item, very few users actually leave ratings for the products. Getting explicit ratings is therefore not scalable for any meaningful prediction exercise.
- **Implicit**: Since explicit ratings are generally not an option, you can decide to deduce the ratings from other user actions. For example, a purchase of a product on a website without a return may indicate that the user has rated the item highly. Similarly a video streaming website may feel that if a user watches the complete video, they have given the movie/video a positive high rating. If they actually decide to end the video in mid-stream, that can be considered a negative rating of a product. The issue with implicit rating is that you can either have a positive or negative rating, but you can't have a high/low rating. For example, a product purchase can indicate a positive rating of a production, and a non-purchase or return can indicate a negative rating. However, you cannot measure this on a scale of 1 (Low) to 10 (High), whether the positive rating was a 5 or a 10.

Predicting unknown from known ratings

Once we have the data available, we can extrapolate unknown ratings from known ratings. The key problem here is that the utility matrix that we had built earlier was sparse, which means that most people had not rated the items. In addition to that we have to deal with the cold start issues, which means that the new items do not have any ratings, while new users have no history based on which you can recommend them new content. There are three major approaches in recommending/predicting unknown from known:

- Content based recommendations
- Collaborative filtering
- Latent factor models

Content-based recommendations

The main concept behind content based recommendations is to recommend the items to a customer that are similar to the items that they have already rated highly. For example, if we talk about movies, we can recommend movies that have similar actors, genres, or directors. If you are a Facebook user, you regularly get friend recommendations, which are basically people that you have some sort of connection with in terms of common friends, common school/college, and so on. Content-based ratings are done based by building an item and a user profile. An item profile is basically the features of an item, for example in the case of a movie, the item profile might include features such as title, actors, and directors, and so on. In case of people, that could be a set of friends, or the places where they lived, studied, or worked together. An item profile is basically a vector containing one or zero depending on if the particular feature is part of an item profile or not.

In the case of blogs and news articles, item profiles are more complex since they are based on the features of the text, which essentially are important words typically identified using **TF-IDF** score (**Term Frequency – Inverse Document Frequency**).

Once you have an item profile, the next step is to build a user profile. Each item with a particular profile build in an earlier step might have been rated by the user. Let's assume that the user has rated n number of items, starting with i_1 to i_n. The simplest way to get a user profile is to average the item profiles. If N is the total number of item profiles, we average the item profiles. This, however, is a very rudimentary approach as it does not take into account if a user has a particular item more than the other items and in that case, we can take the weighted average, where a weight is equal to the rating given by the user. However, from experience we know that certain users are easy raters and certain users are hard raters. What that means is that on a scale of 1-5, some users will only give a rating between 1-3, while others being more generous with their ratings will happily rate a movie as 5 (if it ticks all the right boxes for them). In that particular case, we might want to normalize weights using the average rating of a user. It is important to understand what specific features make the user rate a movie highly, and that could be any number of features.

Once we have a user profile and an item profile, the next task is to make predictions and recommend items to users. The way to approach this is generally looking at a movie that the user has not previously watched and trying to predict the possible ratings that the user will give to that specific movie. Once we look at all the movies, we can recommend the ones that we feel the user will rate highly.

Predicting unknown ratings

Both the user and item profiles are vectors in a high-dimensional space with lots of different features. We need to identify the distance between them and one major distance metric often used is cosine similarity. For any particular user, we compute the cosine similarity between that user and all the items in the catalog, and pick up the highest k items and recommend them to the users.

Pros and cons of content based recommendations

The Pros are:

- Content based ratings are based on content, and a specific user. You do not need other user ratings and hence can start making content-based recommendations from day one.
- Unlike the collaborative filtering approach, you can tailor choices to the unique tastes of users rather than having a generic recommendation.

- Content based recommendations allow for recommending new and popular items as they are based on the profile rather than how many people have watched/rated/bought them previously and this avoids the first-rate problem of collaborative filtering.
- Content-based recommendations allow you to give explanations for every recommendation that you make.

The Cons are

- Feature engineering for relevant features is hard. It is especially difficult to find features for images.
- Since a lot of users rate a small percentage of the movies/items they watch/buy, you could easily miss out on recommendations because the user has never explicitly shown an interest in a similar movie. So you could see a scenario where a popular movie is not recommended because the user has never rated a movie with similar features; for example by actor, genre, and so on.
- Cold-start is still a problem. If a user has never rated any item, it is hard to recommend new products to them. However, generally new users are provided with system-wide popular recommendations. Once the user starts building his profile, we can augment with other recommendation methods.

Collaborative filtering

Collaborative filtering follows a relatively simpler approach for making recommendations. The idea behind collaborative filtering is that suppose you want to make recommendations for a particular user, say X, you would find a group of users that are similar to this user based on their likes and dislikes. Once we have a group of users similar to our user X, we will recommend items that are rated highly by the users in that group. However, the key issue here is to find users that are similar, and certain measures are used to measure this similarity, including:

1. Jaccard similarity
2. Cosine similarity
3. Centered cosine similarity

Let's look at this in a bit more detail, as our code example will follow the collaborative filtering example. We will go with the movies example, since we can easily relate to such an example, and that is what we are using in our code examples as well. We have four users and a set of movies, which have been rated by different users:

	Godfather I	Godfather II	Good Will Hunting	A Beautiful Mind
Roger			5	4
Aznan		5	2	
Fawad	5		1	
Adrian			4	

Roger and Fawad have both rated two movies. In order to understand the similarity between two users, say X and Y, we will need to create a similarity metric that looks at their rating vectors where r_x is the rating vector for user X, and r_y is the rating vector for user Y. If you look at the rating table, you will see that we have a lot of unknown ratings, and that is a key problem while recommending values.

Furthermore, since grouping users is a key objective here, you would like to make sure that users with similar likes are grouped together. From the table if you look at Roger and Adrian, they look similar as both have rated *Good Will Hunting* quite highly; whereas Aznan and Fawad have rated *Godfather I* and *Godfather II* highly while at the same time have given a relatively low rating to *Good Will Hunting*. Furthermore, if you look at Roger and Fawad, they seem to have quite dissimilar tastes as Roger has rated *Good Will Hunting* highly, whereas Fawad has given a low rating. When we group these users together using the previously shared metrics, we would like to make sure that this similarity is captured properly as these groupings will directly impact the recommendations that we make on our websites within our applications.

Jaccard similarity

The **Jaccard Index**, also known as the **Jaccard similarity** coefficient, is a statistic used for comparing similarity and diversity of sample sets. In the interest of this chapter's main objective, we will skip further details of this coefficient. However, you can visit `https://en.wikipedia.org/wiki/Jaccard_index` for more details on this. Jaccard similarity for our specific example can be represented mathematically as follows:

$$Sim(Roger, Fawad) = {|r_{Roger} \cap r_{Fawad}|} / {|r_{Roger} \cup r_{Fawad}|}$$

$$Sim(Roger, Adrian) = {|r_{Roger} \cap r_{Adrian}|} / {|r_{Roger} \cup r_{Adrian}|}$$

So Roger and Fawad have both watched two movies, and we can see that they have quite different tastes:

$$r_{Roger} \cap r_{Fawad} = 1$$

$$r_{Roger} \cup r_{Fawad} = 3$$

$$Sim(Roger, Fawad) = 1/3$$

On the other hand, Roger and Adrian have also watched two movies each and seem to have similar tastes:

$$r_{Roger} \cap r_{Adrian} = 1$$

$$r_{Roger} \cup r_{Adrian} = 3$$

$$Sim(Roger, Adrian) = 1/3$$

This example lays bare the deficiency of Jaccard's similarity coefficient where it takes the number of ratings, but not the actual rating values, which give a very clear insight into the similarities and tastes of both users.

Cosine similarity

Cosine similarity is another measure of similarity between two non-zero vectors and it measures the cosine of the angle between them. You can learn more about cosine similarity at `http://bit.ly/1V8H7Vp`. Essentially, we are treating these ratings from different users as rating vectors. Cosine similarity, however, requires that there are no unknown ratings, and in order to complete the vector and rating matrices we would place zeros in the place of missing values, which means that our rating matrix would look something like this:

	Godfather I	Godfather II	Good Will Hunting	A Beautiful Mind
Roger	0	0	5	4
Aznan	0	5	2	0
Fawad	5	0	1	0
Adrian	0	0	4	0

Calculating cosine similarity between Roger and Fawad results in the following:

Sim(Roger,Fawad) = 0.153

However, when we calculate the cosine similarity between Roger and Adrian, the result is quite different:

Sim(Roger,Adrian)= 0.780

The cosine similarity between these three rating vectors clearly indicates that Roger and Adrian have much more similar interests than Roger and Fawad. This is quite intuitive too. However, there is one slight issue with the cosine similarity assumptions. We have replaced the missing ratings with 0, which due to the ordinal nature of the rating value indicates that all the missing ratings are negative ratings. If Adrian hasn't rated *A Beautiful Mind,* our assumption is that it has to be a negative rating. This is untrue and it will result in false results when we are faced with much bigger and varied datasets.

In addition, we haven't come across easy raters and hard raters, which is an interesting problem. For example, you might have a user who rates a movie that they really like as 5, whereas another user who rates a great movie as only 3 despite the fact that they loved it. How do you measure this? How do you tackle this problem? This problem can be tackled using Centered Cosine, also known as **Pearson Correlation**.

Centered cosine (Pearson Correlation)

In order to calculate the Centered Cosine, we will normalize the ratings for the users, which is generally done by subtracting the average rating from the users. In addition to that we will treat our blank values as zeros, but the interesting thing is that the values would be centered around zero. You can try this for different Datasets.

Predicting unknown ratings

So we have now seen how we can look at users who are similar to each other and users who are dissimilar to each other using various metrics. We can compute the similarity between our user and every other user and select the top k users with the highest similarity values and call that an N set. Once we have this set we can make predictions. We now want to predict how the user will rate a particular item I:

- **Option 1:** The simplest way to do that is to take the average rating from the neighborhood of users for any item I, and use that as an estimate of this users rating.
- **Option 2:** We can use the weighted average. We can weigh the similarity value with the average value. For example, we can look at the neighborhood N and for each user y in the neighborhood N, we weight the y's rating for item I by similarity of x and i. This gives us a rating estimate for the user x and item I.
- **Option 3:** We have just looked at the user-user collaborative filtering here. You can also supplement it with item-item collaborative filtering. The approach is that you pick an item i, identify items similar to item I, and estimate the rating for the item I based on the ratings of similar items. You can use the same similarity metrics as you have used in the user-user model. In practice, most predictions are done using a combination of user-user collaborative filtering and item-item collaborative filtering.

Latent factor methods

The motivation behind latent factor methods is that the ratings on the items are sometimes deeply influenced by some factors that are very specific to a particular domain. For example, the Godfather series of movies are popular because it was the first movie on the Italian Mafia, which is rarely obvious and hard to estimate the impact it has on the popularity of a particular item. The objective is to consider the recommendation as an optimization problem, and infer these so called latent factors using mathematical techniques. In the interest of time, we will not spend too much time on latent factor methods theory in this chapter. If you would like to learn more, I would suggest reading this on SlideShare: `http://bit.ly/2j0mcft`.

Evaluating prediction method

So we have now discussed various approaches to develop a recommendation system, however, we now need to identify if the recommendations are accurate or not. Let's look at the following utility matrix where we have movies on the x-axis and users on the y-axis. As discussed earlier, typically such a utility matrix is sparse. Some users have rated certain movies on a rating scale of 1 to 5.

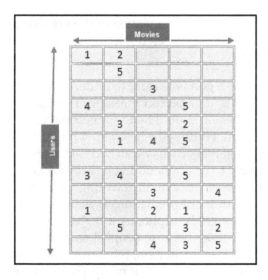

Figure 9.3: Utility matrix

The common method of evaluating a particular recommendation strategy is to take a piece of this matrix and use it as a test set. These sets of ratings are highlighted in a gold color in the preceding matrix. As you can see, some of the users have rated certain movies, but we will treat these ratings as unknown and use our recommendation algorithm to rate these movies. We will then compare our predictions with those given by the users and see how well our recommendation system works. The most common way to measure our accuracy is called **Root Mean Square Error (RMSE)**.

Let's assume that for a test set T and a user u rating an item i with a total number of N withheld ratings:

The predicted rating $= r_{ui}$

The actual rating $= r_{ui}{}^{*}$

The mean squared error for such a set is as follows:

$$RMSE = \left(\sqrt{\frac{\Sigma\left((u,i) \epsilon\, T\ (r_{ui} - r_{ui}{}^{*}) \right)}{N}} \right)$$

So essentially we are just calculating the deviation of the predicted ratings from the actual ratings to understand how well our predicted rating model (our recommendation system) fits to this particular Dataset.

Please note that while RMSE is a good measure to understand how well a recommendation system predicts our ratings, it is not a perfect measure. The reason is that our objective in building a recommendation system should be to suggest better recommendations and not find the best ratings for an item. Finding the best rating might lead us to recommend non-diverse items. For example, if somebody has watched *Godfather I*, based on the rating prediction we are highly likely to recommend them *Godfather II* and *Godfather III*. While these are definitely valuable, we are essentially creating a non-diverse set of ratings. The context of predictions and the order of predictions is as important as the prediction itself. For example, if a person has bought headphones, a typical recommendation system might recommend them other headphones because people browsed them together. The issue is that once a person has already bought an item, the recommendation system should be context aware and recommend them items that might go with headphones.

Finally, the order of predictions is important. For example, if a person is reading a book in a series of books, the recommendation system should recommend those books in sequence rather than in an Ad-hoc fashion. This understanding of order within predictions is important to make the recommendations more worthwhile.

Recommendation system in Spark

We are now going to move ahead with the practical example of building the recommendation system with Spark. Since most users are familiar with movies, we are going to use the Movie Lens data set for building a recommendation system, have a look at the data, and look at some of the options. The theory behind recommendation systems and this practical example should give you a good starting point in building one.

Sample dataset

We are going to use the MovieLens 100k dataset, which at the time of writing was last updated in October 2016. This dataset (ml-latest-small) describes 5-star rating and free-text tagging activity from **MovieLens** (https://movielens.org/), a movie recommendation service. It contains 1,00,004 ratings and 1,296 tag applications across 9,125 movies. This data was created by 671 users between January 09, 1995 and October 16, 2016. This dataset was generated on October 17, 2016 and it can be found at http://bit.ly/24PV0hK. Further details about the data set can be found here: http://bit.ly/2i6yste. We'll just be going through the structure of some of the files in the dataset.

1. Ratings data structure:

    All ratings are present in ratings.csv with each line representing one rating of one movie per user. The format is as follows:

    userID, movieID, rating, timeStamp

    A sample of the ratings file is shown as follows:

    ```
    userId,movieId,rating,timestamp
    1,31,2.5,1260759144
    1,1029,3.0,1260759179
    1,1061,3.0,1260759182
    1,1129,2.0,1260759185
    1,1172,4.0,1260759205
    1,1263,2.0,1260759151
    1,1287,2.0,1260759187
    1,1293,2.0,1260759148
    1,1339,3.5,1260759125
    ```

    Figure 9.4: Ratings CSV file

2. Tags data structure:

All tags are contained in a file called `tags.csv` file. Each line of this file represents a tag applied to one movie by one user; the format of the file is as follows:

userID, movieID, Tag, TimeStamp

A sample of the tags file is shown in the following screenshot:

```
userId,movieId,rating,timestamp
1,31,2.5,1260759144
1,1029,3.0,1260759179
1,1061,3.0,1260759182
1,1129,2.0,1260759185
1,1172,4.0,1260759205
1,1263,2.0,1260759151
1,1287,2.0,1260759187
1,1293,2.0,1260759148
1,1339,3.5,1260759125
```

Figure 9.5: Tags CSV file

3. Movies data structure:

Movie information is contained in the `movies.csv` file. Each line of this file after the header represents one movie and it has the following format:

MovieID, Title, Genres

A sample of the movies file is shown in the following screenshot:

```
userId,movieId,tag,timestamp
15,339,sandra 'boring' bullock,1138537770
15,1955,dentist,1193435061
15,7478,Cambodia,1170560997
15,32892,Russian,1170626366
15,34162,forgettable,1141391765
15,35957,short,1141391873
15,37729,dull story,1141391806
15,45950,powerpoint,1169616291
15,100365,activist,1425876220
```

Figure 9.6: Movies CSV file

How does Spark offer recommendation?

Spark's machine learning library `spark.ml` supports model-based CF in which items are described by latent factors which as we discussed earlier can be used to predict missing entries. Spark's `spark.ml` package provides the **Alternative Least Squares (ALS)** algorithm to learn the latent factors. ALS is basically a matrix factorization algorithm that uses Alternating Least squares. It factors the user-to-item Matrix R into a user to feature Matrix U and Item-to-Feature matrix M and runs the algorithm in a parallel fashion.

The ALS algorithm discovers the latent factors that explain the user-to-item ratings and then tries to find optimal factor weights to minimize the least squares between predicted and actual ratings using an iterative approach. ALS is a very flexible and parallelism-friendly algorithm. The following paper explains this algorithm in much more detail: `http ://bit.ly/2jhXx29` (also available at `http://yifanhu.net/PUB/cf.pdf`).

The API for Spark is based on DataFrames, and the current implementation uses the following parameters. Other parameters are described at `http://bit.ly/2fk8vXh`:

Parameter Name	Description
`numBlocks`	This is a performance tuning option. This option indicates the number of blocks that the users and items will be partitioned into in order to parallelize computation (defaults to 10).
`rank`	Indicates the number of latent factors in the model (defaults to 10).
`maxIter`	As mentioned, ALS is an iterative algorithm, and this parameter controls the number of iterations. Default iterations = 10.

Let's kick start the development of the recommendation system.

Importing relevant libraries

As usual, before starting any program, we will need to import the relevant libraries.

```
import org.apache.spark.ml.evaluation.RegressionEvaluator
import org.apache.spark.ml.recommendation.ALS
import org.apache.spark.sql._
```

```
scala> import org.apache.spark.ml.evaluation.RegressionEvaluator
import org.apache.spark.ml.evaluation.RegressionEvaluator

scala> import org.apache.spark.ml.recommendation.ALS
import org.apache.spark.ml.recommendation.ALS

scala> import org.apache.spark.sql._
import org.apache.spark.sql._
```

Defining the schema for ratings

Ratings, as mentioned previously, are available as `ratings.csv`. We'll be using the DataFrame API to load this data and use the encoders class for schema definition. At the time of writing, it is still experimental. An encoder is actually used to convert a JVM object of type *T* to and from an internal Spark SQL representation. Without encoders, you would need to go through the complex usage of `StructType`, `StructField`, and DataType classes to define a schema for a particular row object:

```
case class Ratings(userId: Int, movieId: Int, rating: Double, ratingTs:
Long)
val ratingsSchema = Encoders.product[Ratings].schema
```

Defining the schema for movies

We'll use the same strategy to define a schema for the movies data before using this while
loading the dataset:

```
case class Movies(moveId: Int, title: String, genre: String)
val moviesSchema = Encoders.product[Movies].schema
```

```
scala> import org.apache.spark.ml.evaluation.RegressionEvaluator
import org.apache.spark.ml.evaluation.RegressionEvaluator

scala> import org.apache.spark.ml.recommendation.ALS
import org.apache.spark.ml.recommendation.ALS

scala> import org.apache.spark.sql._
import org.apache.spark.sql._

scala> case class Ratings(userId: Int, movieId: Int, rating: Double, ratingTs: Long)
defined class Ratings

scala> val ratingsSchema = Encoders.product[Ratings].schema
ratingsSchema: org.apache.spark.sql.types.StructType = StructType(StructField(userId,IntegerType,false), StructField(
movieId,IntegerType,false), StructField(rating,DoubleType,false), StructField(ratingTs,LongType,false))

scala> case class Movies(moveId: Int, title: String, genre: String)
defined class Movies

scala> val moviesSchema = Encoders.product[Movies].schema
moviesSchema: org.apache.spark.sql.types.StructType = StructType(StructField(moveId,IntegerType,false), StructField(t
itle,StringType,true), StructField(genre,StringType,true))
```

Figure 9.7: Imports and defining schemas for ratings and movies

Loading ratings and movies data

Let us now read the ratings and movies data into DataFrames:

```
val ratings = spark.read.option("header","true")
  .schema(ratingsSchema)
  .csv("hdfs://sparkmaster:8020/user/hdfs/sampledata/ratings.csv")
val movies = spark.read.option("header","true")
  .schema(moviesSchema)
  .csv("hdfs://sparkmaster:8020/user/hdfs/sampledata/movies.csv")
```

We'll load the ratings and movies data, and see the top five records to make sure we have loaded the data correctly.

```
scala>  val ratings = spark.read.option("header","true").schema(Encoders.product[Ratings].schema).csv("hdfs://sparkma
ster:8020/user/hdfs/sampledata/ratings.csv")
ratings: org.apache.spark.sql.DataFrame = [userId: int, movieId: int ... 2 more fields]

scala>  val movies = spark.read.option("header","true").schema(Encoders.product[Movies].schema).csv("hdfs://sparkmast
er:8020/user/hdfs/sampledata/movies.csv")
movies: org.apache.spark.sql.DataFrame = [moveId: int, title: string ... 1 more field]

scala> ratings.show(5)
+------+-------+------+----------+
|userId|movieId|rating|  ratingTs|
+------+-------+------+----------+
|     1|     31|   2.5|1260759144|
|     1|   1029|   3.0|1260759179|
|     1|   1061|   3.0|1260759182|
|     1|   1129|   2.0|1260759185|
|     1|   1172|   4.0|1260759205|
+------+-------+------+----------+
only showing top 5 rows

scala> movies.show(5)
+------+--------------------+--------------------+
|moveId|               title|               genre|
+------+--------------------+--------------------+
|     1|    Toy Story (1995)|Adventure|Animati...|
|     2|      Jumanji (1995)|Adventure|Childre...|
|     3|Grumpier Old Men ...|      Comedy|Romance|
|     4|Waiting to Exhale...|Comedy|Drama|Romance|
|     5|Father of the Bri...|              Comedy|
+------+--------------------+--------------------+
only showing top 5 rows
```

Figure 9.8: Ratings and movies data schemas

Data partitioning

As we explained during the initial parts of this chapter, we will divide the data into training and validation. For the purpose of this exercise, we are using a 70/30 proportion for splitting, which is quite common. Some practitioners prefer to go with 80/20 as well. We will be using the randomSplit() method to split the data:

```
val Array(train, test) = ratings.randomSplit(Array(0.7, 0.3))
```

```
scala> val Array(train, valid) = ratings.randomSplit(Array(0.7,0.3))
train: org.apache.spark.sql.Dataset[org.apache.spark.sql.Row] = [userId: int, movieId: int ... 2 more fields]
valid: org.apache.spark.sql.Dataset[org.apache.spark.sql.Row] = [userId: int, movieId: int ... 2 more fields]

scala> train.count()
res7: Long = 69894

scala> valid.count()
res8: Long = 30110
```

Figure 9.9: Data partitioning

Training an ALS model

We are now going to use the Alternating Least Squares Matrix factorization method. We have discussed the theory earlier in this chapter. The key parameters here are:

- The **Max Iterations** parameter defines the maximum number of parameter
- **Regularization Parameter,** which is set to 0.01

As discussed earlier in this chapter, recommendations can be used across a number of industries and typically you have three entities of interest:

- A user who rates an item
- An item that is being rated
- A rating that is given by a user for a particular item

You will need to pass the appropriate column names to the ALS model and fit the training dataset using the parameters to generate a model:

```
val als = new ALS()
  .setMaxIter(15)
  .setRegParam(0.01)
  .setUserCol("userId")
  .setItemCol("movieId")
  .setRatingCol("rating")
val recommendationModel = als.fit(train)
```

```
scala> val als = new ALS().setMaxIter(15).setRegParam(0.01).setUserCol("userId").setItemCol("movieId").setRatingCol("rating")
als: org.apache.spark.ml.recommendation.ALS = als_90dc933faaf7

scala> val recommendationModel = als.fit(train)
recommendationModel: org.apache.spark.ml.recommendation.ALSModel = als_90dc933faaf7
```

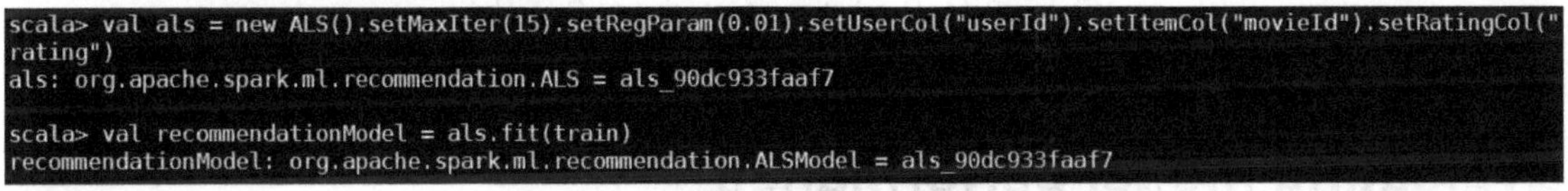

Figure 9.10: Training the model using training data

Predicting the test dataset

Once you have a model, you can then use the transform option to transform the input data set to generate predictions based on the model:

```
val predictions = recommendationModel.transform(test)
```

The resultant data set has an extra column, named **predictions** by default, which contains the prediction from the model. You can then compare your actual ratings against those predicted by the model.

```
scala> test.show(5)
+------+-------+------+----------+
|userId|movieId|rating|  ratingTs|
+------+-------+------+----------+
|     1|   1129|   2.0|1260759185|
|     1|   1172|   4.0|1260759205|
|     1|   1263|   2.0|1260759151|
|     1|   1293|   2.0|1260759148|
|     1|   1343|   2.0|1260759131|
+------+-------+------+----------+
only showing top 5 rows


scala> predictions.show(5)
+------+-------+------+----------+----------+
|userId|movieId|rating|  ratingTs|prediction|
+------+-------+------+----------+----------+
|   311|    463|   3.0|898008246| 3.5355787|
|    85|    471|   3.0|837512312|  2.585321|
|   548|    471|   4.0|857407799| 3.3410475|
|   306|    471|   3.0|939718996| 3.6584222|
|   491|    471|   3.0|940797129| 3.1157556|
+------+-------+------+----------+----------+
only showing top 5 rows
```

Figure 9.11: Predictions from the ALS model

Evaluating model performance

Once we have a model and a set of metrics, we can use the Regression Evaluator to evaluate the results. The Regression Evaluator supports the following metrics:

- RMSE – Root Mean Squared Error (default)
- SE – Mean Squared Error
- MAE – Mean Absolute Error

We have already discussed the details of the Mean Squared Error earlier in this chapter and we will be using that to evaluate the results of the prediction.

```
scala> val evaluator = new RegressionEvaluator().setMetricName("rmse").setLabelCol("rating").setPredictionCol("predic
tion")
evaluator: org.apache.spark.ml.evaluation.RegressionEvaluator = regEval_32f07f86a01d

scala> val rmse = evaluator.evaluate(predictions)
rmse: Double = 0.45236706206901606

scala> println(s"Root-mean-square error = $rmse")
Root-mean-square error = 0.45236706206901606
```

Figure 9.12: Evaluating model performance

This is by no means an optimum model and performance can be optimized by tuning various options. One of the better ways to do that is to pick the boundaries of various parameters; for example, iterations between 10 and 20, Lambda values between 0.1 and 6.0, and so on, and run them through a loop, each time comparing against the best RMSE calculated yet. If your RMSE is less than the previously stored RMSE, you can nominate the current model as the champion and the current RMSE as the best RMSE.

Here's a quick example of how you might attempt something like this for an optimized model. This example has been adapted from the RDD example available at **AmpLab** (http ://bit.ly/2jaFE6i). Full details of this example are available on this book's GitHub page:

```
val ranks = List(1,2,3,4,5,6,7,8,9,10)
val lambdas = List(0.1,0.2,0.3,0.4,0.5,0.6,0.7,0.8,0.8,1,2,3,4,5,6,10.0)
val regParams = List(0.01,0.05,0.1,0.2,0.3,0.4,0.5,0.6,0.7,0.8,0.8,0.10,10)
val numIters = List(5,10,15,20)
var bestModel: Option[ALSModel] = None
var optimalRMSE = Double.MaxValue
var bestRank = 0
var bestRegParam = -1.0
var bestNumIter = -1
/** Iterative Computation - Find best Model*/
for (rank <- ranks; regParam <- regParams; numIter <- numIters) {
  val als = new ALS().setMaxIter(numIter).setRank(rank)
    .setRegParam(regParam).setUserCol("userId")
    .setItemCol("movieId").setRatingCol("rating")
  val model = als.fit(train)
  val predictions = model.transform(valid)
  val currentRMSE = evaluator.evaluate(predictions.filter("prediction <>
'NaN'"))
  println("Metrics => RMSE (Validation) = " + currentRMSE + " :
    Model Metrics(rank = "+ rank + ", regParam = "
   + regParam + ", and numIter = " + numIter + ").")
  if (currentRMSE < optimalRMSE) {
    bestModel = Some(model)
    optimalRMSE = currentRMSE
    bestRank = rank
    bestRegParam = regParam
```

```
        bestNumIter = numIter
    }
}
```

At the end of the iterations, you will have the `bestModel` as the `bestModel` parameter, which can then be used to perform recommendations for your users.

Using implicit preferences

While we have used explicit ratings in our case, if the rating matrix is based on implicit signals that we have discussed earlier, you can set the implicit preferences to true:

```
val als = new ALS()
    .setMaxIter(15)
    .setRegParam(0.01)
    .setImplicitPrefs(true)
    .setUserCol("userId")
    .setItemCol("movieId")
```

Sanity checking

As we have the movies data loaded, we can check if the predictions are accurate as well, and if they make sense. This would traditionally mean cross-checking to see if the movie recommendation actually works. For example, you might want to understand if action movies are being recommended to people who like action movies, and thrillers are recommended to people who have a habit of watching thrillers. This is often an important part of the overall exercise.

Model Deployment

So you build a great model, which gives you a great lift. What next? Surely that can't be the end of it. While building a model that gives a good lift is important, deploying the model into production is crucial. It is important to understand that while your model development environment might happen in Spark, model operationalizing can happen elsewhere.In addition to the operational environment, model scoring can be done in an offline or an online mode. An example of an offline mode could be churn prediction, where you segment your data and identify which customers are likely to churn and hence device a churn-tackle strategy. An online scoring can be when the customer is waiting on the response. An online scoring scenario typically needs low latency e.g. online fraud detection, or bidding on an advertising slot.

Finally, it is important to understand that business continuously evolves, and with that often their needs to be a change to the model itself. You should continuously revaluate your deployed model to understand if changes need to be made. It is important to setup alerts which can update you on the model decay and the subsequent need for revaluation. A model should follow a proper release process between the development, testing and production environments. It is quite common for companies to use A/B testing with different versions of models to understand what works best in a particular scenario.

If you would like to learn more about model deployment, I would suggest starting at `http://bit.ly/SparkModelDeployment`.

References

The following articles, blogs, and videos have been used for the contents of this chapter. They have also been included to provide users with further reading material:

1. Coursera course on *Mining Massive Datasets* by *Stanford University*.
2. The Long Tail – `https://www.wired.com/2004/10/tail/`
3. Harvard CS50 – Recommender Systems – `https://www.youtube.com/watch?v=Eeg1DEeWUjA`
4. `https://en.wikipedia.org/wiki/Cosine_similarity`
5. `https://en.wikipedia.org/wiki/Jaccard_index`
6. 6. F. Maxwell Harper and Joseph A. Konstan. 2015. The MovieLens Datasets: History and Context. ACM Transactions on Interactive Intelligent Systems (TiiS) 5, 4, Article 19 (December 2015), 19 pages. DOI=`http://dx.doi.org/10.1145/2827872`
7. `http://ampcamp.berkeley.edu/big-data-mini-course/movie-recommendation-with-mllib.html`

Summary

This concludes the chapter. We have gone through recommendation systems, including the theory and some practical examples in Scala. I have learned a lot of this theory from some of the courses on data mining at Coursera, which is an amazing platform. I hope we have been able to do justice to the topic. We have tried to focus a lot on the design and the factors involved in a recommendation system as I always believe that engineering the solution is the easy part once you understand what you are up against.

The next chapter is focused on another case study, which is churn prediction, one of the most popular use cases in any customer-driven organization, that understands the cost of acquiring a new customer versus retaining an existing one.

10
Customer Churn Prediction

This is our last chapter for this book, and we have looked at the technology topics around Spark from architecture to the details of the APIs including RDDs, DataFrames, and machine learning and GraphX frameworks. In the last chapter, we covered a recommendation engine use case where we primarily looked at the Scala API. We've primarily used Scala, Python, or R-Shell. In this chapter, we will be using the Jupyter notebook with the Pyspark interpreter to look at the Churn prediction use case.

The chapter covers:

- Overview of customer churn
- Importance of churn prediction
- Understanding the dataset
- Exploring data
- Building a machine learning pipeline
- Predicting Churn

This chapter will hopefully give you a good introduction to churn prediction systems, which you can use as a baseline for other prediction activities.

Let's get started.

Overview of customer churn

I have spent almost 15 years in the telecom and financial industry with some of the major telecom and financial customers, and if there is one business case that makes the business worried it is Customer Churn. So what is customer churn?

According to Wikipedia, Customer attrition, also known as customer churn, customer turnover, or customer defection, is the loss of clients or customers (`http://bit.ly/2kfTHXF`).

Customer churn is such a nightmarish problem for major vendors because:

- Churn affects your customer base and hence profitability and baseline
- Churn impacts your overall business image
- Churn hurts your company's goodwill and market sentiment
- Churn hurts your total addressable market

- Churn gives your competitors a psychological and economic advantage
- Churn affects your overall employee morale

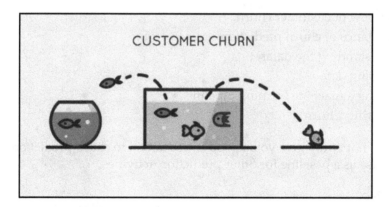

Figure 10.1: Customer churn via http://bit.ly/2iUScln

While you can never reduce the churn rate to zero, you essentially want to:

- Identify who is most likely to churn
- Identify the potential value of the customer, and if it's worth retaining the customer
- Compare the cost of retaining a customer versus divesting an unprofitable customer

Why is predicting customer churn important?

So based on the quick overview of what churn is and how it impacts the organizations, why is it important to predict churn? Well it is as important as predicting any potential bad event happening in the organization. Predicting the customers that are prone to churn will help you to devise a strategy to tackle the potential problem. Remember, not all churn is bad for the bottom line; however, you need to understand the impact of a customer's churn on the revenues and other non-tangible factors mentioned in the previous section. Remember, that until you understand what the problem is, you cannot devise a strategy to resolve the problem. Each customer, or segment of a customer's needs is to be treated differently, and perhaps with a different strategy for each segment. There are various ways by which you can reduce your churn rate, and some of them have been eloquently described in the blog by Ross Beard, which can be accessed here: `http://bit.ly/2jJagwd`.

How do we predict customer churn with Spark?

Predicting customer churn in Apache Spark is similar to predicting any other binary outcome. Spark provides a number of algorithms to do such a prediction. While we'll focus on Random Forest, you can potentially look at other algorithms within the MLLib library to perform the prediction. We'll follow the typical steps of building a machine learning pipeline that we had discussed in our earlier MLLib chapter.

The typical stages include:

- **Stage 1:** Loading data/defining schema
- **Stage 2:** Exploring/visualizing the data set
- **Stage 3:** Performing necessary transformations
- **Stage 4:** Feature engineering
- **Stage 5:** Model training
- **Stage 6:** Model evaluation
- **Stage 7:** Model monitoring

Data set description

Since we are going to target the telecom industry, we'll use one of the popular data sets around generally used for telecommunication demonstrations. It was originally published in *Discovering Knowledge in Data* (http://www.dataminingconsultant.com/DKD.htm) (Larose, 2004). You can download the data directly from http://www.dataminingconsulta nt.com/data/churn.txt. This is a smallish data set with only 3,333 rows, but it is sufficient for our needs. We'll be using the Spark Python DataFrame API and we will use the Jupyter notebook. The reason for using a notebook is because the data needs to be explored, and there is nothing better than bar and Scatter plots to explore the data. We'll discuss setting up Jupyter notebook in the Appendix, *There's More with Spark*, so if you have not setup Jupyter before, don't fret upon it. While some users might want to use Zeppelin notebook (also comes packaged with Hortonworks Data Platform), unfortunately at the time of writing the **Zeppelin** notebook had a few unresolved show-stopper bugs, which meant Zeppelin notebook was not working with Spark 2.0.

Field Name	Sample Values	Description
State	KS, OH	Two letter state
Account Length	128, 107	Account length in months
Area Code	415, 415	Area code
Phone	382-4657, 371-7191	Phone number
Int'l Plan	no, yes	International plan indicator
VMail Plan	yes, no	Vmail plan indicator
VMail Message	25, 26	Vmail messages
Day Mins	265.1, 161.6	Number of day mins

Day Calls	110, 123	Number of day calls
Day Charge	45.07, 27.47	Day airtime charge
Eve Mins	197.4, 195.5	Number of eve mins
Eve Calls	99, 103	Number of eve calls
Eve Charge	16.78, 16.62	Eve airtime charge
Night Mins	244.7, 254.4	Number of night mins
Night Calls	91, 103	Number of night calls
Night Charge	11.01, 11.45	Night airtime charge
Intl Mins	10, 13.7	Number of international dialling mins
Intl Calls	3, 3	Number of international calls
Intl Charge	2.7, 3.7	Charge for international calls
CustServ Calls	1, 1	Calls to customer service centre
Churn?	False, True	Target column indicates churn.

Rather than going into too much theoretical discussion of churn, let's start working on the code examples.

Code example

We will need to import the relevant Spark packages. You'll see them being used in the following code examples:

```
from pyspark.sql import SparkSession
from pyspark.ml.classification import DecisionTreeClassifier,
LogisticRegression, RandomForestClassifier
from pyspark.ml import Pipeline
from pyspark.ml.feature import OneHotEncoder, StringIndexer,
VectorAssembler
from pyspark.ml.evaluation import BinaryClassificationEvaluator
from pyspark.ml.tuning import ParamGridBuilder, CrossValidator
```

Defining schema

If you look closely at the first line of the file, it contains a header that can be used as field names. However, the names are not consistent. It is better from a standardization perspective that we have standard names for the fields. I personally prefer fields without any spaces and all characters in capital case. I know some teams prefer to use camel case notation, so feel free to change the code as per your liking:

```
from pyspark.sql.types import *
schemaString =
"STATE,ACCOUNTLENGTH,AREACODE,PHONE,INTLPLAN,VMAILPLAN,VMAILMESSAGE,DAYMINS
,DAYCALLS,DAYCHARGE,EVEMINS,EVECALLS,EVECHARGE,NIGHTMINS,NIGHTCALLS,NIGHTCH
ARGE,INTLMINS,INTLCALLS,INTLCHARGE,CUSTSERVCALLS,CHURN"

fields = [StructField(field_name, StringType(), True) for field_name in
schemaString.split(",")]
churnSchema = StructType(fields)
```

The reason we define the schema before loading the data is because we can apply the schema while loading the data.

Loading data

We'll now load the data from HDFS onto Spark. We aren't doing anything new here, and rather are using code similar to what we had earlier described/seen. For continuity's sake, we will use the DataFrame API:

```
churnDataset = spark.read.option("header","true")
  .schema(churnSchema)
  .csv("hdfs://sparkmaster:8020/user/hdfs/sampledata/churn.csv")
```

Data exploration

Now that the data is loaded, let's perform some basic exploration of the data, to get a feel of what we are working with. This is an essential component of any analysis irrespective of the tool that you are using.

Spark DataFrames have a `describe()` method that will give you some basic summary statistics about various fields of the dataset. Since our target column is **churn**, let's run some summary statistics to get an insight into what we are dealing with:

```
churnDataset.describe('Churn').show()
```

As mentioned earlier, I am running a Jupyter notebook with Python interpreter:

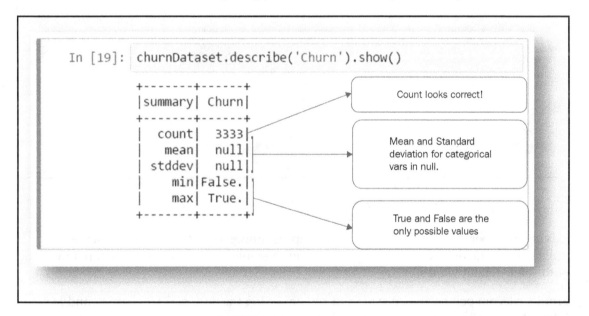

Figure 10.2: Data exploration – churn variable

You may want to look at detailed summary statistics for all the fields together, rather than doing it one by one. Fortunately, the `describe()` method is overloaded and it can accept more than one argument as well.

```
churn.describe('Phone','IntlPlan','VMailPlan','VMailMessage','DayMins','DayCalls','DayCharge','Churn').show()
churn.describe('State','EveMins','EveCalls','EveCharge','NightMins','NightCalls','NightCharge').show()
churn.describe('AccountLength','AreaCode','IntlMins','IntlCalls','IntlCharge','CustServCalls').show()
```

summary	Phone	IntlPlan	VMailPlan	VMailMessage	DayMins	DayCalls	DayCharge	Churn
count	3333	3333	3333	3333	3333	3333	3333	3333
mean	null	null	null	8.099009900990099	179.77509750975116	100.43564356435644	30.562307230723093	null
stddev	null	null	null	13.688365372038598	54.46738920237146	20.069084207300893	9.259434553930495	null
min	327-1058	no	no	0	0.000000	0	0.000000	False.
max	422-9964	yes	yes	9	99.900000	99	9.930000	True.

summary	State	EveMins	EveCalls	EveCharge	NightMins	NightCalls	NightCharge
count	3333	3333	3333	3333	3333	3333	3333
mean	null	200.98034803480346	100.11431143114311	17.083540354035392	200.8720372037204	100.10771077107711	9.039324932493264
stddev	null	50.713844425811985	19.92262529394312	4.310667643110347	50.57384701365836	19.568609346058544	2.275872837660027
min	AK	0.000000	0	0.000000	100.300000	100	1.040000
max	WY	99.500000	99	9.950000	99.300000	99	9.990000

summary	AccountLength	AreaCode	IntlMins	IntlCalls	IntlCharge	CustServCalls
count	3333	3333	3333	3333	3333	3333
mean	101.06480648064806	437.18241824182417	10.237293729372933	4.4794479447944795	2.764581458145804	1.5628562856285628
stddev	39.822105928595676	42.37129048560661	2.7918395484084116	2.4612142705460953	0.753772612663045	1.3154910448664752
min	1	408	0.000000	0	0.000000	0
max	99	510	9.900000	9	5.400000	9

Figure 10.3: Data exploration – summary statistics for the entire table

Having a deeper look into these variables helps us understand that we do not have any nulls in the data. In real life this is generally not possible unless you have prepared the data with some default values.

From a telecom perspective, use of your phone during the day, night, evenings, and for international calls can be a good predictor of a customer segment, and can be a good predictor for churn behavior. Let's visually explore this data, and see if we can find something interesting. We are typically looking at the distribution of the data, as that will help us understand if we need to perform any pre-processing on this data.

Let's start by exploring the data for `DayMins`, `EveMins`, `NightMins`, and `IntlMins`. We'll use the `Matplotlib` library to visualize the data. If you would like to understand how you can configure this with your Spark distribution, please look at the Appendix.

PySpark import code

We are going to import `Matplotlib.Pyplot`, `Pandas`, and `Numpy` for some of the visualization:

```
%matplotlib inline
import random
import matplotlib.pyplot as plt
import pandas as pd
import numpy as np
num_bins = 10
```

Exploring international minutes

The following code snippet is used to explore international minutes within the dataset:

```
n, bins, patches =
plt.hist(np.array(churnDataset.select("IntlMins").rdd.collect()).astype(np.
float), num_bins, normed=0, facecolor='green', alpha=0.5, label="Intl
Mins")
plt.legend(loc='upper right')

plt.show()
```

Exploring night minutes

The following code snippet is used to explore night minutes within the dataset:

```
n, bins, patches =
plt.hist(np.array(churnDataset.select("NightMins").rdd.collect()).astype(np
.float), num_bins, normed=0, facecolor='red', alpha=0.5, label="Night
Mins")
plt.legend(loc='upper right')
plt.show()
```

Exploring day minutes

The following code snippet is used to explore day minutes within the dataset:

```
n, bins, patches =
plt.hist(np.array(churnDataset.select("DayMins").rdd.collect()).astype(np.f
loat), num_bins, normed=0, facecolor='blue', alpha=0.5,label="Day Mins")
plt.legend(loc='upper right')
plt.show()
```

Exploring eve minutes

The following code snippet is used to explore evening minutes within the dataset:

```
n, bins, patches =
plt.hist(np.array(churnDataset.select("EveMins").rdd.collect()).astype(np.f
loat), num_bins, normed=0, facecolor='orange', alpha=0.5,label="Eve Mins")
plt.legend(loc='upper right')
plt.show()
```

We are going to display them separately and then overlay them on each other, to understand the distribution of the variables.

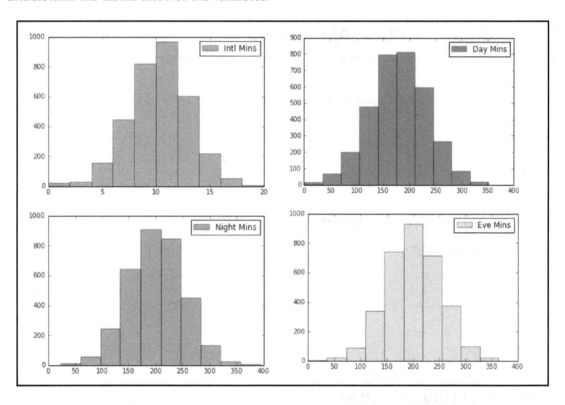

Figure 10.4: Data Exploration – distribution of minutes variables

Comparing minutes data for churners and non-churners

In order to get a better understanding of the data, you may want to compare the Minutes data for churners versus non-churners. We will need to divide the data between churners and non-churners using the Churn-Flag and then use that to plot the difference and comparison:

```
churnDataset.createOrReplaceTempView("churn_tab")
churners = spark.sql("select * from churn_tab where churn = 'True.'")
churners.count()
nonChurners = spark.sql("select * from churn_tab where churn = 'False.'")
nonChurners.count()
```

We now have two DataFrames: **Churners** and **Non-Churners**. The following code examples would be helpful in exploring the data for churners and non-churners.

```
n, bins, patches =
plt.hist(np.array(churners.select("IntlMins").rdd.collect()).astype(np.floa
t), num_bins, normed=0, facecolor='green', alpha=0.5, label="C Intl Mins")
plt.legend(loc='upper right')
plt.show()

n, bins, patches =
plt.hist(np.array(nonChurners.select("IntlMins").rdd.collect()).astype(np.f
loat), num_bins,
normed=0, facecolor='green', alpha=0.5, label="NC Intl Mins")
plt.legend(loc='upper right')
plt.show()

n, bins, patches =
plt.hist(np.array(churners.select("NightMins").rdd.collect()).astype(np.flo
at), num_bins, normed=0, facecolor='red', alpha=0.5, label="C Night Mins")
plt.legend(loc='upper right')
plt.show()

n, bins, patches =
plt.hist(np.array(nonChurners.select("NightMins").rdd.collect()).astype(np.
float), num_bins, normed=0, facecolor='red', alpha=0.5, label="NC Night
Mins")
plt.legend(loc='upper right')
plt.show()

n, bins, patches =
plt.hist(np.array(churners.select("DayMins").rdd.collect()).astype(np.float
), num_bins, normed=0, facecolor='blue', alpha=0.5,label="C Day Mins")
```

```
plt.legend(loc='upper right')
plt.show()

n, bins, patches =
plt.hist(np.array(nonChurners.select("DayMins").rdd.collect()).astype(np.fl
oat), num_bins, normed=0, facecolor='blue', alpha=0.5,label="NC Day Mins")
plt.legend(loc='upper right')
plt.show()

n, bins, patches =
plt.hist(np.array(churners.select("EveMins").rdd.collect()).astype(np.float
), num_bins, normed=0, facecolor='orange', alpha=0.5,label="C Eve Mins")
plt.legend(loc='upper right')
plt.show()

n, bins, patches =
plt.hist(np.array(nonChurners.select("EveMins").rdd.collect()).astype(np.fl
oat), num_bins, normed=0, facecolor='orange', alpha=0.5,label="NC Eve
Mins")
plt.legend(loc='upper right')
plt.show()
```

We can see major behavioral differences between how churners and non-churners use their calling minutes, and hence they seem to be an important variable in predicting churn.

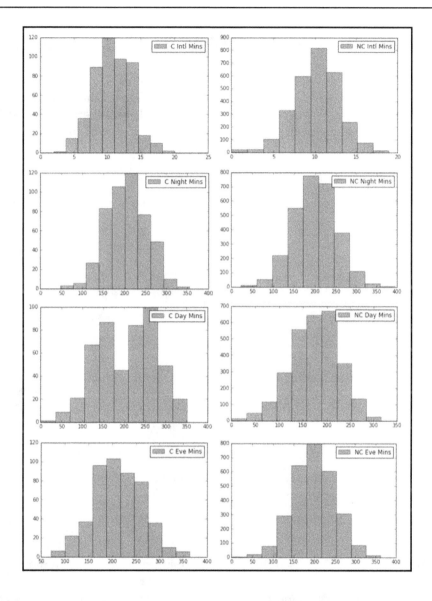

Figure 10.5: Data Exploration-Distribution of minutes variables – churners versus non-churners

Legend: C =churners, NC=non-churners

Comparing charge data for churners and non-churners

Similar to our earlier approach, we'll now compare the charge for day, evening, night, and international calls between churners and non-churners and see if there is any relationship between the charge applied and the relevant churn. The code to plot this is quite similar to the code that we have seen earlier:

```
n, bins, patches =
plt.hist(np.array(churners.select("IntlCharge").rdd.collect()).astype(np.fl
oat), num_bins, normed=0, facecolor='red', alpha=0.5, label="C Intl Chrg")
plt.legend(loc='upper right')
plt.show()

n, bins, patches =
plt.hist(np.array(nonChurners.select("IntlCharge").rdd.collect()).astype(np
.float), num_bins, normed=0, facecolor='green', alpha=0.5, label="NC Intl
Chrg")
plt.legend(loc='upper right')
plt.show()

n, bins, patches =
plt.hist(np.array(churners.select("NightCharge").rdd.collect()).astype(np.f
loat), num_bins, normed=0, facecolor='red', alpha=0.5, label="C Night
Chrg")
plt.legend(loc='upper right')
plt.show()

n, bins, patches =
plt.hist(np.array(nonChurners.select("NightCharge").rdd.collect()).astype(n
p.float), num_bins, normed=0, facecolor='green', alpha=0.5, label="NC Night
Chrg")
plt.legend(loc='upper right')
plt.show()
```

For brevity's sake, we have just used the code for the international and night charge. The code for `DayCharge` and `EveCharge` will look very similar. Let's have a look at the frequency histograms to understand the structure of the data, and if there is any correlation between the charge data and the churn variable.

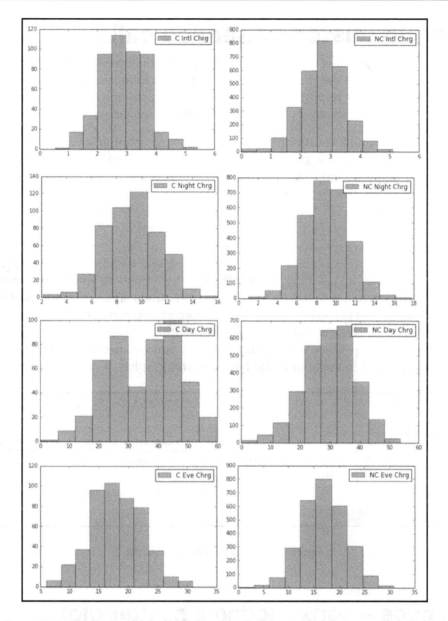

Figure 10.6: Data Exploration – distribution of call charges-churners versus non-churners

Legend:- **C** = Churners, **NC** = Non-Churners

Exploring customer service calls

Based on past experience, in a typical churn scenario, customers who churn would typically make more calls to the customer service centers compared to those who don't churn. Calls to customer service center imply a problem faced by the customer, and multiple calls to the customer service center indicate a persistent unresolved problem.

We've used **Plotly** to build a scatter plot for calls made to customer services. Plotly, also known by its URL, Plot.ly, is an online analytics and data visualization tool providing online graphing, analytic, and statistics tools for individuals and collaboration, as well as scientific graphing libraries for **Python** (https://en.wikipedia.org/wiki/Python_(progr amming_language), **R** (https://en.wikipedia.org/wiki/R_(programming_language)), **MATLAB** (https://en.wikipedia.org/wiki/MATLAB), **Perl** (https://en.wikipedia.org /wiki/Perl), **Julia** (https://en.wikipedia.org/wiki/Julia_(programming_language)), **Arduino** (https://en.wikipedia.org/wiki/Arduino), and **REST** (https://en.wikipedia .org/wiki/REST). You can use Plotly within the Jupyter notebook, and the community edition is free for personal use. It does have some restrictions on usage in terms of the number of calls that you can make, but if you are doing basic exploratory work, the limit should suffice. You can register for the community edition at https://plot.ly/accounts /login/?action=signup. Once you sign up to Plotly, you will need to generate an API key, which can then be used to make calls and build "*pretty*" graphs:

```
In [173]: %%sh
          pip install plotly

Collecting plotly
  Using cached plotly-1.13.0.tar.gz
Requirement already satisfied (use --upgrade to upgrade): requests in ./anaconda3/lib/python3.5/site-packages (from plotly)
Requirement already satisfied (use --upgrade to upgrade): six in ./anaconda3/lib/python3.5/site-packages (from plotly)
Requirement already satisfied (use --upgrade to upgrade): pytz in ./anaconda3/lib/python3.5/site-packages (from plotly)
Building wheels for collected packages: plotly
  Running setup.py bdist_wheel for plotly: started
  Running setup.py bdist_wheel for plotly: finished with status 'done'
  Stored in directory: /root/.cache/pip/wheels/bf/98/1a/34852baa1b15825ee6a1368880cd019932e008daf561466d35
Successfully built plotly
Installing collected packages: plotly
Successfully installed plotly-1.13.0
```

Figure 10.7: Installation of Plotly via pip

Scala code – constructing a scatter plot

We will now see the sample Scala code for constructing a scatter plot to explore the correlation between customer service calls and the churn variable

You will need to perform a few data transformations while building a scatter plot with `Plotly` and Spark DataFrames. Here are a few important points:

- The Python API for Plotly visualizations expects you to provide an array of numbers for the visualization. You would need to use `Numpy` or a similar library for this.
- Since the visualization will be rendered on the client side, make sure you limit the data before bringing it in.
- The visualizations, for example scatter plots, need two series of numbers. You've got to be clever in creating a similar series from randomly generated numbers to plot it on the same canvas.

The code for this visualization is available on the GitHub page of this book:

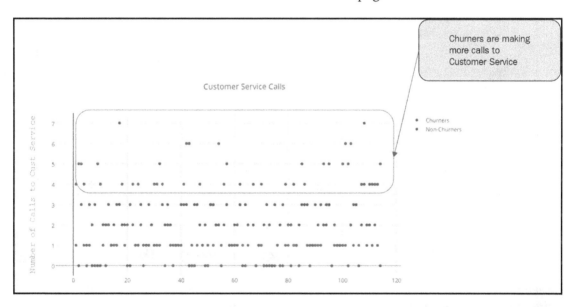

Figure 10.8: Scatter Plot of customer service calls versus customer churn (trace0=Churn, trace1=Non-churn)

As you can see from the scatter plot, customers who have churned (red-dots) have generally made more calls to the customer service center compared to the ones who have not churned (green-dots). We see this variable being a significant predictor of churn.

Exploring the churn variable

We want to perform a simple exploration to see the frequency chart of our Churn variable, and see if there is a need for separate sampling. This is usually done when the secondary outcomes are over represented in the data set, thus affecting the ability to predict outcomes of unknown data by the model. Let's start by looking at the code for the visualization before looking at the actual histogram:

```
#Imports
import plotly.plotly as py
import plotly.graph_objs as go

#Separating the data into Churn and Non-Churn Data Set
churnDataset.createOrReplaceTempView("churn_tab")
churners = spark.sql("select * from churn_tab where churn='True.'")
nonChurners = spark.sql("select * from churn_tab where churn='False.'")

#Getting the Count for churners/Non-Churners
churnCnt = churners.count()
nonChurnCnt = nonChurners.count()

data = [go.Bar(
            x=['Churners', 'Non-Churners'],
            y=[churnCnt, nonChurnCnt]
    )]

py.iplot(data, filename='Churn-NonChurn Plot')
```

Figure 10.9: Code for the visualization of the churn variable

It seems that non-churners are overly represented in this data set, by a factor of 1:5, which is quite typical and we will need to make a few adjustments to our data to make sure that non-churners are not overly represented in the predictive model.

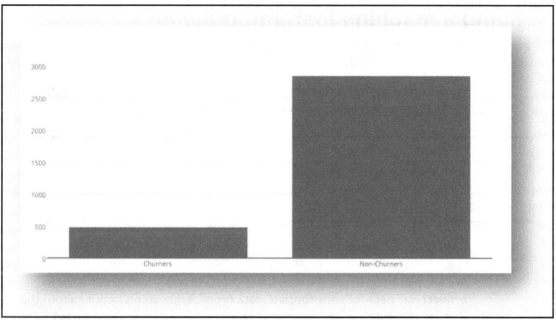

Figure 10.10: Histogram of the churn variable

Data transformation

We have explored the contents of our data set, and it looks good. However, for use with Spark we need to perform various transformations for certain variables. The type of transformations we'll perform include:

- Data type conversions, some of the algorithms we use for prediction expect the data to be in numerical format. We will need to convert the data that was loaded as strings into a numerical format.
- Indexing of categorical variables.
- Transforming the churn variable with labels.
- Converting the categorical variables into binary sparse vectors.
- Transforming all features into a vector.
- Splitting the data into training and validation.

Building a machine learning pipeline

We are now going to build a machine learning pipeline, which involves data transformation, training, and prediction.

1. Data type conversions: Earlier in the *Loading data* section, we loaded the data as a Spark DataFrame. By default, this will load all data as strings:

```
In [55]:  churnDataset.schema

Out[55]:  StructType(List(StructField(STATE,StringType,true),StructField(ACCOUNTLENGTH,StringType,true),StructField(AREACODE,StringType,tr
          ue),StructField(PHONE,StringType,true),StructField(INTLPLAN,StringType,true),StructField(VMAILPLAN,StringType,true),StructField
          (VMAILMESSAGE,StringType,true),StructField(DAYMINS,StringType,true),StructField(DAYCALLS,StringType,true),StructField(DAYCHARGE,
          StringType,true),StructField(EVEMINS,StringType,true),StructField(EVECALLS,StringType,true),StructField(EVECHARGE,StringType,tru
          e),StructField(NIGHTMINS,StringType,true),StructField(NIGHTCALLS,StringType,true),StructField(NIGHTCHARGE,StringType,true),Struc
          tField(INTLMINS,StringType,true),StructField(INTLCALLS,StringType,true),StructField(INTLCHARGE,StringType,true),StructField(CUST
          SERVCALLS,StringType,true),StructField(CHURN,StringType,true)))
```

Figure 10.11: Schema of churn dataset.

We are planning to use the Random Forest classifier and hence need to convert our data into appropriate data types. You can read more about the Random Forest classifier here: `http://bit.ly/2kdJMVL`. The data set comprises of numerical columns and categorical columns. We'll first convert the numerical columns into `double`.

```
in [45]:  churnDataset = churnDataset.withColumn("ACCOUNTLENGTH", churnDataset["ACCOUNTLENGTH"].cast("double"))
          churnDataset = churnDataset.withColumn("AREACODE", churnDataset["AREACODE"].cast("double"))
          churnDataset = churnDataset.withColumn("VMAILMESSAGE", churnDataset["VMAILMESSAGE"].cast("double"))
          churnDataset = churnDataset.withColumn("DAYMINS", churnDataset["DAYMINS"].cast("double"))
          churnDataset = churnDataset.withColumn("DAYMINS", churnDataset["DAYMINS"].cast("double"))
          churnDataset = churnDataset.withColumn("DAYCALLS", churnDataset["DAYCALLS"].cast("double"))
          churnDataset = churnDataset.withColumn("DAYCHARGE", churnDataset["DAYCHARGE"].cast("double"))
          churnDataset = churnDataset.withColumn("EVEMINS", churnDataset["EVEMINS"].cast("double"))
          churnDataset = churnDataset.withColumn("EVECALLS", churnDataset["EVECALLS"].cast("double"))
          churnDataset = churnDataset.withColumn("EVECHARGE", churnDataset["EVECHARGE"].cast("double"))
          churnDataset = churnDataset.withColumn("NIGHTMINS", churnDataset["NIGHTMINS"].cast("double"))
          churnDataset = churnDataset.withColumn("NIGHTCALLS", churnDataset["NIGHTCALLS"].cast("double"))
          churnDataset = churnDataset.withColumn("NIGHTCHARGE", churnDataset["NIGHTCHARGE"].cast("double"))
          churnDataset = churnDataset.withColumn("INTLMINS", churnDataset["INTLMINS"].cast("double"))
          churnDataset = churnDataset.withColumn("INTLCALLS", churnDataset["INTLCALLS"].cast("double"))
          churnDataset = churnDataset.withColumn("INTLCHARGE", churnDataset["INTLCHARGE"].cast("double"))
          churnDataset = churnDataset.withColumn("CUSTSERVCALLS", churnDataset["CUSTSERVCALLS"].cast("double"))
```

Figure 10.12: converting numeric columns into double.

2. Indexing categorical columns and binary sparse vectors: Spark MLLib provides feature transformation functions to convert a categorical column into an indexed value. We'll be using two main functions for this conversion:

   - StringIndexer: StringIndexer as discussed during the MLlib chapter encodes a string column of labels into a column of label indices. The more frequent categories get indexed before the lower frequency categories.

   - OnHotEncoder: OneHotEncoder is also a very useful feature transformation function that allows transformation of a column of label indices (can be output of StringIndexer) into a column of binary vectors, with at most a single one-value. The function is valuable because it allows algorithms such as Logistic Regression to use categorical features, which is not possible by default, as Logistic Regression expects only continuous features.

Code example for the categorical transformation is:

```
stages = [] # Creating Stages array for our pipeline
#Declaring Categorical columns
categoricalColumns = ["PHONE","STATE", "INTLPLAN", "VMAILPLAN"]
#Looping through the categoricalcolumns for feature transformation
for categoricalCol in categoricalColumns:
# Category Indexing with StringIndexer
stringIndexer = StringIndexer(inputCol=categoricalCol,
  outputCol=categoricalCol+"Index")
# Use OneHotEncoder to convert categorical variables into binary
SparseVectors
encoder = OneHotEncoder(inputCol=categoricalCol+"Index",
  outputCol=categoricalCol+"classVec")
# Add stages to the stages array. We'll pass these stages
 to the pipeline.
stages += [stringIndexer, encoder]
```

3. Transforming the churn variable: The next step is to transform the churn variable. Again we'll be using the StringIndexer function to transform the values True/False into indexed values. Random Forest and certain other machine learning algorithms require two input columns:

   - A features column – feature vector
   - A label column – label to predict.

We'll rename the churn column as label.

Code example for the churn column transformation:

```
#Using String indexer to transform Chrun variable
label_stringIdx = StringIndexer(inputCol = "CHURN",
  outputCol = "label")
#Adding the Churn transformation to our pipeline stages
stages += [label_stringIdx]
```

4. Assembling all features: We now have completed the relevant transformations. Remember, feature engineering is where the art of modeling happens, so some of you might be inclined to perform further complex analysis and enhance the features by combining information from other sources. However, for the purpose of this exercise we will not do any further transformation to the data set.

In order to combine the categorical vectors and numerical columns, we will now use the VectorAssembler, which is a very handy utility to combine the raw features with those generated through other feature transformers. You can read more about VectorAssembler at http://bit.ly/2kBF5CR.

Code example for churn assembling raw and transformed features is:

```
# Transform all features into a vector using VectorAssembler
numericCols =
  ["ACCOUNTLENGTH","AREACODE","VMAILMESSAGE",
    "DAYMINS","DAYCALLS","DAYCHARGE",
    "EVEMINS","EVECALLS","EVECHARGE",
    "NIGHTMINS","NIGHTCALLS","NIGHTCHARGE",
    "INTLMINS","INTLCALLS","INTLCHARGE",
    "CUSTSERVCALLS"]
#Pick up all the transformed categorical variables
categoricalVectorColumns = [*map(lambda c: c +
  "classVec", categoricalColumns)]

#Add transformed categorical variables and numberical columns
to the assmebler input
assemblerInputs = categoricalVectorColumns + numericCols
#Use Vector assembler to combine raw numerical features
with transformed categorical inputs
assembler = VectorAssembler(inputCols=assemblerInputs,
  outputCol="features")
#Add the feature assembling part to the pipeline stages
  stages += [assembler]
```

5. Building the ML pipeline: We discussed the Pipeline API in `Chapter 6`, *Machine Learning with Spark*. We are going to make use of the concepts we studied, and essentially we are going to use the stages that we have built up until now to create a pipeline, and then fit the churn dataset to build a pipeline model.

```
In [132]:  pipeline = Pipeline(stages=stages)
           pipelineModel = pipeline.fit(churnDataset)
           churnDataset = pipelineModel.transform(churnDataset)

In [135]:  pipelineModel

Out[135]:  PipelineModel_43af97ff485f28804637

In [136]:  churnDataset

Out[136]:  DataFrame[label: double, features: vector, STATE: string, ACCOUNTLENGTH: double, AREACODE: double, PHONE: string, INTLPLAN: stri
           ng, VMAILPLAN: string, VMAILMESSAGE: double, DAYMINS: double, DAYCALLS: double, DAYCHARGE: double, EVEMINS: double, EVECALLS: do
           uble, EVECHARGE: double, NIGHTMINS: double, NIGHTCALLS: double, NIGHTCHARGE: double, INTLMINS: double, INTLCALLS: double, INTLCH
           ARGE: double, CUSTSERVCALLS: double, CHURN: string]
```

Figure 10.13: Building a pipeline

If you view the transformed dataset, you'll see that we have two additional columns, a `label` and a `features` column. While you still have all the original columns, we will not need them while training the model, or even validating it as they are the base columns based on which the features vector has been calculated. If you take a quick look at the features vector, which is what your model is going to use to make predictions, it looks like a bunch of vectors:

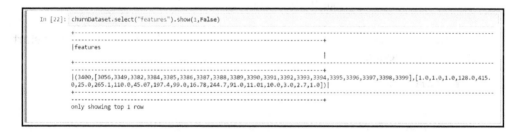

Figure 10.14: Feature vector sample

6. Training the model: We are going to demonstrate the training of a model as a separate step. You might see in some cases, the training of the model as a part of the pipeline as well. Since we are using `RandomForestClassifier`, we only need two input parameters for our model:
   - Label
   - Features

We'll simply select these columns from the full column list, which at the moment includes all columns in addition to these two:

```
selectedcols = ["label", "features"] + cols
churnDataset = churnDataset.select(selectedcols)
```

The next step is to split the data into training and validation sets. We are using 70% of the data for training, and leaving the remaining 30% for testing of our model. In practice, people often use the 80/20 rule as well.

Code example for model training is:

```
### Randomly split data into training and validation sets
(trainingData, testData) = churnDataset.randomSplit([0.7, 0.3],
  seed = 78799)
```

Splitting the data in this way will leave us with around 2,333 rows for training, and around 1,000 for the validation.

```
In [23]:  ### Randomly split data into training and validation sets
          (trainingData, testData) = churnDataset.randomSplit([0.7, 0.3], seed = 78799)

In [26]:  print("===================================================")
          print("Training size: [" + str(trainingData.count())+"] === Test Size: ["+str(testData.count())+"]")
          print("===================================================")


          ===================================================
          Training size: [2333] === Test Size: [1000]
          ===================================================
```

Figure 10.15: Feature vector sample

Now that we have split our data sets into training and validation, we can start training our model:

```
# Start timer
start_time = time.time()
# Create an initial RandomForest model.
rf = RandomForestClassifier(labelCol="label",
featuresCol="features", maxDepth=5, maxBins=32, numTrees=20)
# Train model with Training Data
rfModel = rf.fit(trainingData)
# Calculate total time
train_time = time.time() - start_time
print("Training time is " + str(train_time) + "s")
```

```
In [16]:   # Start timer
           start_time = time.time()

           # Create an initial RandomForest model.
           rf = RandomForestClassifier(labelCol="label", featuresCol="features", maxDepth=5, maxBins=32, numTrees=20)

           # Train model with Training Data
           rfModel = rf.fit(trainingData)

           # Calculate total time
           train_time = time.time() - start_time
           print("Training time is " + str(train_time) + "s")

           Training time is 10.90792441368103s
```

Figure 10.16: Model training

We have used certain parameters for our Random Forest classifier: for example, numTrees=20. You may want to play around with certain parameters as we saw in Chapter 9, *Building a Recommendation System,* in order to identify an optimum model.

```
In [27]:   rfModel

Out[27]:   RandomForestClassificationModel (uid=rfc_2832c50151b2) with 20 trees
```

Figure 10.17: Random Forest model

7. Validating the model: We now have a model that we have trained successfully. We want to make predictions on test data to identify how well our model has performed.

Code example for model validation:

```
# Start timer
start_time = time.time()
# Make predictions on test data using the
Transformer.transform() method.
predictions = rfModel.transform(testData)
# Evaluate model. Default metric is Area under the curve
evaluator = BinaryClassificationEvaluator()
auc = evaluator.evaluate(predictions)
# Calculate total time
eval_time = time.time() - start_time
print("Evaulation time is " + str(eval_time) + "s")
# Print total time for training + evaulation
print("Total time for training and evaulation is " +
  str(train_time + eval_time) + "s")
```

```
In [28]:  # Start timer
          start_time = time.time()

          # Make predictions on test data using the Transformer.transform() method.
          predictions = rfModel.transform(testData)

          # Evaluate model. Default metric is areaUnderROC
          evaluator = BinaryClassificationEvaluator()
          auc = evaluator.evaluate(predictions)

          # Calculate total time
          eval_time = time.time() - start_time
          print("Evaulation time is " + str(eval_time) + "s")


          # Print total time for training + evaulation
          print("Total time for training and evaulation is " + str(train_time + eval_time) + "s")

          Evaulation time is 1.014225721359253s
          Total time for training and evaulation is 11.922150135040283s

In [29]:  print("Area under the curve is : "+str(auc)+"s")

          Area under the curve is : 0.8701236787621239s
```

Figure 10.18: Validation of the model

You can view the predictions made by the model along with the probability by which the prediction has been made:

```
In [32]:  selected.show(5,False)

          +-----+----------+------------------------------------------+
          |label|prediction|probability                               |
          +-----+----------+------------------------------------------+
          |0.0  |0.0       |[0.8617317493137119,0.1382682506862881]   |
          |0.0  |0.0       |[0.8658637362350545,0.13413626376494553]  |
          |0.0  |0.0       |[0.8530759766580674,0.1469240233419326]   |
          |0.0  |0.0       |[0.7845468788124232,0.2154531211875767]   |
          |0.0  |0.0       |[0.8729465847681863,0.12705341523181374]  |
          +-----+----------+------------------------------------------+
          only showing top 5 rows
```

A sample of the results shows that the predictions are fairly accurate. While we have used Random Forest classifier, you may want to use another algorithm, or a number of different algorithms to identify the champion model, and deploy that into production. We are hoping that this would give you a good starting point into building your own applications.

References

We've referenced the following blogs, articles, and videos during the creation of this chapter. You may want to refer to them for further reading:

1. `http://sixteenventures.com/churn-hurts`
2. `https://www.livechatinc.com/blog/churn-rate/`
3. `https://docs.databricks.com/spark/latest/mllib/binary-classification-mllib-pipelines.html`

Summary

This concludes the chapter. We have gone through a churn prediction example using the PySpark and the Jupyiter notebook. I hope this gives you a good starting point for building your own applications. The full code and the Jupyter notebook are available on this book's GitHub page.

This was the last major chapter of this book. As a part of this book our intention was to take the users who are beginning to learn Spark on a journey where they can start from the very basics to a level where they feel comfortable with Spark as framework and also about writing their own Spark applications. We've covered some interesting topics including RDDs, DataFrames, MlLib, GraphX and also how to set up Spark in a cluster mode. Any book cannot do justice to Spark as a framework, as it is continuously evolving with new and exciting features added in every release.

We hope you have enjoyed this journey and look forward to hearing from you on your experience and feedback. In the `Appendix`, *There's More with Spark*, we'll cover some of the topics that we deem to be important, but didn't fit into the main chapters of this book. This includes a variety of topics including performance tuning, setting up Jupyter notebooks, sizing up your cluster and some key security topics.

There's More with Spark

We've covered some of the hottest areas in Spark from the new Catalyst optimizer to RDDs and DataFrames. We have covered the MLLib and GraphX library before looking at some use cases to see how an application can be built on Spark. However, as this book is just an introduction, we have skipped various important topics along the way. This was intentional as we wanted to keep the book at a readable level to help you get started, but with pointed references along the way that can help you master a particular topic. However, there are certain key areas which we would like to cover as a part of an Appendix, which we believe are important for you to develop and deploy your Spark applications.

In this Appendix, we would like to cover

- Performance tuning Spark
    - Data serialization
    - Memory management
    - Sizing up your executors
    - Handling skew
- Security
- Key configuration properties
- Configuring Jupyter with Spark
- Shared variables: advanced

Let's get started.

Performance tuning

Most of you would have heard of the old adage "*Good, Fast, Cheap – Pick any two*". That adage is still true, though the scales have shifted slightly with the open source model where the software is free but does need a relevant skillset to make the best use of it. That skillset comes at a cost, and performance tuning is one area where that specialized skillset is a must-have. When you talk about performance tuning, the underlying assumption is that your system is already working, fully functional.

Figure 11.1: Good – Fast and Cheap

You are not happy with the response rates. However, that does not have to be so all the time. You can take certain key decisions that can help you build a relatively optimized system early on.

So what are the key areas for consideration? Each distributed application has to work with five major computing resources:

- Network
- Disk
- I/O
- CPU
- Memory

For an application to perform at its optimum level, it has to make sure it makes the best of all these resources. We'll look at areas that allow you to improve computation efficiency across all these resources. The key topics of concern are:

- Data serialization
- Memory tuning

Data serialization

Serialization is the process of converting an object into a sequence of bytes which can then be:

- Persisted to disk
- Saved to a database
- Sent over the network

The reverse of converting bytes back to an object is therefore called **Deserialization**. As you can imagine Serialization and Deserialization are fairly common operations, especially during caching, persistence or shuffle operations in Spark. The speed of your application will depend on the serialization mechanism you choose, and those of you with a Java background will know that Java provides a Serializable interface. Java Serialization is the default serialization mechanism in Spark, but is not the fastest serialization mechanism around. The main reasons Java Serialization is slow are:

- Java Serialization uses excessive temporary object allocation.
- Java Serialization makes use of Reflection to get/set field values.

So while Java Serialization is flexible it is slow and hence you should use **Kyro** serialization which is an alternate serialization mechanism in Spark. You would need to set the new serialization in the Spark configuration.

Let us start by setting up the serializer:

```
conf.set( "spark.serializer",
"org.apache.spark.serializer.KyroSerializer")
```

For any network intensive application, it is recommended that you use the **Kyro Serializer**. Since Spark 2.0, the framework had used Kyro for all internal shuffling of RDDs with simple types, arrays of simple types and so on. However, you will still need to use your custom classes with Kyro, which can be done using `registerKyroClasses` method:

```
conf.registerKyroClasses(Array(classOf[MyCustomClass]))
```

The following are Spark related Kyro serialization properties, which you can set in the configuration object (`http://bit.ly/2khlxCv`).

Property Name	Default	Meaning
`spark.kryo.classesToRegister`	(none)	If you use Kryo serialization, give a comma-separated list of custom class names to register with Kryo. See the tuning guide for more details.
`spark.kryo.referenceTracking`	TRUE	Specifies whether to track references to the same object when serializing data with Kryo, which is necessary if your object graphs have loops and useful for efficiency if they contain multiple copies of the same object. Can be disabled to improve performance if you know this is not the case.
`spark.kryo.registrationRequired`	FALSE	Specifies whether to require registration with Kryo. If set to True, Kryo will throw an exception if an unregistered class is serialized. If set to false (the default), Kryo will write unregistered class names along with each object. Writing class names can cause significant performance overhead, so enabling this option can enforce that a user has not omitted classes from registration.
`spark.kryo.registrator`	(none)	If you use Kryo serialization, give a comma-separated list of classes that register your custom classes with Kryo. This property is useful if you need to register your classes in a custom way, and so on to specify a custom field serializer. Otherwise `spark.kryo.classesToRegister` is simpler. It should be set to classes that extend `KryoRegistrator`.
`spark.kryo.unsafe`	FALSE	Specifies whether to use unsafe based Kryo serializer. Can be substantially faster by using Unsafe Based IO.

spark.kryoserializer.buffer.max	64m	Maximum allowable size of Kryo serialization buffer. This must be larger than any object you attempt to serialize. Increase this if you get a *buffer limit exceeded* exception inside Kryo.
spark.kryoserializer.buffer	64k	Initial size of Kryo's serialization buffer. Note that there will be one buffer *per core* on each worker. This buffer will grow up to `spark.kryoserializer.buffer.max` if needed.

Memory tuning

Data serialization is key during all persistence and shuffle operations, but since Spark is an in-memory engine, you can expect that memory tuning will play a key part in your application's performance. Spark has improved since its earlier versions in terms of handling contention between various elements within the framework for memory, which is a scarce resource (certainly scarcer than disks). The three major types of contentions include:

- Execution and storage
- Tasks running in parallel
- Operators within the same task
- Memory management configuration options
- Memory tuning key tips

Execution and storage

Memory required for execution of tasks, for example shuffles, joins, sorts and aggregations is called execution memory, whereas memory required for caching data sets and propagating internal data across the cluster is known as Storage memory. Since Spark 1.6 with the advent of unified memory management, memory is shared between execution and storage, which means that if execution requires more memory, it can get it from storage. As we know that both execution and storage can grow, while the need for more execution memory can evict storage from memory using the LRU mechanism, the need for storage will not evict execution memory.

Tasks running in parallel

Since Spark 1.0, dynamic memory assignment is considered where, if you have an N number of tasks running, the memory will be divided among the tasks. If you are running a very memory intensive task, say `Task1`, it will consume all the available memory. If another task, say `Task2` is scheduled, `Task1` will need to spill some of its data to disk to ensure that `Task2` gets fair share of the resources.

Operators within the same task

If you have a number of operators within the task, since Spark 1.6, they will use cooperative spilling to share memory resources. For example, if you are running a query that needs to aggregate data before it sorts it, the aggregate operator would get all the available memory. However, when the sort operator runs, it will ask the *aggregate* to share some memory, which might result in *aggregate* spilling some pages.

Memory management configuration options

Spark provides a number of memory management configuration options documented on the Apache Spark configuration page at `http://bit.ly/2kgDDtk`.

Memory tuning key tips

The following are some tips to help you understand memory management within Spark:

1. The best way to understand your storage requirements is to either look at the Spark Web UI to see how a cache object consumes memory: or for specific objects, you can use the `SizeEstimator()` (`http://bit.ly/sizeestimator`) estimate method.

2. If you have less than 32 GB of RAM you can conserve memory by making your pointers only 4 bytes instead of 8 using the JVM `-XX:+UseCompressOops` flag. This enables the use of compressed 32 bit OOPs in a 64-bit JVM without scarifying the heap size advantage. These can be set in the `spark-env.sh` file.

More memory tips can be found at `http://bit.ly/2lkV4s6`. If you would like to spend some more time in understanding memory management within Spark, I urge you to have a look at the following talk: http://bit.ly/2lkZorEx`.

I/O tuning

I/O is critical when you are reading data to/from disk. The major things that you need to consider are:

Data locality

The closer your computer is to your data, the better the performance for your jobs. Moving compute to your data is more optimal compared to moving data to your compute, and therein lies the concept of data locality. Process and data can be quite close to each other, or in some cases on entirely different nodes. The locality levels are defined as follows:

- PROCESS_LOCAL: This is the best possible option where data resides in the same JVM as the process, and hence is called local to the process.
- NODE_LOCAL: This indicates that the data is not in the same JVM, but is on the same node. This provides a fast way to access the data, despite it being slower than PROCESS_LOCAL, since the data has to be transferred from either the disk or another process.
- RACK_LOCAL: There can be multiple servers in the RACK. This option indicates that the data is on the same rack as the current node.
- ANY: This indicates that the data is elsewhere on the network but on the same Rack.
- NO_PREF: No preference is given to the locality of the data and it is accessed quickly from anywhere. This is especially true in cases where Spark is unable to determine preferred locations.

Spark realises the importance of data locality and hence tries its best to schedule tasks with optimum data locality. However, this cannot be guaranteed and hence Spark offers configuration options for you to configure alternate options. Here's what Spark can do:

- Try to schedule a task on the node where the data is resident.
- In the case of the node being busy, wait until n number of seconds before trying to configure the task on another node with free CPU.
- Don't wait – Simply start the task wherever it gets a chance and accepting the performance penalty of data movement.

The relevant data locality configuration options are documented at the following link `http://bit.ly/21RX60u`.

Property Name	Default	Description
`spark.locality.wait`	3s	How long to wait to launch a data local task before giving up and launching it on a less local node. The same wait will be used to step through multiple locality levels (process-local, node-local, rack-local and then any). It is also possible to customize the waiting time for each level by setting `spark.locality.wait.node`, and so on. You should increase this setting if your tasks are long and see poor locality, but the default usually works well.
`spark.locality.wait.node`	`spark.locality.wait`	Customize the locality wait for node locality. For example, you can set this to 0 to skip node locality and search immediately for rack locality (if your cluster has rack information).
`spark.locality.wait.process`	`spark.locality.wait`	Customize the locality wait for process locality. This affects tasks that attempt to access cached data in a particular executor process.
`spark.locality.wait.rack`	`spark.locality.wait`	Customize the locality wait for rack locality.

Optimum data caching can have a dramatic impact on performance. For a data set that you would need to access multiple times, instead of recreating it from scratch it is best to cache it. However, please don't go overboard with caching: you will be amazed to see how many times we see this in practice. Use this option judiciously.

Data caching goes hand in hand with serialization, so make sure you pick up the best serialization mechanism available for your objects.

Sizing up your executors

When you set up Spark, executors are run on the nodes in the cluster. To put it simply, executors are the processes where you:

- Run your compute
- Store your data

Each application has its own executor processes and they will stay up and running until your application is up and running. So by definition, they seem to be quite important from a performance perspective, and hence the three key metrics during a Spark deployment are:

- **–num-executors:** How many executors you need?
- **–executor-cores:** How many CPU cores would you want to allocate to each executor?
- **–executor-memory:** How much memory will you like to assign to each executor process?

So how do you allocate physical resources to Spark? While this may generally depend on the nature of the workload, you can vary between the following extreme parameters.

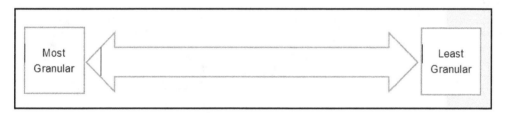

Figure 11.2: Executor granularity

Extreme approaches are generally a bad option except for very specific workload situations. For example, if you define very small sized executors for example, 1 core/executor or 4GB/executor you will not be able to execute multiple tasks within the same executor and hence will not benefit from cache sharing.

Similarly, in other cases where you have extremely large executors for example, on a 16-core machine having a 16-core executor with the maximum amount of RAM possible (e.g. 128 GB). This will obviously mean you won't have any space for anything else to run on that machine which can include OS and other daemons. Even if you leave space for other daemons, this is still not a good way to size your machine. while Spark-on-YARN can dynamically help you configure the number of executors, it still can't help you with the number of cores per executor and the memory to be allocated.

So how do you configure your cluster?

Calculating memory overhead

We are going to assume you are using YARN. However, this will hold true for other cluster managers too. The hierarchy of memory properties of Spark and YARN is shown in the following screenshot (Reference: `http://bit.ly/2lUQUEQ`).

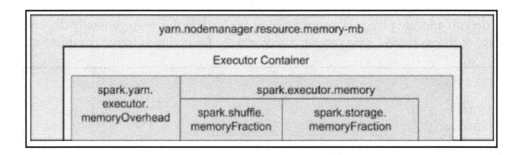

Figure 11.3: Memory hierarchy – Spark on YARN

You will need to allocate memory for the executor overhead, which typically includes VM overhead, internalized string: (`http://bit.ly/21UQ2Ad`) and so on. The `Spark.yarn.executor.memoryOverhead` property controls the amount of off-heap memory to be allocated for each Executor. This can either be a minimum of 384 MB or 10% of your executor memory (whichever is larger). So let's assume you have 128 GB of RAM per node, and you ask for 128 GB from YARN Resource Manager, you'll actually be making a request for 140.8 GB (*128 * 1.10 = 140.8 GB*). This is actually more than the memory available on the node. So a better way to deal with this is to request at least 10% lesser memory, so that after the addition of overhead, you still do not exceed the total memory on the node.

Setting aside memory/CPU for YARN application master

As we have seen earlier you can run Spark in either a client deployment mode or a cluster deployment mode. In the cluster deployment mode, your driver program will run as a part of the YARN Application Master, which means one core assigned to the AM. You will need to make sure you allocate this properly. Hence if you have a 5 node cluster with 16 core /128 GB RAM per node, you need to figure out the number of executors; then for the memory per executor make sure you take into account the system over head.

I/O throughput

In the case of having a least granular executor, where you allocate all the cores to the executor, you will suffer by not getting adequate I/O throughput. If you are using HDFS, most practitioners (including Cloudera's official documentation) recommend a maximum of 5 tasks per executor, which should be the number of cores you allocate to your executor.

Sample calculations

Let us take a look at the following sample calculations:

- 5 node cluster
- 128 GB RAM / Node
- 16 cores per node
- Total cores Available= *16 * 5 = 80*
- Total cores Usable (1 core for OS) = *15 * 5 = 75*
- Total RAM available per node = 128 GB

We leave out 2 GB RAM per Node for OS, leaving us with 126 GB of RAM to work with.

Typical configuration:

- **–executor-cores:** Based on the 5 cores per executor, we can have a maximum of 15 executors and 3 executors per node (75/5=15)
- **–executor-memory:** For the RAM allocation, we will allocate 126/3=41 GB RAM per executor
- **–num-executors:** Since we have to leave out one executor for AM, we will have only 14 total executors (15 – 1 = 14)

Please do understand that while these are typical configurations, your configuration might change based on your cluster configuration and your typical workload. You need to see if your applications are making full use of the resources, and if not you can always reconfigure based on the feedback that you receive from your cluster.

The skew problem

Distributed systems just like teams of people working on an activity perform at the most optimum level when the work is evenly distributed among all the members of the team or the cluster. Both suffer, if the work is unevenly distributed and the system performs only as fast as the slowest component.

In the case of Spark, data is distributed across the cluster. You might have come across cases where a map job runs fairly quickly by your joins or shuffles take an excessive time. In most real life cases you would have popular keys or null values in your data, which would result in some tasks getting more work than others, thus resulting in a system skew. In the database world, original keys would actually be used to create new keys with random values such that the resultant keys would be fairly unique and thus allow the system to distribute the data more evenly across the system. Of course, you would need to do a multiple stage aggregation, but this would in most cases be faster than in the case of a system working with a skewed system.

A typical pipeline would need to be transformed as follows:

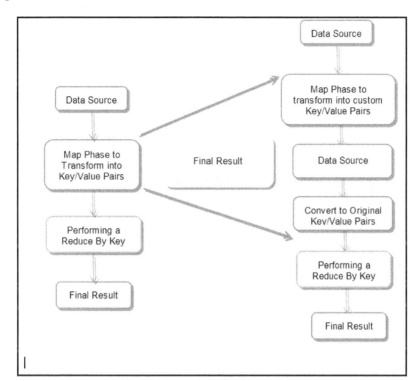

Figure 11.4: Multistage Map/Reduce to solve the skew problem

Security configuration in Spark

Spark currently supports two methods of authentication:

- Kerberos
- Shared Secret

Kerberos authentication

It is recommended to use **Kerberos** authentication when using Spark on YARN.

A Kerberos Principal is used in a Kerborized system to represent a unique identity. Kerberos can assign tickets to these identities, which helps them identify themselves while accessing Hadoop clusters secured by Kerberos. While the principals can generally have an arbitrary number of components, in Hadoop the principals are of the following format: username/FQDN@REALM.com. Your user name here can refer to an existing account like HDFS, Mapred, or Spark.

You will need to follow the following steps:

Creation of the Spark Principal and Keytab file – You will need to create a Spark Principal and the Spark keytab file using the following commands:

FQDN is your **Full Qualified Domain Name**

- **Creating the Principal**:

    ```
    kadmin: addprinc -randkey spark/fqdn@your-realm.com
    ```

- **Creating the Keytab file**:

    ```
    kadmin: xst - spark.keytab spark/fqdn
    ```

- **Relocating the keytab file to the Spark configuration directory**:

    ```
    mv spark.keytab /etc/spark/conf
    ```

- **Securing the Keytab file**:

    ```
    chown spark /etc/spark/conf/spark.keytab
    chmod 400 /etc/spark/conf/spark.keytab
    ```

Add Principal and Keytab properties to the spark-env.sh file – You have to configure the Spark history server to use Kerberos, and this can be done by specifying the Principal and Keytab created above in the Spark-env.sh file. The Spark-env.sh file is typically located in the conf directory.

```
vi /etc/spark/conf/spark-env.sh
  SPARK_HISTORY_OPTS=-Dspark.history.kerberos.enabled=true \
  -Dspark.history.kerberos.principal=spark/FQDN@REALM \
  -Dspark.history.kerberos.keytab=/etc/spark/conf/spark.keytab
```

Kerberos options for `Spark-submit` – When you are submitting applications using `Spark-submit`, you have the following options available for use on a secure cluster:

- **–proxy-user**
- **–principal**
- **–keytab**

The help system for these commands will give you a fairly good idea of what these are used for:

```
--proxy-user NAME          User to impersonate when submitting the application.
                           This argument does not work with --principal / --keytab.
--principal PRINCIPAL      Principal to be used to login to KDC, while running on
                           secure HDFS.
--keytab KEYTAB            The full path to the file that contains the keytab for the
                           principal specified above. This keytab will be copied to
                           the node running the Application Master via the Secure
                           Distributed Cache, for renewing the login tickets and the
                           delegation tokens periodically.
```

Figure 11.5: Kerberos related options in Spark-Submit

A `keytab` is a file that consists of your Kerberos prinicpals and your encrypted keys. A `keytab` file is used to authenticate a Kerberos principal on a host to Kerberos without human interaction or storing a password in a plain text file. If you have access to a `keytab` file, you can act as the principal whose credentials are secured in the `keytab` file, which makes them an asset of high importance and hence creates a greater need for them to be secured.

Shared secrets

Spark supports authentication via shared secret. The parameter used to configure the authentication is `spark.authenticate`, which controls the authentication via shared secret. The authentication process is quite simply a handshake between Spark and the other party to ensure that they have the same shared secret and can be allowed to communicate.

Shared secret on YARN

Configuring `spark.authenticate` to true will automatically handle generating and distributing shared secret. Each application will use a unique shared secret.

Shared secret on other cluster managers

For other types of Spark deployment, `spark.authenticate.secret` should be configured on each of the nodes. This secret will be used by all the Master/Workers and applications.

You can read more about shared secrets on the Apache Spark documentation pages (`http://bit.ly/2kyWkZo`).

Setting up Jupyter Notebook with Spark

In this section we will look at how to setup a Jupyter notebook with Spark. For those of you who haven't yet been able to grasp the concept of the notebook environment, it is important to understand the benefits as opposed to a traditional environment. Please do note that Jupyter Notebook is one of the many options that users have.

What is a Jupyter Notebook?

A Jupyter Notebook is an interactive computational environment which can combine execution of code, integrating rich media and text and visualizing your data with numerous visualization libraries. The notebook itself is just a small web application that you can use to create documents, and add explanatory text before sharing them with your peers or colleagues. Jupyter notebooks are being used at Google. Microsoft, IBM, NASA, and Bloomberg among many other leading companies.

Setting up a Jupyter Notebook

Following are the steps to set up a Jupyter Notebook:

- Pre-requisites – You would need Python 2.7 or Python >=3.3 for installing Jupyter Notebook.

- Install Anaconda – Anaconda is recommended as it will install Python, Jupyter Notebook and other commonly used packages for scientific computing and data science. You can download Anaconda from the following link: https://www.continuum.io/downloads.

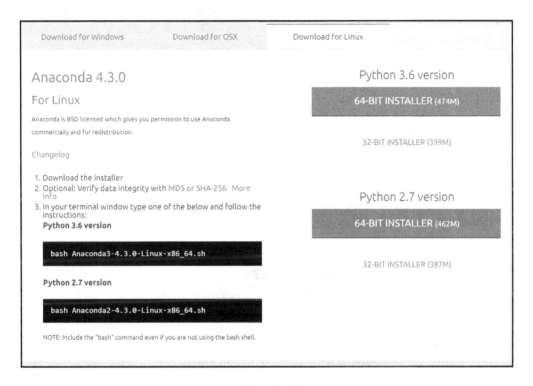

Figure 11-6: Installing Anaconda-1

You can click the link to get access to the installer and download it on your Linux system:

```
[root@m1580420 anaconda]# wget https://repo.continuum.io/archive/Anaconda3-4.3.0-Linux-x86_64.sh
--2017-02-19 06:43:44--  https://repo.continuum.io/archive/Anaconda3-4.3.0-Linux-x86_64.sh
Resolving repo.continuum.io... 104.16.19.10, 104.16.18.10, 2400:cb00:2048:1::6810:130a, ...
Connecting to repo.continuum.io|104.16.19.10|:443... connected.
HTTP request sent, awaiting response... 200 OK
Length: 496412001 (473M) [application/x-sh]
Saving to: "Anaconda3-4.3.0-Linux-x86_64.sh"

100%[==============================================================================>] 496,412,001 4.97M/s   in 2m 49s

2017-02-19 06:46:33 (2.80 MB/s) - "Anaconda3-4.3.0-Linux-x86_64.sh" saved [496412001/496412001]
```

Figure 117: Installing Anaconda-2

Once you have downloaded Anaconda, you can go ahead and install it.

```
[root@m1580420 anaconda]# ls -ltr
total 484784
-rw-r--r-- 1 root root 496412001 Feb  1 20:13 Anaconda3-4.3.0-Linux-x86_64.sh
[root@m1580420 anaconda]# sudo Anaconda3-4.3.0-Linux-x86_64.sh
```

Figure 11.7: Installing Anaconda-3

The installer will ask you questions arbout the install location, and walk you through the license agreement, before asking you to confirm of installation and weather it should add the path to the `bashrc` file. You can then start the notebook using the following command:

```
jupyter notebook
```

However, please bear in mind that by default a notebook server runs locally at `127.0.0.1:8888`. If this is what you are looking for, then this is great. However, if you like to open it to the public, you will need to secure your notebook server.

Securing the notebook server

Notebook server can be protected by a simple single password by configuring `NotebookApp.password` setting in the following file: `Jupyter_notebook_config.py`.

This file should be located in your home directory: `~/.jupyter`. If you have just installed Anaconda, you might not have this directory. You can create this by executing the following command:

```
jupyter notebook --generate-config
```

Running this command will create a `~/.jupyter` directory and will create a default configuration file:

```
[root@m1580420 anaconda]# jupyter notebook --generate-config
Writing default config to: /root/.jupyter/jupyter_notebook_config.py
[root@m1580420 anaconda]# ls /root/.jupyter/
jupyter_notebook_config.py
```

Figure 11.9: Securing Jupyter for public access

Preparing a hashed password

You can use Jupyter to create a hashed password or prepare it manually.

Using Jupyter (only with version 5.0 and later)

You can issue the following command to create a hashed password:

```
jupyter notebook password
```

This will save the password in your ~/.jupyter director in a file called jupyter_notebook_config.json.

Manually creating hashed password

You can use Python to manually create the hashed password:

```
[root@m1580420 anaconda3]# python
Python 3.6.0 |Anaconda 4.3.0 (64-bit)| (default, Dec 23 2016, 12:22:00)
[GCC 4.4.7 20120313 (Red Hat 4.4.7-1)] on linux
Type "help", "copyright", "credits" or "license" for more information.
>>> from notebook.auth import passwd
>>> passwd()
Enter password:
Verify password:
'sha1:cd7ef63fc00a:2816fd7ed6a47ac9aeaa2477c1587fd18ab1ecdc'
```

Figure 11.10: Manually creating a hashed password

You can use either of these passwords in your jupyter_notebook_config.py and replace the parameter value for c.NotebookApp.password.

```
c.NotebookApp.password =
u'sha1:cd7ef63fc00a:2816fd7ed6a47ac9aeaa2477c1587fd18ab1ecdc'
```

```
## Hashed password to use for web authentication.
#
#  To generate, type in a python/IPython shell:
#
#    from notebook.auth import passwd; passwd()
#
#  The string should be of the form type:salt:hashed-password.
c.NotebookApp.password = u'sha1:cd7ef63fc00a:2816fd7ed6a47ac9aeaa2477c1587fd18ab1ecdc'
```

Figure 11-11: Using the generated hashed password

By default the Notebook runs on port 8888; you'll see the option to change the port as well.

Since we want to allow public access to the notebook, we have to allow all IP's to access the notebook using any of the configured network interfaces for the public server. This can be done by making the following changes:

Before Change

```
## The IP address the notebook server will listen on.
#c.NotebookApp.ip = 'localhost'
```

After Change

```
## The IP address the notebook server will listen on.
c.NotebookApp.ip = '*'
```

Figure 11.12: Configuring Notebook server to listen on all interfaces

You can now run Jupyter, and access it from any computer with access to the notebook server:

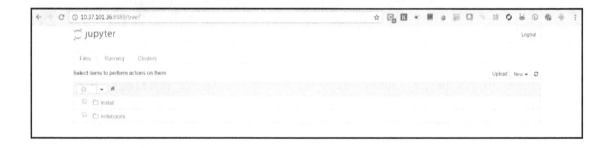

Figure 11-13: Jupyter interface

Setting up PySpark on Jupyter

The next step is to integrate PySpark with Jupyter notebook. You have to do following steps to setup PySpark:

1. Update your `bashrc` file and set the following variables:

```
# added by Anaconda3 4.3.0 installer
export PATH="/root/anaconda3/bin:$PATH"
PYSPARK_PYTHON=/usr/bin/python
PYSPARK_DRIVER_PYTHON=/usr/bin/python
SPARK_HOME=/spark/spark-2.0.2/
PATH=$PATH:/spark/spark-2.0.2/bin
PYSPARK_DRIVER_PYTHON=jupyter
PYSPARK_DRIVER_PYTHON_OPTS=notebook
```

2. Configure PySpark Kernel: Create a file `/usr/local/share/jupyter/kernels/pyspark/kernel.json` with the following parameters:

```
{
  "display_name": "PySpark",
  "language": "python",
  "argv": [ "/root/anaconda3/bin/python", "-m", "ipykernel",
  "-f", "{connection_file}" ],
  "env": {
    "SPARK_HOME": "/spark/spark-2.0.2/",
    "PYSPARK_PYTHON":"/root/anaconda3/bin/python",
    "PYTHONPATH": "/spark/spark-2.0.2/python/:/spark/
    spark-2.0.2/python/lib/py4j-0.10.3-src.zip",
    "PYTHONSTARTUP": "/spark/spark-2.0.2/python/pyspark/
     shell.py",
    "PYSPARK_SUBMIT_ARGS": "--master spark://sparkmaster:7077
     pyspark-shell"
  }
}
```

3. Open the notebook: Now when you open the Notebook with `jupyter notebook` command, you will find an additional kernel installed. You can create new Notebooks with the new Kernel:

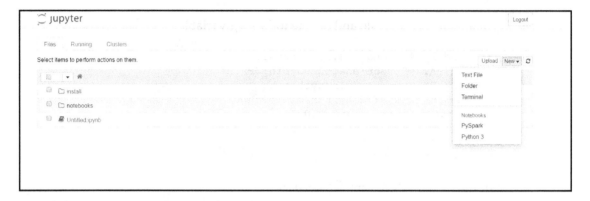

Figure 11.14: New Kernel

Shared variables

We touched upon shared variables in `Chapter 2`, *Transformations and Actions with Spark RDDs*, we did not go into more details as this is considered to be a slightly advanced topic with lots of nuances around what can and cannot be shared. To briefly recap we discussed two types of Shared Variables:

- Broadcast variables
- Accumulators

Broadcast variables

Spark is an MPP architecture where multiple nodes work in parallel to achieve operations in an optimal way. As the name indicates, you might want to achieve a state where each node has its own copy of the input/interim data set, and hence broadcast that across the cluster. From previous knowledge we know that Spark does some internal broadcasting of data while executing various actions. When you run an action on Spark, the RDD is transformed into a series of stages consisting of TaskSets, which are then executed in parallel on the executors. Data is distributed using shuffle operations and the common data needed by the tasks within each stage is broadcasted automatically. So why do you need an explicit broadcast when the needed data is already made available by Spark? We talked about serialization earlier in the `Appendix`, *There's More with Spark*, and this is a time when that knowledge will come in handy. Basically Spark will cache the serialized data, and explicitly deserializes it before running a task. This can incur some overhead, especially when the size of the data is huge. The following two key checkpoints should tell you when to use broadcast variables:

1. Tasks across multiple stages need the same copy of the data.
2. You will like to cache the data in a deserialized form.

So how do you Broadcast data with Spark?

Code Example: You can broadcast an array of string as follows.

```
val groceryList =
sc.broadcast(Array("Biscuits","Milk","Eggs","Butter","Bread"))
```

You can also access its value using the `.value` method:

```
scala> val groceryList = sc.broadcast(Array("Biscuits","Milk","Eggs","Butter","Bread"))
groceryList: org.apache.spark.broadcast.Broadcast[Array[String]] = Broadcast(0)

scala> groceryList.value
    def value: Array[String]

scala> groceryList.value
res0: Array[String] = Array(Biscuits, Milk, Eggs, Butter, Bread)
```

Figure 11.15: Broadcasting an array of strings

It is important to remember that all data being broadcasted is read only and you cannot broadcast an RDD. If you try to do that Spark will complain with the message Illegal Argument passed to `broadcast()` method. You can however call `collect()` on an RDD for it to be broadcasted. This can be seen in the following screenshot:

```
scala> val readmeBroadcast = sc.broadcast(sc.textFile("README.md"))
java.lang.IllegalArgumentException: requirement failed: Can not directly broadcast RDDs; instead, call collect() and broadcast the re
sult.
  at scala.Predef$.require(Predef.scala:224)
  at org.apache.spark.SparkContext.broadcast(SparkContext.scala:1385)
  ... 48 elided

scala> val readmeBroadcast = sc.broadcast(sc.textFile("README.md").collect())
readmeBroadcast: org.apache.spark.broadcast.Broadcast[Array[String]] = Broadcast(4)
```

Figure 11.16: Broadcasting an RDD

Accumulators

While broadcast variables are read only, Spark Accumulators can be used to implement shared variables which can be operated on (added to), from various tasks running as a part of the job. At a first glance, especially to those who haven a background in MapReduce programming, they seem to be an implementation of MapReduce style counters and can help with a number of potential use cases including for example debugging, where you might to compute the records associated to a product line, or number of check-outs or basket abandonments in a particular window, or even looking at the distribution of records across tasks.

However, unlike MapReduce they are not limited to `long` data types, and user can define their own data types that can be merged using custom merge implementations rather than the traditional addition on natural numbers. Some key points to remember are:

1. Accumulators are variables that can be added through an associate or commutative operation.
2. Accumulators due to the associative and commutative property can be operated in parallel.
3. Spark provides support for:

Datatype	Accumulator creation and registration method
double	doubleAccumulator(name: String)
long	longAccumulator(name: String)
CollectionAccumulator	collectionAccumulator[T](name: String)

4. Spark developers can create their own types by sub classing Accumulator V2 abstract class and implementing various methods such as:
   - `reset()`: Reset the value of this accumulator to a zero value. The call to is `Zero()` must return true.
   - `add()`: Take the input and accumulate.
   - `merge()`: Merge another same-type accumulator into this one and update its state. This should be a merge-in-place.

5. If the updates to an accumulator are performed inside a Spark action, Spark guarantees that each task's update to the accumulator will only be applied once. So if a task is restarted the task will not update the value of the accumulator.

6. If the updates to an accumulator are performed inside a Spark Transformation, the update may be applied more than once of the task or the job stage is reexecuted.

7. Tasks running on the cluster can add to the accumulator using the add method, however they cannot read its value. The values can only be read from the driver program using the value method.

Code Example – You can create an accumulator using any of the standard methods, and then manipulate it in the course of execution of your task:

```
//Create an Accumulator Variable
val basketDropouts = sc.longAccumulator("Basket Dropouts")
//Reset it to ZerobasketDropouts.reset
//Let us see the value of the variable.
basketDropouts.value
//Parallelize a collection and for each item, add it to the Accumulator
variable
sc.parallelize(1 to 100,1).foreach(num => basketDropouts.add(num))
//Get the current value of the variable
basketDropouts.value
```

Let's look at the following screenshot where we see the above programming example in action:

```scala
scala> val basketDropouts = sc.longAccumulator("Basket Dropouts")
basketDropouts: org.apache.spark.util.LongAccumulator = LongAccumulator(id: 45, name: Some(Basket Dropouts), value: 0)

scala> basketDropouts.reset

scala> basketDropouts.value
res4: Long = 0

scala> sc.parallelize(1 to 100,1).foreach(num => basketDropouts.add(num))

scala> basketDropouts.value
res6: Long = 5050
```

Figure 11.17: Accumulator variables

The Spark Driver UI will show the accumulators registered and their current value. As we can see on the driver UI, we have a `BasketDropouts` registered in the Accumulators section, and the current value is 5050. While this is a relatively simple example, in practice you can use it for a range of use cases.

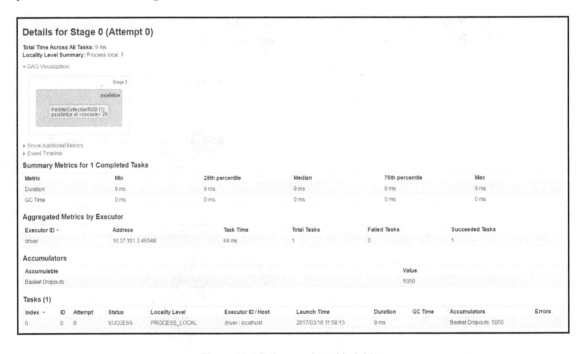

Figure 11-18: Accumulator Variables

References

1. http://spark.apache.org/docs/latest/tuning.html.
2. https://www.youtube.com/watch?v=dPHrykZL8Cg.
3. https://www.youtube.com/watch?v=vfiJQ7wg81Y.
4. http://spark.apache.org/docs/latest/security.html.
5. http://stackoverflow.com/questions/19447623/why-javas-serialization-slower-than-3rd-party-apis.
6. https://www.youtube.com/watch?v=vfiJQ7wg81Y&t=398s.
7. https://web.mit.edu/kerberos/krb5-1.5/krb5-1.5.4/doc/krb5-user/What-is-a-Kerberos-Principal_003f.html.
8. https://web.mit.edu/kerberos/krb5-1.5/krb5-1.5.4/doc/krb5-user/What-is-a-Kerberos-Principal_003f.html.
9. http://ramhiser.com/2015/02/01/configuring-ipython-notebook-support-for-pyspark/.
10. http://imranrashid.com/posts/Spark-Accumulators/.

Summary

This concludes our *Appendix* where we covered some topics based on performance tuning, sizing up your executors, handling data skew, configuring security, setting up a Jupyter notebook with Spark and finally broadcast variables and accumulators.

There are many more topics still to be covered, but we hope that this book has given you an effective quick-start with Spark 2.0, and you can use it to explore Spark further. Of course, Spark is one of the fastest moving projects out there, so by the time the book is out there will surely be many new features. One of the best places to keep up-to-date on the latest changes is http://spark.apache.org/documentation.html, where you can see the list of releases and the latest news.

Index

K

Kerberos authentication 309
key abstractions, ML Pipeline
  DataFrames 170
  estimator 171
  Evaluator 172
  parameter 172
  pipeline 172
  PipelineModel 172
  Transformer 170
key issues, with recommendation systems
  about 247
  known input data, gathering 247
  unknown, predicting from known ratings 248
KMeans clustering 159
Kyro 84
Kyro serialization 299
Kyro Serializer 299

L

Label propagation 13
latent factor methods
  prediction method, evaluating 255, 256
levels, data locality
  ANY 303
  NO_PREF 303
  NODE_LOCAL 303
  PROCESS_LOCAL 303
  RACK_LOCAL 303
LongTail phenomenon
  reference 243
Lucene 91

M

Machine Learning (ML) 10
machine learning algorithms
  about 162
  semi-supervised learning 164
  supervised learning 162
  unsupervised learning 163
machine learning
  about 158, 160
  need for 161
  references 158

use cases 162
manual recommendations 244
map transformation 50
Markov Decision Process 164
Massively Parallel Processing (MPP) 11
MasterUI
  applications, running 222
  cluster overview 221
  completed applications 223
  drivers overview 222
  workers overview 221
MATLAB
  reference 284
Mean Squared Error (MSE) 172
memory management configuration options,
    Apache Spark
  reference 302
memory overhead
  calculating 306
  I/O throughput 307
  sample calculations 307
memory tuning
  about 301
  execution, and storage 301
  key tips 302
  memory management configuration options 302
  operators, within same task 302
  reference, for tips 302
  tasks, running in parallel 302
memory/CPU
  setting, aside for YARN application master 307
Mesos configuration properties
  spark.mesos.coarse 239
  spark.mesos.executor.memoryOverhead 239
  spark.mesos.extra.cores 239
  spark.mesos.mesosExecutor.cores 239
  spark.mesos.principal 239
  spark.mesos.uris 239
Mesos run modes
  Coarse Grained 238
  Fine Grained 238
Mesos
  about 235
  modes of operation 236
  reference 236